MORE MAKESHIFT WORKSHOP SKILLS

MORE MAKESHIFT WORKSHOP SKILLS

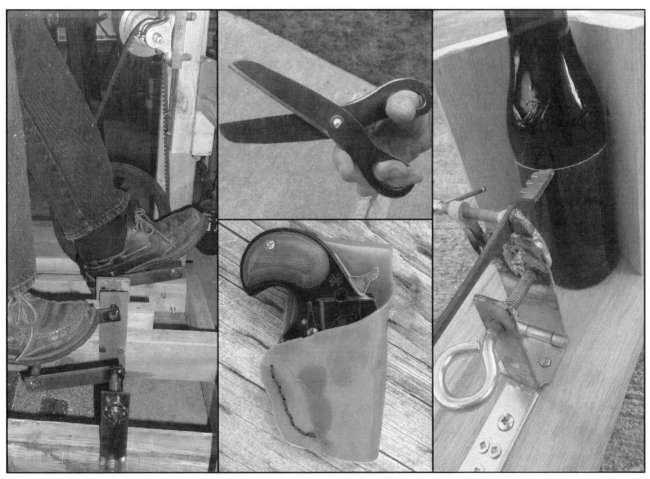

James Ballou

Foreword by Jim Benson

PALADIN PRESS • BOULDER, COLORADO

Also by James Ballou:
Long-Term Survival in the Coming Dark Age
Makeshift Workshop Skills for Survival and Self-Reliance

More Makeshift Workshop Skills
by James Ballou

Copyright © 2011 by James Ballou

ISBN 13: 978-1-58160-746-8
Printed in the United States of America

Published by Paladin Press, a division of
Paladin Enterprises, Inc.
Gunbarrel Tech Center
7077 Winchester Circle
Boulder, Colorado 80301 USA
+1.303.443.7250

Direct inquiries and/or orders to the above address.

Visit our website at www.paladin-press.com

Warning

The information in this book is based on the experiences, research, and beliefs of the author and cannot be duplicated exactly by readers. The author, publisher, and distributors of this book disclaim any liability from any damage or injury that a reader or user of information contained in this book may incur from the use or misuse of said information. This book is *for academic study only*.

Contents

Chapter 1: More Improvised Homemade Tools   1

The Simplest Tool   1

The Spearhead Dagger Digging Trowel   2

The Ancient Adze   3

The Essential Awl   5

A Pricking Wheel for Leather   8

The Useful Crooked Knife   11

A PVC Pipe Bucksaw   14

Making a Saw Blade from Scratch   17

Homemade Screwdrivers   20

Homemade Scissors   21

Chapter 2: Manually Powered Machines You Can Build   29

Build Your Own Handcart   31

Foot-Treadle Machines   37

Spring-Pole Machines   40

Machines Powered by Foot Pedals or Hand Cranks   41

Chapter 3: Useful Things from Discarded Plastic Products   49

Ready-Made Plastic Containers   49

Plastic Bottles   51

Plastic Buckets   53

Plastic Bags   60

A PVC Scoop for Digging in Sand 62
Make Use of Those Free Credit Card Offers 64
Commonly Overlooked Sources of Plastic Raw Materials 64

Chapter 4: More Odd Things Adapted from Common Household Items 67
The Versatility of Ordinary Cans 67
Cutting and Breaking Glass Jars and Bottles 71
Making Things Out of Empty Ammunition Cartridge Cases 81
Alternate Uses for Ordinary Books 85

Chapter 5: Additional Uses for Duct Tape 87
Which Brand to Use? 87
Duct Tape Cordage 88
An All Duct Tape Bag 90
A Duct Tape Handgun Holster 93
A Duct Tape Knife Sheath 95
A Duct Tape Belt 96
Duct Tape Moccasins 97
Functional Duct Tape Arrow Fletching 99
Other Useful Makeshift Applications for Duct Tape 100

Chapter 6: Handy Little Makeshift Tricks 103
Attach Ropes to a Sheet or Tarp with No Grommets 103
Inflate Tubeless Tires 104
Neat Ways to Use Sections of Garden Hose 105
Drill Bit Depth Gauge 106
Drill Press Safety Tip 107
Practical Soldering Techniques 108
Repairs with a Natural Adhesive 108
Dovetailed Joints, Wedge Keys, and Plugs 108
Protect Wooden Ax Handles with Cord 111
Clamps and Vises from Sections of PVC Pipe 112
Handy Tricks for Joining Leather 113
Sharpen Your Dull Drill Bits 115
Expedient Guides, Stops, Jigs, Pushers, and Fences 118
Cover the Jaws of Your Vise 122
Circles for the Makeshift Hobbyist 122

Chapter 7: When You Can't Get to the Hardware Store 129
Making Your Own Nuts, Bolts, and Screws 130
Homemade Wood Screws 136
More Common Hardware Items That Are Easy to Make 140
When the Needed Parts are Missing or Broken 142
The More Tools You Have, the More You Can Do 145

Chapter 8: Makeshift True Stories 149
Makeshift Camping on Loop Creek 149
Changing a Flat Tire without a Jack Handle 151
Makeshift Repair to a Pair of Eyeglasses 152

Contents

Makeshift Windshield Wiper Repairs 152
Expedient Ammunition Hand-Loading 154
Makeshift Toy Repairs 155

Chapter 9: Useful Charts and Data for Makeshift Projects 157

Melting Temperatures of Common Metals 157
Fractions to Decimals 157
Useful Mathematical Formulas for Calculating Area and Volume 158
Traditional Units of Measurement 159
Handy Gauge References 160
Some Popular and Useful Engineering Formulas 164

Appendix: Useful Mechanical Principles for the Makeshifter 169

Mechanical Advantage 169
Gear Ratios 171
Belt-Driven Pulleys 176
Sprocket and Chain Drives 178
Dealing with Friction 178
Affixing Wheels to Shafts 179

Suggested Resources for Further Study 181

Foreword

To the uninitiated—that is, those millions of people who live their lives without thinking about their total dependence on modern conveniences and services—Jim Ballou's *More Makeshift Workshop Skills* and his earlier work, *Makeshift Workshop Skills for Survival and Self-Reliance*, might seem odd, even bizarre.

Why should anyone be interested in making their own tools, clothes, or appliances? Why would anyone be concerned about not having essential equipment and raw materials on hand to manufacture or repair things on their own? All you have to do is go to the nearest store and buy what you need whenever you need it . . . so the conventional wisdom goes.

What Jim refers to as the "makeshifter's mindset" is a way of thinking that goes hand in hand with the philosophy of self-reliance and survival. It comes down to the idea that you can do a lot with ordinary items that are often considered junk to those unenlightened souls who are utterly dependent on the rest of society for every aspect of their existence.

But a little resourcefulness goes a long way, and

for those of us open to new and unconventional ideas about making and repairing things ourselves, the rewards can be great indeed. It can mean the difference between doing without and suffering along, or having a much more comfortable and enjoyable existence. Sometimes, it can mean the difference between life and death.

As Jim says, *More Makeshift Workshop Skills* is essentially an expansion on the basic theme of his earlier work, *Makeshift Workshop Skills for Survival and Self-Reliance.*

That first book had a lot to do with applying basic skills in makeshift ways and the improvised tools, fixtures, and machines that can be produced with those skills. This included illustrated discussion about creating homemade glue, repairing a damaged cabinet or broken gunstock, and making items ranging from simple screwdrivers and other common hand tools to an improvised welding machine or your own anvil and forge. Jim showed how all of this can be accomplished with expedient materials found all around us today—materials, he notes, that are often tossed out as garbage. "You will start to see a lot of what we normally consider trash in a whole new light," he observes.

While I found *Makeshift Workshop Skills for Survival and Self-Reliance* very interesting and loaded with unique and useful information, Jim's new book is even more valuable in the sense that it ties together and expands upon the ideas and techniques in the earlier work, as well as introduces a slew of new concepts for making and repairing things we might need or want. Just some of the valuable skills you are about to learn include making a foot-powered treadle to operate a homemade grinding wheel or sewing machine; making a stove out of a used can; making moccasins, belts, sheaths, and holsters out of common duct tape; making your own nuts, bolts, and screws; and obtaining or making many types of tools with which to perform these operations.

Some people may see the ideas and products in Jim's books as useful only in an apocalyptic survival scenario—the proverbial "end of the world as we know it."

In reality, the instructions and concepts in *More Makeshift Workshop Skills* have great value for our everyday world—a world where, for millions of people on various occasions, the end of the world as we have known it has actually come about for extended periods. In these occurrences, people have been left to fend for themselves with few, if any, modern conveniences and essentials. Think about it: What would *you* do without access to commercial food suppliers, heating or cooling, electricity, and the like? More importantly, what *could* you do under such circumstances? Jim shows what you *can* do.

For those of us who have experienced natural and manmade disasters, poverty, war, rioting, or related emergencies, or for those who understand that such situations can occur at any time, this book is a godsend. It is packed with highly valuable and thought-provoking information that could make a critical difference in an emergency situation. But it is also a treasure trove of ideas even if there is no crisis. We can certainly utilize the knowledge it imparts to save a lot of money by making and repairing things ourselves. More importantly, we can use it to develop the resourceful mindset it takes to live a self-sufficient life.

—Jim Benson

For 16 years, Jim Benson served as the editor of the influential magazine *American Survival Guide*, the pioneering publication that helped usher in today's prepper and self-reliance movement. For the past 10 years, he was the publisher and editor of its online successor, *Modern Survival* magazine.

Preface

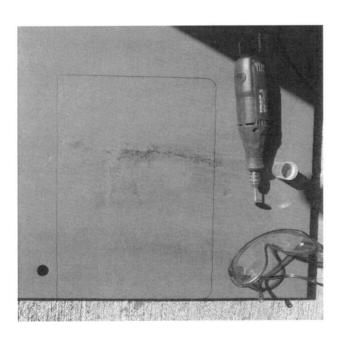

Everything a makeshift craftsman needs: safety gear, the right tool for the job, and raw material.

This book is essentially an expansion on the basic theme of my previous book, *Makeshift Workshop Skills for Survival and Self-Reliance*—employing expedient or alternative methods for fabricating and repairing all sorts of interesting things. The continuing flow of new ideas, combined with the popularity of the first book, begged for a second volume, so here we will be exploring even more intriguing makeshift concepts.

In my view, a makeshift approach to building and repairing things goes hand in hand with a kind of "possibilities philosophy." By seeking alternative ways of doing things, we tend to reject the limitations of convention, preferring instead to find other possibilities whenever situations call for them. And that is my goal with these books: to help readers develop a "makeshifter's" mindset, or at least to awaken in readers an existing knack for improvising and adapting.

If you don't already, after reading this book you will start to see a lot of what we normally consider trash in a whole new light. You'll think of how you might be able to use normally discarded items and contemplate what kinds of interesting things can be made out of them. And you will open your mind to some unconventional and intriguing ideas for the workshop.

Many, but not all, of the skills and techniques discussed in this book are completely conventional. In other words, a lot of common workshop tools and techniques lend themselves well to nonstandard projects. You might invent a whole new mechanical device but use age-old processes to build it. This won't always be the case, of course, but very often workshop projects and expedient repairs are accomplished most easily with proven methods.

Enjoy!

CHAPTER 1

More Improvised Homemade Tools

In the first volume of *Makeshift Workshop Skills for Survival and Self-Reliance* (hereafter referred to as *Makeshift I*), we explored a variety of ways to improvise miscellaneous hand tools. Here we will study even more examples.

THE SIMPLEST TOOL

Perhaps the simplest tool ever created by human hands is the digging stick. Primitive toolmakers discovered, presumably very early on, that a sharpened stick of hardwood, or a stick with a chisel-shaped edge abraded on one end, would do a much better job of digging up roots and excavating small holes in the ground than human fingernails were capable of (especially when the point was fire-hardened for durability). Sharpening a stick with rocks is not terribly difficult, and this same fundamental technology can be applied in a modern-day emergency survival situation to the fabrication of crude spears, garden fences, booby traps, fire pokers, and tent/teepee poles.

Using a sharpened stick as a tool may seem basic and obvious, but it is mentioned here merely

Digging with only a sharpened stick.

1

to remind you that such a simple device has a lot of practical merit under certain conditions and therefore should never be overlooked.

THE SPEARHEAD DAGGER DIGGING TROWEL

A wooden digging stick is certainly superior to human hands when it comes to excavating hard ground, but it cannot match the strength and durability of iron. If you need a decent digging tool for survival gardening or camp tasks, consider attaching a steel tip to your stick.

A large, dagger-shaped spearhead made of steel is indeed a versatile instrument. This primitive device can be used as a large knife for hacking through rope or tree limbs, for chopping firewood kindling, or as an expedient pry bar or digging trowel. In a situation of desperate survival, it could be used on the end of a pole as a spearhead for stabbing at large, dangerous animals for meat or as an effective close-range defensive weapon.

Such a spearhead-shaped instrument is surprisingly simple to fabricate, either by hammer-forging over an anvil or grinding its shape out of a long, rigid piece of strap iron, a big flat bastard file, a flattened end on a section of rebar, or from almost any long piece of steel flat stock that is hefty enough for the task. It need not be fancy; it only has to be sharply pointed at the tip or have sharp cutting edges, sturdy enough for the task at hand, and well secured to whatever tough material is used as a handle. To attach the steel head to its handle, fit it into a slot cut into the business end of the shaft and bind it tightly with strong cord, heavy wire, or wet rawhide. (Why wet? Because it will stretch slightly when applied that way, and when it dries it will shrink and get tighter than you could pull by hand.)

A spear shaft need not necessarily be a wooden pole, although a straight, sturdy shaft of hardwood is usually a practical choice, being relatively lightweight (compared with a steel pipe for example), fairly tough, durable, and readily available in nature. But any straight, rigid pole or pipe, whether of steel, aluminum, or plastic, could serve the same purpose. With any of these alternate materials, consider wrapping some tape around the shaft for a more secure and comfortable gripping surface. The head might even be secured with tight wrappings of duct tape in a pinch.

Interchangeable survival tools, top to bottom: iron-tipped spear, Indian-style dagger, and homemade garden trowel.

Digging a hole in the ground with a steel spearhead.

THE ANCIENT ADZE

Adzes have been around for a very long time—since the Stone Age, in fact. This ancient tool doesn't seem to garner as much attention in our modern society as such similar hand tools as axes or hatchets, even though an adze can be a very practical tool for certain chores.

For those not familiar with the tool, an adze is somewhat similar to an ax except that its bit extends crosswise from its handle, as opposed to vertically like an ax bit. A garden hoe is a similarly configured type of tool. Adzes are useful for removing bark from logs, trimming and notching tree logs in log construction, shaping squared timbers or planks, converting round poles or tree trunks into flat boards the primitive way, channeling out a large tree log for making a dugout boat, scraping animal hides, or for general shaping of wood by hand.

It is truly fascinating to watch craftsmen who are skilled with an adze as they work. In a NOVA documentary on the modern construction of an ancient Egyptian pharaoh's ship, traditional Egyptian craftsmen are shown helping shape the large hardwood planks for the skin of the vessel with their adzes, swinging the sharp bits with impressive precision as they trim the wood within inches of their bare feet.

A simple adze configuration is not terribly difficult to create. Suitable makeshift materials include tree branches, tough roots, deer and elk antlers, hip bones of large mammals, or even iron, as long as the material is sturdy enough and provides the basic L shape. On several occasions, I have attached homemade hide scraper blades to L-shaped wooden handles to form a kind of adze. A heavy tree branch with a slightly smaller limb branching off at an angle can often be adapted as a handle to fit a steel blade to create an adze. The branching limb provides a supporting arm to which the blade can be lashed or otherwise secured. Similarly, a heavy piece of antler can serve as a primitive adze handle.

The cutting edge of a homemade primitive-style adze.

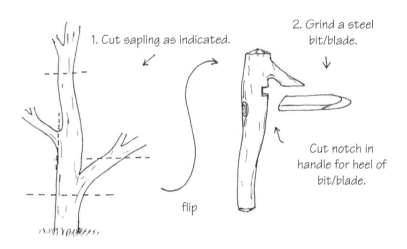

1. Cut sapling as indicated.

2. Grind a steel bit/blade.

Cut notch in handle for heel of bit/blade.

flip

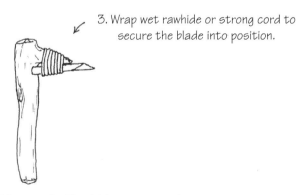

3. Wrap wet rawhide or strong cord to secure the blade into position.

Making a primitive hide scraper adze.

Adze at left is homemade with a piece of file for its bit, secured with rawhide. At right is a modern manufactured adze.

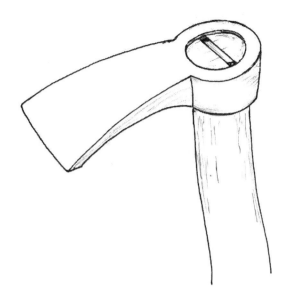

Contemporary system for attaching the adze's handle.

An adze blade (or bit) can be almost any sharpened wedge-shaped piece of steel, as long as its dimensions are proportional to the handle to which it will be fitted and secured. A usable chunk of steel can be obtained from a heavy bastard file by tightening the file in a large vise with the needed section extending beyond the jaws and, with a hard strike from a heavy hammer, snapping the piece off. (Wear safety glasses.)

Form the bevel on the bit's edge at the grinding wheel or with files before securing it to the handle. An adze bit used for scraping animal hides should have a rounded profile, with no sharp corners that could rip holes in the hide. A bit for shaping lumber will typically have a straighter cutting edge, much like the edge of a butt chisel.

An adze head can be secured to its handle in a number of ways. One basic method that was employed routinely in the Stone Age (when bits were of stone) and even well into the early Iron Age is to use cord or rawhide to haft a mostly flat, rectangular piece of steel, such as a section broken off a heavy flat bastard file, to a piece of wood. Notch or chisel the wooden handle so it conforms to the bit for a snug fit.

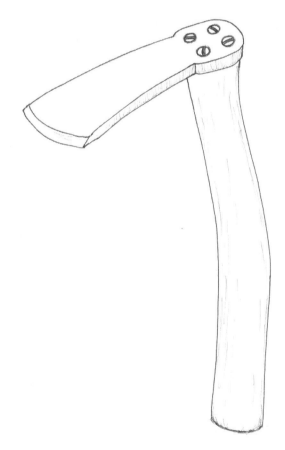

Adze head screwed to its handle.

The most common type of adze head today has an eye through which the top of the handle fits and is held fast with a tapered wedge driven into the wood, exactly as most modern axes, hatchets, mauls, and tomahawks are configured. This may be the most reliable system for attaching the head to the handle.

Another approach would be to drill several holes through a flat adze blade and attach it with screws to the top of the wooden handle. This would be a simple and convenient alternative for a light-duty tool, if not necessarily the most secure way to attach an adze bit to its handle.

Another expedient possibility for creating an adze is to grind or forge the bit on one end of a large steel corner bracket. The 90-degree bend in the bracket would make attaching it to a handle especially convenient, either by binding with cord or rawhide, attaching with screws or bolts, or some

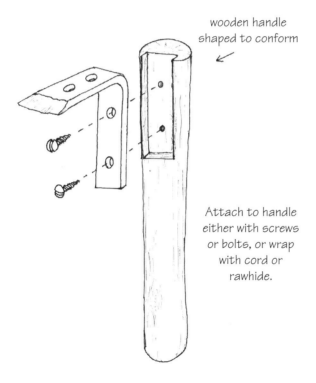

wooden handle shaped to conform

Attach to handle either with screws or bolts, or wrap with cord or rawhide.

Adze bit forged from corner bracket.

combination of methods for joining them together. An adze bit really should have some weight to it, so your corner bracket should be of sufficient size and thickness (say, 1/4-inch thick) for the work it will perform. An ordinary bookshelf bracket might work if it is the only choice available, but it might only be practical for light-duty work.

THE ESSENTIAL AWL

The awl is another one of the early tools used by primitive people, when they clothed themselves primarily with animal skins. Today, the art of hand-stitching leather invariably involves the use of a stitching awl, which in its most basic form is nothing more than a pointed instrument that pierces the leather to create the holes that allow a needle and thread to pass through. But awls and such similar tools as scribes and picks can be used for other purposes as well, such as scratching lines in metal or other materials, serving as a center punch, piercing or chipping ice, stabbing holes in a potato before baking to allow steam to escape, splicing rope, starting screw holes in wood, or even as a substitute for a small drill bit for punching holes in soft wood, among who knows how many other applications.

This is a very easy tool to manufacture, especially with the help of a bench grinder, bastard file, honing stone, or even a belt sander. The objective is to simply shape a tapered point onto one end of a thin metal rod.

People of primitive societies used natural materials such as stones, bones, or even porcupine quills for their awls, because those were the materials they had to work with. Steel is the preferred material for this purpose today.

You can achieve the tapered configuration with steel in several ways. One way is to heat the metal to a glowing red or orange with either a torch or forge (or possibly even in an open campfire) and then draw out (i.e., thin down with hammer blows) the end of the rod into a pointed taper. This should be easy for anyone who has experience working with hot metal.

Another easy way to achieve the same basic result, as was noted in *Makeshift I*, is called stock removal, which simply entails grinding or filing down the end of the rod to the desired point. Think

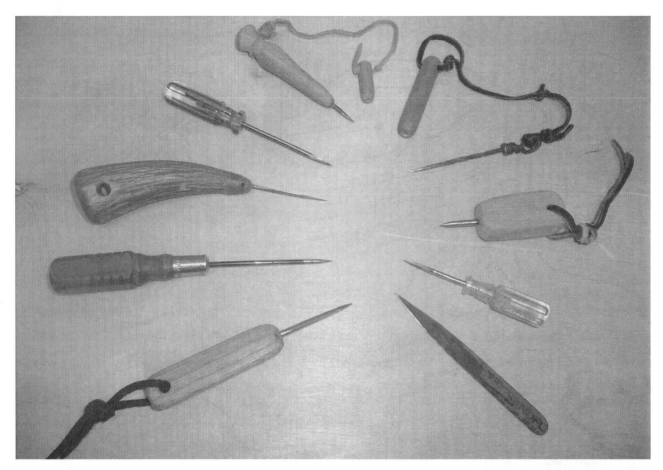

Miscellaneous homemade awls.

of this approach as kind of like sharpening a pencil—literally cutting a point onto the end of a rod. It is called stock removal because the unwanted material is removed from the workpiece (in this case ground or filed away) to obtain the desired shape, as opposed to the material-displacement process that occurs when drawing out the material with hot-forming/forging.

You can create functional awls out of several kinds of common things. I've made them out of nails, slivers of sheet metal, small drill bits, thin hacksaw blades, and even large sewing needles traditionally used in sail rigging. Just about any piece of steel of the appropriate size can serve as suitable raw material for this tool.

Excellent awls for leather stitching can be made very easily from small screwdrivers. A screwdriver already has a shaft set into a perfect handle, so it lends itself very well as an awl. Simply grind the shaft to a gradually tapered point using a bench

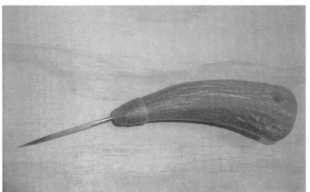

Here a large sewing needle is set into a piece of cow horn with epoxy to create an awl for leather.

grinder or files. I have made several awls this way, and they appear to be as good in every way as the best awls you can buy.

Keep a can or jar of water somewhere near the grinding wheel for periodically dipping the workpiece to prevent it from overheating. (Some craftsmen prefer to keep the wheel itself wet while

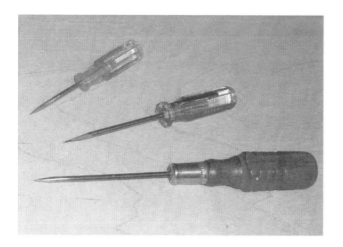

Awls made out of screwdrivers.

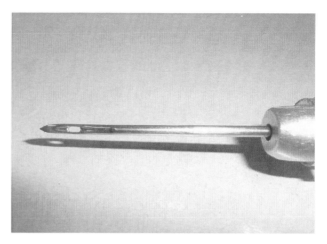

Close-up of the eye near the tip on a factory-made sewing awl.

they grind.) If you don't keep the work adequately cool (and this is especially tricky near the thin point), the metal will quickly overheat and be destroyed. The overheating will be evident when the steel starts turning dark colors. Dip the workpiece in water every few seconds, and perform the grinding slowly, without applying much pressure against the fast-spinning grinding wheel.

A three-cornered tapered shaft is generally considered the best awl configuration for poking holes through leather. These seem to pierce the material more easily than a simple tapered cylindrical rod. This triangular shape is fairly easy to achieve by careful grinding. I even make some of my homemade awls with a squared tapered shaft, which still seems to work better than a round-shafted awl for leatherwork. (For piercing materials like cotton canvas, I suspect a rounded shaft would be preferable; it would cause the least amount of damage to the natural fibers in the material.)

Once the grinding stage is completed, the awl's tip—the flat surfaces along the triangular taper all the way to the point—can be smoothed up with either an oilstone or fine-grit sandpaper to clean up as many of the grind marks as possible. You might even want to polish the surface—simply rubbing the surface over a scrap of rough leather can do wonders. This will make the tool easier to use by minimizing friction, especially when stitching tough cowhide.

Another variation of the awl, sometimes referred to as a sewing awl, has an eye near the point to allow thread to be drawn through the stitch holes while lock stitching. The awl looks something like a large needle with a handle.

A sewing awl can be fabricated from a screwdriver as well. If you are making one from a screwdriver with a handle that isn't easily removed without sawing or grinding it off, and you want to heat the metal to flatten it before drilling the hole for the eye, first apply a heat-block paste to the base of the rod where it sets into the handle to prevent burning or melting the handle. (Brownells sells a product called Heat Stop Heat Control Paste.) Heat the steel rod in the area for the eye with the flame from a small propane torch until it glows orange, while avoiding burning or melting the handle. Then, quickly move the piece to the anvil and hammer the rod somewhat flat with a few moderate blows. One of the keys to success is to apply the heat to only a limited area and for only a brief period of time on the rod, since you won't need to flatten it paper thin. You only need a small, flat surface to drill into.

If you don't happen to have a blacksmith anvil to hammer on, the small anvil surface on most bench vises or any thick, flat bar of steel will usually do. It might be easier for some people to simply grind an area flat on the rod where you will drill the hole, but one advantage to hammering out a flat area is that you can obtain a wider spot that is better for drilling than you would by simply grinding it flat on both sides. Either way, you'll want that part of the rod flattened just enough to make it easier to drill the eyehole.

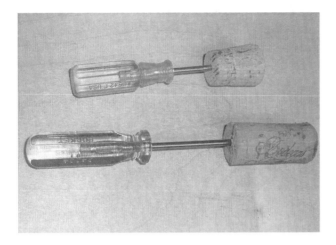

Two awls shown here with their handy cork tip protectors.

Using a homemade pricking wheel to mark wet leather for stitch holes.

Once a small hole is drilled through the awl, it can be elongated if desired, like the eye of a sewing needle, in one of two easy ways. The first is to use tiny round needle files, if the hole is large enough to accommodate them. The other (easier) way to elongate an eye is to drill the round hole of slightly larger diameter than you want the final diameter to be, and then simply hammer both sides of the hole's circumference just enough to make the hole narrower and longer. I've used this trick when making the eyes in homemade sewing needles as well.

In any case, you might find it easier to drill the eye *before* tapering the point to ensure there will be enough material for drilling the hole, which can actually be the trickiest part of the whole project. After the eye is the way it needs to be, the tapered point can then be ground or filed into shape as described above.

Pointed instruments like awls, needles, and picks generally warrant some type of tip protector, and the long cylindrical stoppers from wine bottles are excellent for this. I discovered that the synthetic variety serves this task even better than the traditional cork stoppers do, being more rubbery, durable, and less apt to chip or soften if they get wet, as cork stoppers will.

A PRICKING WHEEL FOR LEATHER

While we're on the topic of making our own leather tools, here is one more that can be a particularly handy little device for marking evenly spaced stitch intervals in the surface of the leather, called a pricking wheel. The basic tool somewhat resembles a tiny boot spur rowel, and it works by rolling its toothed wheel along the stitch line, causing the points of the teeth to press evenly spaced impressions into the hide. This provides a leather worker with consistent spacing for his stitch holes, which he can then punch more accurately with that awl he made after reading the previous section.

A pricking wheel is easy to fabricate from an appropriately sized steel washer. (I find 1-inch-diameter washers to be the perfect size for my wheels.) A large, flat fender washer is not only a perfectly shaped disk of the ideal outside diameter and thickness, but it also already has a hole through its center for whatever kind of pin or screw you use for the axle. All you have to do is mark and then cut the star points or teeth around the circumference of the wheel with a small hacksaw, which I found to be much easier than I had expected.

I carefully measured and marked the pattern on paper for my first homemade pricking wheel, then cut out the pattern with scissors and glued it onto

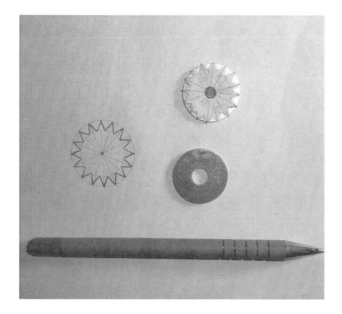

Draw a pattern on paper, cut it out, and glue it to the side of a washer before sawing.

Saw out the pointed teeth all the way around the washer while it's held in a vise.

Finished star-shaped wheel with the small hacksaw used to cut the teeth.

The first pricking wheel tool I made.

the side of the washer before sawing the metal with a small hacksaw. Once I had my star-shaped wheel cut out, it was then a simple matter to mount it onto a wooden handle with a screw and smaller washer such that it created a functional tool.

The pricking wheels available through leather supply catalogs normally sport a metal head, carriage, or housing for the little wheel, but you can make most of that part out of hardwood (as I did) and it will work just fine.

The paper pattern approach worked well, but it

was perhaps more trouble than necessary. I learned later, during my second pricking wheel project, that it is not terribly difficult to estimate the spacing of the pointed teeth and draw them freehand directly onto the washer with a fine-point felt marker.

I wanted my second wheel to space the impressions in the leather slightly farther apart, so I cut the points accordingly on that washer. I also decided to design a different handle to house the wheel, merely as an experiment in variety. For this one I used a section of common hardwood dowel for

The parts and tools used to create the second pricking wheel.

The teeth on this washer are marked freehand with a felt-tipped marker. No pattern was used.

the handle and set the wheel into a slot cut into one end. The center pin for the wheel, or its axle, is a steel pin I found in my junk drawer that conveniently already had a hole near its end, which perfectly accommodated a modified nail to hold the wheel in place.

Although both of my star-shaped wheels appear rather crude up close, in my opinion, I was surprised how well they actually track fairly evenly spaced impressions in the surface of the leather. Absolute perfection is not essential when pressing indentations into leather anyway—you merely want the points on your wheel to be dimensionally as even as you can make them.

The wheel should be mounted to the handle so it can turn freely with a minimum of friction, but also with a minimum of wobble in order to track the most consistent stitch line in the leather. If your wheel exhibits excessive side-to-side play, you might be able to shim it on one side or the other with a small washer, as I did with my second pricking wheel.

Close-up view showing how the wheel of the second tool is held in the handle. I later added a washer on one side to eliminate wobble.

Side view of second tool.

Using the second pricking wheel to form impressions in leather.

THE USEFUL CROOKED KNIFE

A crooked knife is a handy tool that makes it easier to carve out the concave depressions in wooden spoons, ladles, dishes, ashtrays, noggins, cups, and bowls than either flat or straight-bladed knives or the typical gouge chisels used a lot in woodcarving. The basic configuration of the tool has a bent blade—actually curled upward, most often with a J-shaped hook. These knives vary to some extent in shape and style, but they all have the characteristic curved blade.

The curved hoof knives used by farriers can be used as crooked knives. They are slightly similar in design, though usually with a tighter curve or hook near the end of their blades. You can also buy crooked knives from a number of commercial sources (as well as scorps and inshaves—two more woodworking tools used in carving bowls and shaping wood in similar ways), but they aren't as widely available as more conventional straight-bladed knives. Besides, it is much more fun to make your own. It might take some experimentation to obtain the desired curve and edge, but it can be done.

Three variations of homemade crooked knives.

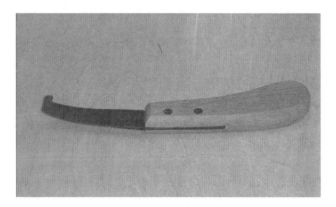

An example of a factory-made hoof knife.

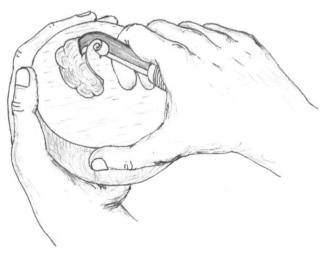

Scooping out the inside of a bowl with a crooked knife.

A crooked knife can be made from a straight-bladed knife by heating and bending the area of the blade for the crook, and then rehardening (and ultimately retempering) the steel such that it will continue to hold an edge. This works best with a narrow blade. You would normally want to perform any heating operations on a blade *before* adding the handle, or you can remove any existing handle first.

Another excellent material for making a crooked knife is a small flat file. This is good, hard steel that will hold an edge well. Simply grind the teeth off, grind a bevel on one side to create a cutting edge, heat it with a small torch until it is glowing red, and bend where desired using pliers. Once it is shaped to your liking, you can then use whatever heat-tempering process you want to restore some of the hardness and finish up by fashioning any sort of handle you like.

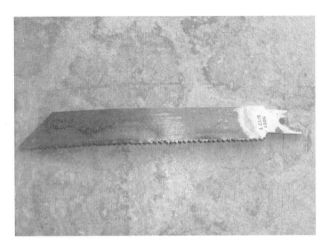

Discarded reciprocating saw blade before being made into a crooked knife.

Heating the reciprocating saw blade with a torch flame to facilitate bending.

The saw blade after being bent into a crooked knife blade.

Homemade crooked knife with wooden handle attached.

A crooked knife made from a flat file, with a piece of antler for a handle.

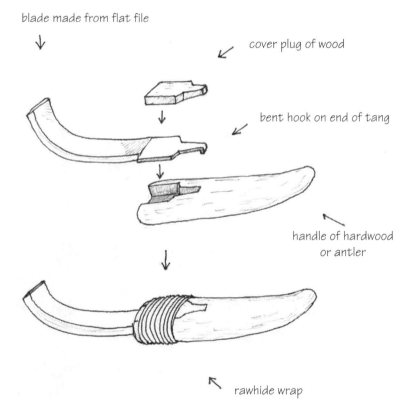

blade made from flat file

cover plug of wood

bent hook on end of tang

handle of hardwood or antler

rawhide wrap

The Northern Indian method for attaching a crooked knife blade to its handle.

One of the secrets I discovered to making the most functional crooked knife design is to keep the blade relatively short. I have had a tendency to make my blades too long, and they are more awkward to use in woodcarving. A crooked knife blade longer than about 1 1/2 to 2 inches now seems impractical to me, after having tested various lengths.

A good article titled "Scrap Metal Tools" in *Backwoodsman* magazine (Jan./Feb. 2009, Volume 30, No. 1) describes how author Rodney Terry makes his own crooked knives out of worn-out Sawz-All blades. He grinds away the dull saw teeth and shapes the metal the way he wants it, then heats it with a small gas torch to a glowing red and forms the desired curve in the blade before quenching only about 3/8-inch depth along the edge. In this way, Terry explains, he is able to produce a hardened cutting edge on the thin steel while maintaining the softer, mostly annealed state in the rest of the blade that isn't quenched. This keeps it from being too brittle.

Just as with conventionally styled knives, there are several possibilities for attaching the handle to a crooked knife. You could cross-pin or rivet the tang of the blade to one solid handle piece, or you could rivet handle slabs made of antler, wood, or bone to both sides of a tang. Alternatively, you can set the tang into a hole in the end of a one-piece handle and secure it in place with epoxy.

A blade-to-handle attachment method for crooked knives common among Northern Indians entails inletting the tang into the side of the handle piece and then fitting a filler plug into the space over it before tightly wrapping that section of the handle with cord or rawhide to hold it all together. This method is particularly practical with blades made from traditional metal files, as their narrow tangs can be heated and bent into an L-shaped hook near their end and set into a smaller, deeper hole in the corresponding end of the cutout space in the side of the handle. The bent part acts as a kind of catch or anchor to lock the blade more securely against being pulled out of the handle after everything is wrapped together with a strip of rawhide or twine.

A PVC PIPE BUCKSAW

PVC pipe products are available in virtually every hardware store, and just a few basic components are all you will need to make a small but very functional bucksaw frame. I got the inspiration for this project from my editor, who offered the suggestion about using PVC pipe after considering the wood-frame bucksaw featured in *Makeshift I*. I didn't expect that a plastic saw frame would be rigid enough for this purpose until I built an example. To my surprise, the PVC pipe serves this task quite well.

Everything you need to assemble your own bucksaw (other than the tools you will use, of course) can be purchased new for under $10.

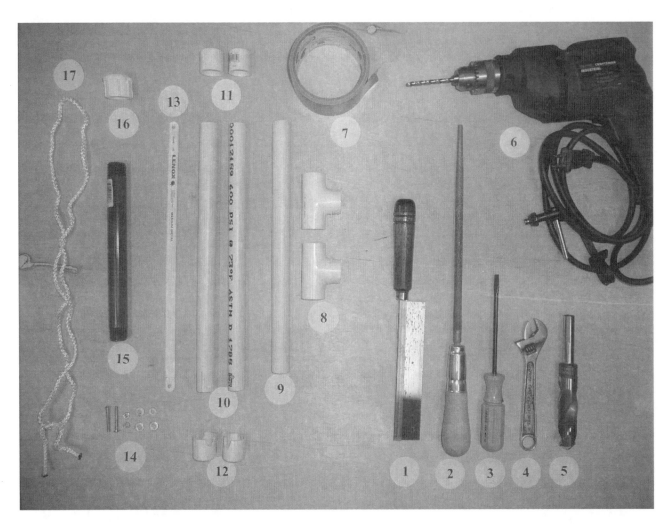

Everything you need to assemble a PVC-frame bucksaw: 1) lightweight saw for cutting the plastic pipe, 2) rattail file, 3) screwdriver, if using screws, 4) wrench for turning nuts—not necessary if you use wing nuts or screws instead of bolts, 5) 7/8-inch-diameter drill bit for boring out the T sections, or you could use the rattail file, 6) drill, 7) duct tape, 8) 1/2-inch PVC T sections, 9) 1/2-inch PVC pipe section to serve as spreader bar, 10) 1/2-inch PVC pipe handle sections, 11) end caps for top of handles, 12) end caps for handle bottoms (optional), 13) saw blade, 14) cross bolts, washers, and nuts, 15) PVC pipe tourniquet bar, 16) end cap for tourniquet bar (optional), and 17) tension cord.

Depending on where you shop, all the PVC products for this project should together cost less than $4. The saw blade, depending on what kind you choose, will likely cost anywhere from $1.50 to $3. The two machine screws, nuts, and washers, if you have to buy them, shouldn't cost much more than a dollar for all. The only other materials required are a few short strips of duct tape and a 2-foot length of bootlace or clothesline.

The bucksaw is very simple in concept. Two vertical sections serve both as handles and mounts for the blade. A horizontal bar, or spreader bar, of slightly shorter length than the length of the blade fits between the two handles at the desired height, serving to brace the frame at that point. The handles essentially pivot over the ends of this horizontal bar (i.e., drawing the tops of the handles inward pivots their bottom ends outward where they attach to the blade). A strong cord looped over the tops of the handles and twisted up tight with a small tourniquet bar (in this case, a short section of PVC pipe) provides the tension that keeps the whole frame and blade rigid for use.

The principle is exactly the same when using PVC pipe as when using wood. The horizontal piece is nothing more than a section of the pipe roughly an inch shorter than the length of the saw blade, and it is secured in position at both ends by the T fittings that slide over the handle pieces (see photos).

Unfortunately, the T fittings sold for 1/2-inch plastic pipe are not designed such that a pipe can slide all the way through, as would be desired for fitting over the handle pieces. The inside diameter steps down in their middle section. You can buy larger T fittings, but I found that the next size larger actually fits too loosely over the 1/2-inch pipe. My solution to this was to simply open up the inside diameter of the hole through the 1/2-inch T fitting so that a section of pipe will slide all the way through it.

The easiest way I could find to bore out the hole through the T fitting was to drill through it with my drill press and a twist bit of 7/8-inch diameter. I wouldn't recommend using a flat spade bit to open up the existing hole inside any plastic tube or pipe, because it most likely won't follow the smaller hole as evenly as will a common twist bit, and it will have more of a tendency to grab and mangle the inside surface of the pipe.

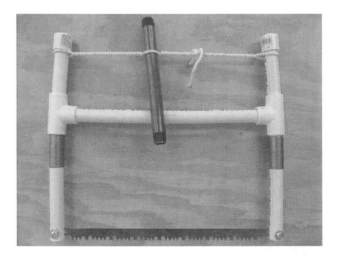

PVC-frame bucksaw with bow saw blade mounted for cutting branches.

Drilling through the center of the T fitting with 7/8-inch bit so it will slide over the handle piece.

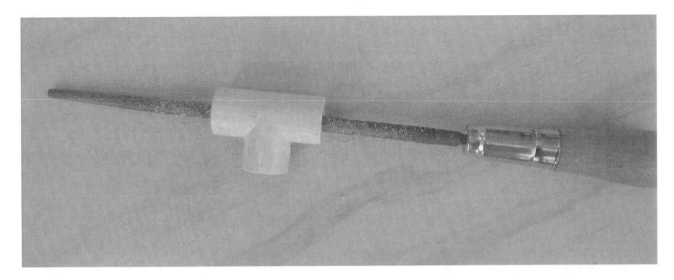

Opening up the center of the T with a rattail file instead of using the drill press and 7/8-inch bit.

Not everyone will have access to a drill press, but I discovered that the same goal is achievable (although much more slowly) by hand using a rattail file. No matter which method you use, the goal is to make sure the pipe sections used for the handle pieces can slide all the way through the T fittings.

Next, cut a slot into the bottom end of each handle piece to accept the saw blade, and drill holes

perpendicular to these slots for the machine screws or bolts that will secure the blade to the frame. PVC plastic is relatively soft and easy to cut, and I cut my slots with a coping saw. I then drilled the holes for the 1/4-inch screws perpendicular to the slots such that the screws would line up with the holes in the saw blade at each end.

Now, slide the T fittings over the handle

Cut a slot into the bottom ends of the handle pieces to accept the saw blade, and drill a hole for the cross bolt that secures the blade in position.

sections to the desired position for the horizontal crossbar. I prefer having the crossbar at anywhere from about two-thirds to three-quarters of the way up on the handles, which gives a reasonably deep cutting throat for the blade, yet it's still centered enough to keep the frame rigid. Hold the T fittings firmly in position where they sit on the handle with a few strips of duct tape.

My first prototype of this saw had longer handles than needed, and I discovered that shortening the handles an inch or so made a slight improvement in the rigidity of the frame. The handle pieces should be capped at the top so the tourniquet cord won't slide off the ends of the pipes. It is not necessary to customize caps for the bottoms of the handle pieces where the saw blade mounts, but you might prefer the way it looks, and it probably adds a degree of strength at those ends.

While I preferred using 1/4-inch-diameter carriage bolts to secure the blades to the wooden handles of my previous bucksaw frames, 1/4-inch machine screws seem more appropriate with PVC. They can be tightened with hex or wing nuts over flat washers. In a pinch, sections of nails of the correct diameter might serve this purpose, as the

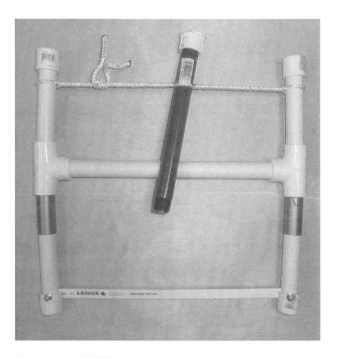

The second PVC bucksaw prototype with shorter handles, mounted with a hacksaw blade. The first prototype (not pictured) had slightly longer handles.

tension provided by the twisted cord will help hold them in place.

A lightweight bucksaw such as described here is economical and functional, fun to build, and quick and easy to assemble for use in the woods or garden, and then just as easy to disassemble for storage in a backpack. The whole works will fit into a piece of 3-inch-diameter PVC pipe (or even a short section of 4-inch with space to spare). You might want to keep a few extra blades in the kit with their teeth protected by a folded strip of thick cardboard held in place with a couple wraps of the tourniquet cord. The cross bolts or screws, nuts, and washers can be stored in a small bag or container in the kit (e.g., 35mm film canister) to keep them together.

MAKING A SAW BLADE FROM SCRATCH

In *Makeshift I*, we explored methods of fabricating a saw blade that entailed using another saw to cut the teeth in a bar of steel. Since conducting those experiments, I've become somewhat obsessed with the idea of creating a functional saw blade *without* the help of another saw or without even a file for cutting the teeth. My thinking on this is that if you already have a saw blade to cut the teeth for the new saw blade, then chances are you shouldn't really need the crude and generally inferior homemade saw all that much, because you'd already have a better one. It just seems like it defeats the whole purpose to need a saw to make a saw. I wanted to figure out how to create a usable saw blade some other way.

My initial experiments produced some almost completely ineffective prototypes. In one of my earlier efforts many years ago, I somehow found the notion to take a strong, thin, braided synthetic cord and glue fine sand to its surface in order to create a kind of sandpaper-like "blade" that I envisioned functioning something like a survival wire saw. Despite several attempts to create this kind of string saw, I was never able to produce a tool capable of cutting through a medium-sized tree branch.

First of all, I found it very difficult to glue an even coating of sand onto the cord—the sand tended to stick to the string in clumps, regardless of the type of glue or gluing methods I used. Also, it only took a few passes over the branch before the glued-on sand was almost completely worn off the cord. The string itself also did not hold up well to this kind of friction, and after limited rubbing over the wood, it started to fray badly and would eventually break.

This experiment, though it seemed like a reasonable idea at first, ultimately proved to be a total disaster in terms of function. I found that it simply would not even begin to cut wood (or probably anything harder than hot butter, I would guess). Okay, I admit that in hindsight, this idea does seem obviously impractical, but I had to try it for myself to find out, and that's usually the way I learn what *not* to do.

A more recent homemade saw blade experiment—though still a long way from being perfected, as we shall see—resulted in a blade that is in fact capable of cutting wood. Those who have read *Makeshift I* will remember my saw blades made from bars of mild steel, with their sharp teeth cut to shape using a hacksaw. Those actually turned out to be more effective for cutting wood than I had anticipated. But again, this time I wanted to get away from having to use another saw to make a usable saw blade.

It seemed that the logical next approach in this pursuit was to forge the saw—to somehow form the teeth in a bar of malleable heated steel. My first thought was to drive the edge of a sharp chisel into the heated metal at intervals along the experimental saw's cutting edge to create narrow,

teeth-like tines. The whole idea here was that a person could easily hammer-forge the chisel he needed to forge the saw teeth, so this methodology would perfectly fit the make-it-from-scratch concept I was hoping to achieve.

I tried this method first using a flat file for the saw blade blank, thinking that the hard file steel would produce a better cutting tool. However, it became apparent fairly quickly that the file didn't lend itself very well to this process, or at least not with my methods. The necessary forge heating, cooling, and reheating of the relatively thin, high-carbon file steel eventually took its toll on the blank, and pretty soon I started to notice distortion and cracking. Also, driving the edge of the chisel into the edge of the blank to form the teeth tended to deform the edge without producing the kind of raised, sharp saw teeth I envisioned, and I was struggling to maintain any degree of consistency with the size and shape of the resulting teeth. I ended up with a somewhat flat slab of hard, brittle steel having a more or less jagged edge that, while capable of sawing through wood given a lot of sweat and perseverance, was a far cry from what I had in mind.

Now it was back to the drawing board, but this time with a narrower flat bar of softer mild steel (1/2-inch wide by 1/8-inch thick) for my new blank. To form the teeth, I decided to start the indentation lines in the edge while the steel was still cold and

Using a hammer and chisel to form saw teeth on a heated blank of steel.

A very crude first prototype of a hand-forged saw blade. It was not very efficient at all.

Using hammer and chisel (ground out of an old file) to cut saw teeth into the edge of a cold piece of mild steel.

There was no need to heat the mild steel in the forge for this project. It worked essentially the same way as when I raised burrs in the face of a flat bar of mild steel with a pointed punch and hammer to create a wood rasp, as I explained in detail in *Makeshift I*.

I also discovered about halfway into the teeth-forming process that it was easy to alternate the angular direction of my chisel's edge to form offset teeth leaning to one side and then the other. This results in a blade that makes a wider cut than the thickness of the blade's body, which provides better clearance and less binding and thus an easier cut.

easy to handle. The idea was to give myself a quick reference for chisel placement later, when the metal would be glowing hot and time would be critical.

However, almost as soon as I began driving the sharp chisel into the edge of the cold saw blank, I discovered that this whole process of separating teeth-like tines was easy enough without even heating the material. I merely secured the blank firmly in the jaws of my bench vise and began using the hammer and chisel freehand to wedge the steel apart at about 1/8-inch intervals to create the teeth.

Once I got into the swing of it, with only that small amount of practice I discovered that, using a sharp cold chisel, only about one or two brisk hammer blows per notch on each side of a tooth were all that was necessary, and the entire saw blade could be created in a short amount of time—maybe five or ten minutes per every 12 inches of blade.

This new saw blade was made to the same dimensions as the bucksaw I had created for *Makeshift I*, so I mounted it to that hardwood frame and proceeded to give it a performance test.

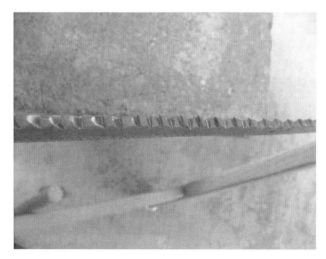

Close-ups of hand-chiseled saw teeth in the experimental blade. Note how they are offset from center for better sawing action.

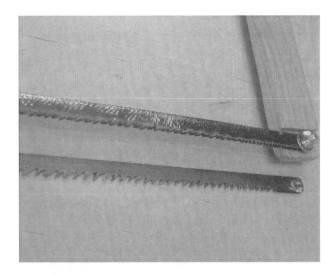

Comparing the teeth on two homemade saw blades; one with its teeth sawn (bottom), the other with teeth chiseled (top).

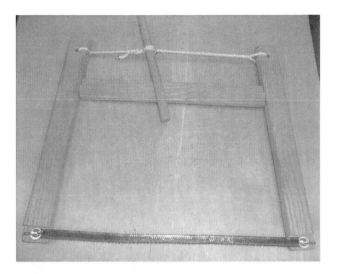

Homemade bucksaw frame with new homemade saw blade mounted.

I have to say that, even though this crude blade wasn't perfectly straight after all the hammering to form the teeth—and it looks to be nearly impossible to straighten this type of blade back out once the teeth are made (without smashing or dulling them, anyway)—I was quite impressed with how well it actually performs. Its steel is pretty soft, but its teeth are nevertheless quite sharp. I had no trouble at all sawing through a 3-inch-diameter tree branch. This type of saw is very easy to fabricate, even without the help of another saw, yet it obviously cuts wood without a struggle. My goal was achieved!

HOMEMADE SCREWDRIVERS

I won't pretend that any of the screwdrivers I have ever made were any better (or even as good, in most cases) as regular store-bought screwdrivers, but any of them will turn a screw with the corresponding slot size under normal circumstances.

One of the biggest problems with homemade screwdrivers in many instances is that they're too soft. Mild steel is easy to cut and shape—very easy to make a screwdriver out of, but it won't sustain very much torque before it becomes deformed. Hard tool steel, on the other hand, can be difficult to cut with a file, and it's typically more expensive and harder to find a common source for it. Hard steel can be annealed to soften it for working on, and then rehardened in the final stages. If the material

Homemade saw blade easily cuts through wood.

selected were much harder than tool steel, as is a file, it might actually be prone to fracture under the stress of heavy torque.

Flat-tipped screwdrivers are commonly known as standard, flathead, or slotted (different sources identify them in different ways). No matter what you call them, they are the easiest tool to make because of their simple shape. They can be quickly fabricated by heating and hammering the tip to the flat shape on an anvil, or by grinding out of larger material at the grinding wheel using the stock-removal method.

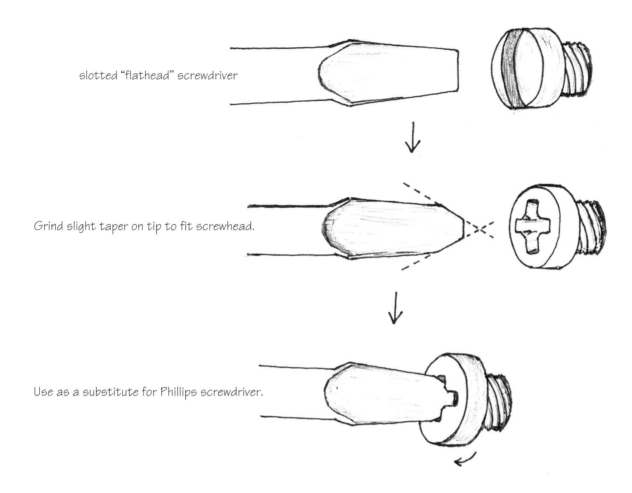

slotted "flathead" screwdriver

Grind slight taper on tip to fit screwhead.

Use as a substitute for Phillips screwdriver.

Makeshift adaptation of a screwdriver.

Phillips tips are more intricate. Facing the tip of the Phillips screwdriver, one sees a + shape. A side view shows the tapered profile of the tip. Creating this configuration from a solid piece of steel presents some challenges. I attempted to shape the end of a steel bar into a Phillips tip using small triangular files, but I came to the conclusion that this awkward pursuit will likely be a waste of time for most readers.

A simplified substitute for a Phillips screwdriver could merely be a slotted screwdriver with a modified tip that tapers to fit either of the two crisscrossing slots in a Phillips screw head. This is certainly expedient and, while not exactly the best kind of tool for turning a screw with a Phillips head, it will normally work much better in a pinch than would the point of your pocket knife.

HOMEMADE SCISSORS

I've been intrigued with the idea of making my own scissors ever since I read about how to do it in Alexander Weygers' book, *The Complete Modern Blacksmith*. Scissors, or shears, are incredibly versatile. They are essential tools for the shop, kitchen, or camp in my view, as they are almost indispensable for cleanly cutting sandpaper, plastic sheet, cardboard, loose thread or cord, thin leather, rubber, plant stems, small tree branches, twigs, and many other materials.

My own research on the Internet and reading numerous how-to books turned up surprisingly little information about how to fabricate steel scissors. Weygers does provide specific instructions on how to create several types of shears in his book, but of course I initially elected to go about it in a completely different way.

Weygers describes using the stock-removal method to obtain the basic shape of both halves of the shears—grinding or hacksawing the pieces out of 3/16-inch-thick steel from either an old car bumper or a section of plow disk. He describes making a cardboard pattern for each half, using one as a pattern for the other to get equal dimensions for both, and then pinning the two together with a thumbtack to test their design before scribing their shapes on the steel. He recommends hollow-grinding the scissor blades and then heat-treating them in the latter stages of production.

I wanted to try hammer-forging my scissor parts out of rebar stock. I had some expectation that common rebar would be a suitable material for general-purpose cutting tools after watching Jason Hawk's *Making Do, Volume One* DVD, available from Paladin Press, wherein he demonstrates his methods for producing decent hand-forged knives out of rebar.

I am mindful that a major factor in determining how well the scissor blades turn out will be the specific heat-treatment process applied. Hawk obviously has this down to a pretty good science, whereas I did not determine precisely the percentage of carbon in the rebar I used. A spark test at my grinding wheel suggested that the amount of carbon was not great, but I decided to give it a try all the same.

I built my first pair of scissors out of 3/8-inch-diameter rebar. I repeatedly heated and hammered the handle end of each piece to draw it out so I could curl the ends and create stylish finger loops. After that phase was completed to my satisfaction, I proceeded to flatten out both the blade end of each piece and the area for the pin where the two halves of the scissors would pivot against each other.

Rather than drill the pivot pinhole in each half, I decided to punch those holes hot over the anvil. Drilling tends to produce a hole with little or no visible deformation to the surrounding area, unlike hole punching in hot metal, but I wanted to complete all of the fundamental stages at the anvil. I made the pivot pin out of a section of a large nail. It actually functions more like a solid rivet because I domed both ends with hammer blows to hold the scissor parts together.

The final steps of this project involved grinding and sanding the bevel on each blade to create the sharpest cutting edges. Although the final product is undeniably crude in appearance, and this pair of scissors is not the smoothest functioning tool I have ever used, it will actually cut paper . . . sometimes.

As it turned out, my design for scissors out of rebar had its flaws. Although the blades will cut cardboard and heavy paper fairly cleanly most of the time, the handles don't pivot smoothly for about an inch and a half of the blades' cutting length. As a

Two sections of 3/8-inch-diameter rebar ready to be forged into a pair of scissors.

The parts of the rebar scissors roughly shaped by forging and with the pivot hole punched.

result, the hand has to work harder than average to operate this particular pair of scissors. I had a devil of a time trying to get the blades to slide flat enough against each other in operation or to close consistently to properly shear material. Also, I

Final work on the blades' edges at a belt sander.

discovered that using a rivet as a pivot pin is not the best idea because it holds the two parts together either too tight, making the scissors difficult to use, or the connection becomes too loose and the blades won't cut. Additionally, the rivet is not as easily removable as a machine screw or small bolt would be in the event the scissors needed to be disassembled for adjustments.

I did not detect any degree of increased hardness in the steel after heating and then quenching in water, so I assume the amount of carbon in that particular source of rebar is pretty low. The steel is relatively soft, and I suspect that this would affect the blades' ability to cut certain materials, although it doesn't seem to make a perceptible difference when shearing things like paper or cardboard.

Of more consequence than the steel's alloy and hardness, I believe, is the design and finish of the final product. In this example, the scissors are crudely finished and, I will admit, of basically poor design. The steel in these scissors is soft enough that the relatively thin blades are not difficult to bend cold, and I messed around for some time tweaking them into various positions trying to find the best arrangement. As I've said, sometimes I am able to get them to cut pretty well, and other times not at all.

I decided to try a completely different approach

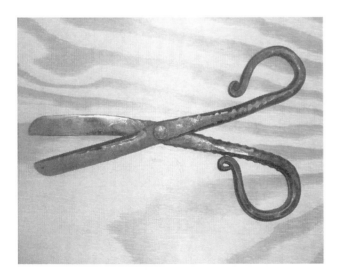

The finished pair of scissors made from rebar.

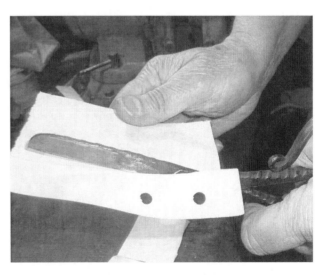

Cutting paper with the rebar scissors.

for my next set of homemade scissors—simply cut the parts out of plate steel and not even use the forge or anvil at all. This approach would follow Weygers' instructions more closely, at least in the beginning.

Weygers recommends making pattern templates out of cardboard and testing the configuration before marking and cutting the pieces out of metal, and that is what I did. This phase is obviously the best time to make any desired corrections or adjustments to the design or shape of the individual pieces. Once I had a pretty good basic pattern for each half of my conceptual scissors, I decided to build a prototype out of wood to test any potential problem areas. I was later glad I took this extra step.

As it turned out, the blades of my wooden model would actually pivot *apart* from each other—as much as an eighth of an inch—as the handles were closed rather than sliding across each other in continuous contact, as is required to shear material. It soon became apparent that the inside surface areas around the pivot pin on both pieces were angled incorrectly. I learned that those surfaces needed to be on as flat a plane in relation to one another as possible—flat surface against flat surface, so to speak, in order to keep the blades in continuous contact during opening and closing. This can be tricky when you are trying to grind or file material away on each blade in order to get the handles into better alignment.

So this wooden model was worth the time spent building it, because now I knew how *not* to shape the insides of the pieces. I was also quite pleased with the outside shape and style of this pair of scissors, so my pattern templates worked out perfectly.

I found a 3/16-inch-thick mild steel plate in my scrap metal pile from which to cut out the parts for the scissors. I traced around the cardboard templates on the steel to mark their outlines and proceeded to cut out the general shape of both halves.

I started removing material in the spaces within the finger loops by drilling rows of small holes close together just inside the line. This way I eventually created openings for the hacksaw blades to fit through in order to saw out the majority of the material that needed to be removed. I finished removing the material inside the finger loops using both half-round and rat-tail files.

The next step was to hacksaw the scissor pieces out of the steel plate. This was when the real work

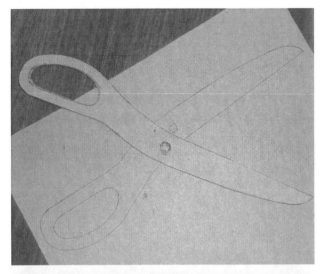

Creating and testing pattern templates of cardboard for second pair of homemade scissors.

24

The wooden prototype to test the function of the design.

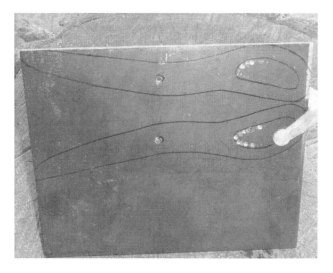

Patterns marked onto steel plate and plate clamped to block of wood so it can be held in vise.

began. For those readers who have never tried it, I am here to tell you that hacksawing scissor parts out of 3/16-inch steel plate by hand is no quick and easy endeavor. You will earn your prize. I did manage to accomplish the task within the lifespan of two new hacksaw blades, however. I recommend saw blades with 18 teeth per inch (TPI) for this, as they cut faster than either 24 or 32 TPI blades. (I used 24 TPI blades because they were what I had on hand.)

When I finally had both pieces cut out of the steel plate, it was time to grind, file, and sand them

to the final dimensions. Initially I had planned to shape their inside surfaces to replicate conventional factory-made scissors as much as possible, with the usual step-down thickness variances to allow for thinner blades, and also to put the handles into better alignment. But when I joined the two completely flat (and proportionately thick) pieces with a small bolt and nut to see how these blanks would fit together, I discovered that they were actually capable of shearing material quite well just as they were.

Drilling holes in a line to remove material from inside the finger loops.

Finger loop spaces opened up by drilling lots of tiny holes inside the line.

The hacksaw work commenced.

Scissor parts rough sawn from steel plate.

I have only started to grind the bevel on the blades' edges—on the sides facing out only, as is appropriate for shear blades (as opposed to conventional knife blades, which are normally beveled on both sides of their cutting edge). I have not progressed very far as of this writing, since I discovered that they will shear material surprisingly well even as blunt as their edges presently are. By contrast, the blades of my rebar scissors possess sharp edges. The biggest factor in how well the blades function seems to be how closely they slide across one another. Even the fact that this pair of scissors is composed of relatively soft low-carbon steel does not seem to hinder its ability to neatly shear paper.

I joined this prototype together with a small bolt and nut, tightened down over washers, which makes the parts easy to disassemble for modifications and then reassemble for repeated testing. This is a clear advantage over the rivet used to hold the rebar scissors together.

Two potentially undesirable features of this rudimentary design are that (1) the handles are not in direct alignment with one another, and (2) there is nothing to prevent over-travel of the blades as they slide past each other during the closing action. A small bead of weld could be added to the inside of one or both handles as a stop to cure the second item, if it were to be considered too much of a nuisance. Despite these minor issues, this pair of scissors does perform its intended function as a cutting tool, and for now that works for me.

The plain flat steel scissor pieces joined together and tested for their ability to cut paper.

Makeshift but functional handmade steel scissors.

CHAPTER 2

Manually Powered Machines You Can Build

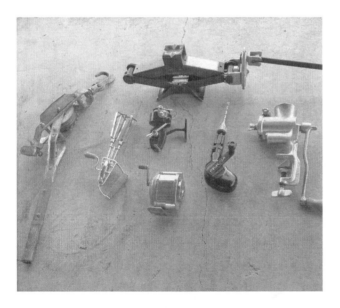

Some manually powered machines are still commonplace even in our modern high-tech world. Machines like these are economical because they require no electricity at all.

There was a time not so awfully long ago when manually powered machines were much more commonplace than they are today. They were used to good effect, and seemingly endless tasks were accomplished with them. Some of the most common examples that have survived to the present are the pedal bicycle, the hand-turned eggbeater, the spinning reel for fishing, any hand-pushed type of cart, and the common hand-cranked pencil sharpener, to name a few.

In this chapter we will study various manually powered machines that we can build and use to our advantage whenever electricity or gasoline engines may not be convenient or available. For our discussion, we might divide this topic into four general classifications of manual machines:

- Wheeled carts. This category includes such things as wheelbarrows, hand trucks, specialty dolly carts, pull wagons, shopping carts, and wheeled travois. This will be our simplest group to consider in this chapter.
- Machines powered by foot treadles with connecting rods and cranks and usually having

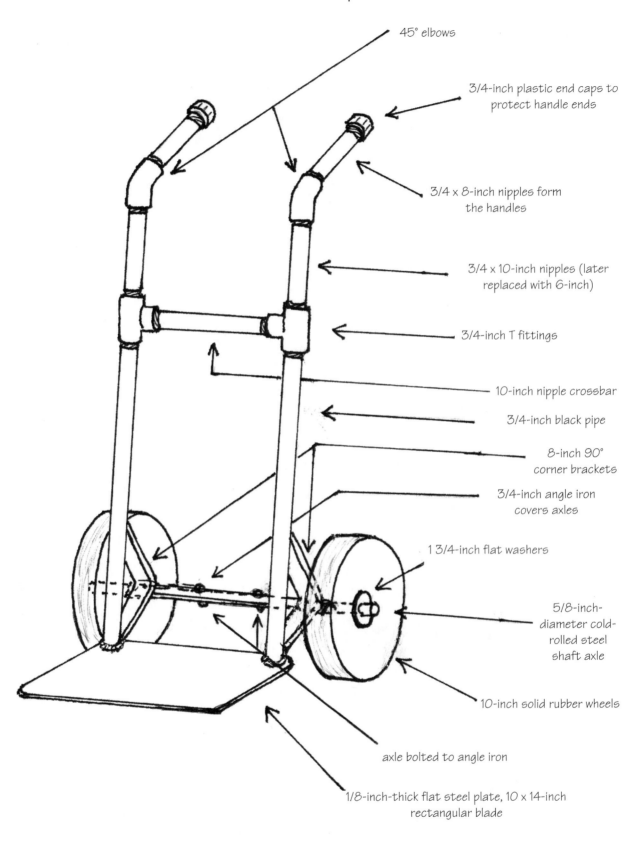

45° elbows

3/4-inch plastic end caps to protect handle ends

3/4 x 8-inch nipples form the handles

3/4 x 10-inch nipples (later replaced with 6-inch)

3/4-inch T fittings

10-inch nipple crossbar

3/4-inch black pipe

8-inch 90° corner brackets

3/4-inch angle iron covers axles

1 3/4-inch flat washers

5/8-inch-diameter cold-rolled steel shaft axle

10-inch solid rubber wheels

axle bolted to angle iron

1/8-inch-thick flat steel plate, 10 x 14-inch rectangular blade

The initial homemade hand truck—basic design and components.

flywheels. This category includes pre-electric sewing machines, as well as many of the old yarn-spinning wheels.

- Spring-assisted treadle machines, such as spring-pole lathes and reciprocating saws.
- Machines powered by turning hand cranks or foot pedals, such as bicycles, manual hand drills, fishing reels, and endless other machines.

As a supplement to this chapter, I have included an appendix at the end of this book where we examine some of the mechanical principles involved with gearing, pulleys, chain drives, and so forth. The reasoning here is that with a solid understanding of some basic mechanical principles, even with just a few important fundamentals, you will be able to more freely invent and build beyond the assortment of contraptions detailed in the space of this one chapter.

Even if you tend to be bored with the more technical elements of mechanics, or if you are already familiar with these basic principles, I encourage you to at least scan the appendix and its illustrations to better understand the fascinating world of these fun machines!

BUILD YOUR OWN HANDCART

I decided to build a hand truck for this chapter because, not only is this a reasonably simple and totally practical project for the average reader of this type of book, but also because I have needed a hand truck around the house on more than one occasion to help me move heavy objects and have just never gotten around to buying one. In the end, I preferred building one according to my own specifications.

The standard configuration of a conventional hand truck design comprises two wheels, an axle, a deck or blade, and the frame that holds everything together. The design and materials should be sturdy enough to handle a relatively heavy load. I had no intentions of moving a full-sized refrigerator up a flight of stairs or anything like that, but I wanted the strongest device I could build on my limited budget.

To begin my project, I bought new 10-inch solid wheels at the local hardware store. I suppose I could have eventually found a complete used hand truck at a yard sale for what I paid for just those two wheels, but they are very good wheels. In a more primitive

The parts of the hand truck before being assembled into a functional product.

environment, I might have even tried to fabricate my own wheels, but for this project the store-bought wheels certainly made everything more convenient and most likely resulted in a superior final product. I also bought a 5/8-inch-diameter cold-rolled steel shaft for the axle.

The deck has to be thick enough to have plenty of strength for lifting the heavy cargo without bending, but not so thick that it won't conveniently slide under items to be moved. I decided to make mine from 1/8-inch-thick flat plate steel, which seems to be close or identical to what you'll find on most of the strongest hand trucks.

In my stockpile of materials, I had some steel racks that someone had welded up from 1/8-inch flat plate with angle iron around some of the edges. The plate was more than large enough for the size of deck I wanted (10 x 14 inches), but I had to cut out the piece to the required dimensions.

There are easier and faster methods for doing this than those that I chose to use. Probably the best way would be with a plasma cutter, or even an oxyacetylene torch with a cutting tip. While I do have a little oxyacetylene torch outfit, I realize that not everyone will have access to welding supplies. Hacksaw blades, on the other hand, are relatively inexpensive.

First I explored several other methods for this cutting phase. I actually started with my Dremel tool and heavy-duty cutoff disks, but I eventually

Starting the cut in the steel plate for the hand truck deck using the Dremel tool.

The task of cutting the deck out of the larger plate was greatly assisted with this homemade hacksaw.

switched to hand hacksaws because the disks progressed too slowly and were consumed too rapidly in the process. I found I was able to go only about a quarter of an inch with the cut before I would have to add a new disk to the tool. The little Dremel is a bit light for making lengthy cuts in such heavy gauge steel, but it did help make the corner cuts a lot easier.

Although it can be time consuming, hacksawing through 1/8-inch-thick mild steel plate is not particularly difficult if the cutting throat of your saw frame is deep enough to accommodate your project. However, most handsaw frames are too shallow for allowing the blade to reach more than about 4 or 5 inches into the plate from any edge. You could try (as I did) to use a compass-saw style of hacksaw blade holder, but I found this to be a very awkward way to cut thick steel because it's difficult to apply enough working pressure on a partially unsupported, thin hacksaw blade. I bent and broke a number of blades trying to make this method work, with very limited success. I finally created my own expedient, deep, bucksaw-type frame out of sturdy yard branches and twisted cord for supporting my hacksaw blades and was finally able to get the task accomplished with this crude setup.

I decided to make the frame for my hand truck out of 3/4-inch black steel plumbing pipe. A fairly rigid structure can be fabricated from steel pipe, and the wide assortment of available pipe lengths and

connection types makes plumbing pipe especially convenient for numerous makeshift projects, including this one. A good number of the frame connections can be made with the pipe by simply screwing the prethreaded pieces together. I chose to use black as opposed to galvanized pipe, because I wanted to avoid any potential safety hazards associated with heating zinc where I planned to weld certain connections—although to be honest, I am not 100 percent convinced that heating zinc is necessarily as dangerous as some say. My advice to readers is that it is always better to be safe than sorry, so do your research before heating any metal coated with zinc.

I used 8-inch 90-degree corner brackets, roughly a quarter-inch thick and very rigid, for the wheel brackets. These were zinc coated, but I welded on them anyway after grinding the contact areas to the contours of the pipe and deck where necessary. I'll never win any prizes for my beautiful welds done with my tiny 70-amp stick welder, with all of its spatter and inefficiency; I simply made sure that I melted enough metal to fuse things permanently. For this project I used what was convenient and economical, and my little stick welder runs on ordinary 110 to 120V house current. Better-looking and potentially stronger welds can be achieved with either a MIG or TIG welder, or at least a larger stick welder.

The integrity of the weld joints at any of the

Preparing to weld the frame pipes to the deck.

Close-up of welded connections.

Corner brackets welded to the frame for the wheel mounts.

high-stress points is particularly important, such as where the ends of the pipe meet the top of the deck plate, so you want to make sure to form a sufficient puddle of molten metal to fuse those connections, regardless of welder type. (In fact, I later added weld to many of these connections for more strength.) If you see any suspicious cracks or weak spots there afterwards, grind it all off and weld it again.

The axle is a cold-rolled steel round bar of 5/8-inch diameter. I bolted it to the inside of a section of 3/4-inch angle iron that I had welded onto the corner brackets to form a horizontal axle housing. The positioning of all of these parts is important and requires a bit of planning, because once everything is welded together, it isn't easily disassembled.

You'll note that the axle housing is positioned on the frame so that the wheels keep the back of the deck raised about an inch or so off the ground. I did it this way to allow clearance when tilting the truck back during use. Plus, I thought the increased incline would provide me with more of a leverage advantage when lifting loads, similar to the way a block of wood placed under a claw hammer provides a leverage advantage when pulling nails. I've since discovered that many commercial hand trucks encompass much less of an incline here—somewhere from about 1/4 to 3/8 inch, to the point where they appear virtually parallel to the ground. The latter design may make it easier to rest a tall or stacked load flat on the ground without having it fall forward, but really, either approach will result in a functional tool.

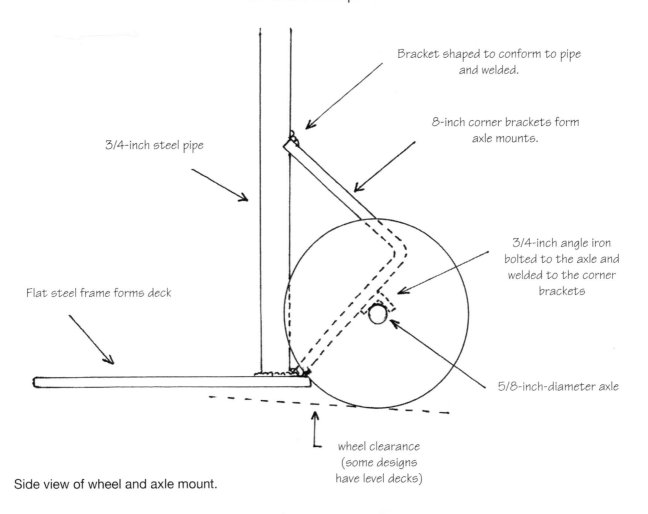

Bracket shaped to conform to pipe and welded.

8-inch corner brackets form axle mounts.

3/4-inch steel pipe

3/4-inch angle iron bolted to the axle and welded to the corner brackets

Flat steel frame forms deck

5/8-inch-diameter axle

wheel clearance (some designs have level decks)

Side view of wheel and axle mount.

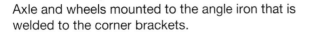

Axle and wheels mounted to the angle iron that is welded to the corner brackets.

Close-up of the end of the axle and retaining cotter pin.

Backside view of the deck and axle mount showing where more welds and another plate of steel were added to reinforce that area.

The basic configuration of the homemade hand truck, before it was improved.

The wheels are trapped onto the shaft with large washers and cotter pins on the ends of the axle. I also placed large washers (1 3/4-inch outside diameter) between the wheels and the ends of the angle iron. Since the wheels turn freely on the axle, there is no need to have a free-turning axle. It should be fixed into position.

The simple design seen in the illustration and photos shows only the very basics of the framework for this hand truck. If I had left it at that, it would probably work fine for a while with light loads—possibly even as well as those typical little variety dollies you can get at the local hardware store for about $40. This is assuming the hideous-looking welds of mine prove trustworthy, though they seem to be holding surprisingly well thus far.

A really good hand truck should have more reinforcement, so I recommend bracing everything up as much as possible. I eventually welded on an additional narrow plate of steel to the back of the deck at an angle and to the lower portions of the corner brackets to strengthen that area, and I also welded the axle to the angle iron axle housing so that it wouldn't be dependent upon just the two little bolts to hold those parts together.

I later changed the height of the frame slightly by replacing the 10-inch pipe sections under the handle elbows with 6-inch sections, giving the unit a more comfortable working size. This shortened the total height from slightly over 55 inches to 52 inches, which I believe is about perfect for a hand truck. It seems that no matter how much planning one puts into a project like this, there are always a few more details that are learned later, after the project is well underway. These things more or less have a way of evolving into the final product.

A hand truck such as described here acts as a first-class lever. In other words, it is a lever with its fulcrum (the lever's pivot point) between the resistance load (i.e., whatever it is you are hauling) and the effort force (i.e., you or, more precisely, your muscle power). With this type of lever, the longer the effort arm, or that portion of the lever from the fulcrum to the effort force, in

Hand truck after reinforcing its frame by welding sections of 3/4-inch angle iron to the frame and axle housing.

Using the homemade hand truck.

relation to the length of the resistance arm, which is that portion from the fulcrum to the center of the resistance load, the greater will be the mechanical advantage for lifting heavy objects. The handles of a typical hand truck design are long enough to provide a very effective mechanical advantage, because the truck's unique L shape puts the fulcrum (the wheel base, in this case) so close to the resistance load. Hence the greater will be the effort-arm to resistance-arm ratio, and the greater the mechanical advantage. (More about this in the appendix.)

Before leaving the subject of wheeled handcarts, it might be worth noting that a wheelbarrow, just like a travois, is an example of a second-class lever, because its fulcrum is at one end where the wheel is positioned, its effort force is applied at the other end, and the resistance load is in between. In this case, the effort arm would be measured from the ends of the handles to the center

of the front wheel, while the resistance arm would be the length from the center of the wheel to the center of the load being carried in the tray. As you might observe, the second-class lever also provides a mechanical advantage.

By contrast, a third-class lever (where the fulcrum is at one end, the resistance load is at the other end, and the effort force is somewhere in the middle) provides a mechanical *disadvantage*, because this type of simple machine requires more input force to move the resistance load than the actual weight of the load, or the resistance (output) force. However, a third-class lever does facilitate an increase in speed as compared to the other two types of levers. An example of a third-class lever is your forearm pivoting at your elbow and pulled up by your biceps muscle when you lift something in your hand. Your muscle pulls with considerable force to raise a modest weight in your hand, but with a strong biceps muscle it can do this very quickly.

FOOT-TREADLE MACHINES

At a craft fair recently, I watched with fascination as a couple of women dressed in early 1800s vintage clothing spun yarn on their traditional foot-treadle spinning wheels. There is something hypnotizing about watching a large wheel being turned by a small crank arm that is connected to a connecting rod pinned at its other end to a pivoting foot pedal that pumps the rod up and down. This method for manually powering machines has been used for literally hundreds of years.

The traditional pre-electric sewing machine works on this same principle, and occasionally one of these will turn up at a farm sale or antique auction, as will such other old treadle-operated tools as grinding wheels, lathes, looms, and forge blowers. The foot treadle effectively powers such machines with an amazingly simple mechanism: by transmitting reciprocating motion at the foot pedal to rotary motion at the wheel.

This type of mechanism consists of a foot pedal fastened over a bar such that one end of the pedal can be pumped up and down comfortably with one foot; a connecting rod that links the pedal with the crank; the crank mechanism that turns the wheel; and a flywheel or pulley that facilitates inertia for sustained rotation. That is all there is to it, other than the drive shaft the wheel or wheels would be mounted on and whatever other gears or pulleys might comprise the system.

An early 1900s New Home treadle sewing machine.

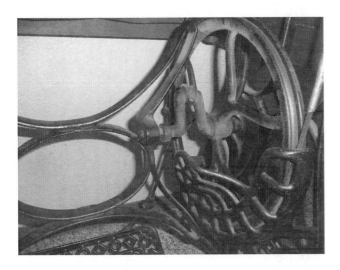

Close-up of treadle sewing machine's mechanism.

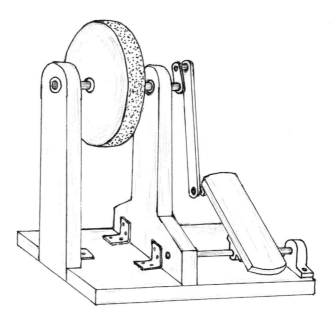

Grinding wheel powered by a foot treadle.

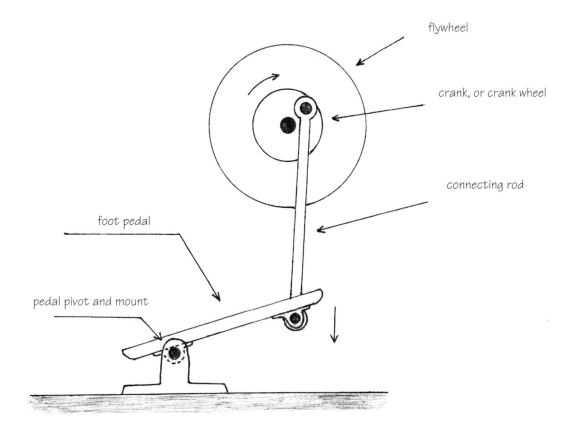

Parts of a basic treadle mechanism.

I decided to build a treadle-operated grinding wheel for this next project, and I had the perfect candidate for the business end of the machine: a small, antique, hand-cranked bench grinder that clamps onto the edge of a table or workbench. I picked up the grinder at a yard sale years ago for $6, if memory serves. The idea here was that the little hand-cranked grinder already had the crank mechanism and gearing in place, so I wouldn't have to worry about making a flywheel, pulleys, gears, crankshaft, or crank; all I needed to provide was the treadle mechanism and link it to the existing crank handle. Changing this hand-cranked tool into a foot-operated setup has the obvious advantage of allowing the user to keep both hands free during its use—a valuable feature whenever attempting to grind on things like ax bits or other blades that require careful and accurate grinding.

The treadle system itself is relatively basic, but the positioning and mounting of the parts are important considerations. It is of paramount importance to allow adequate clearance for the up-and-down swing of the foot pedal.

The hand-crank bench grinder with its handle removed to allow the attachment of the connecting rod.

38

Looking under the 2 x 4 foot pedal at the makeshift U bolts, pipe, and brackets.

Grinder clamped to workbench and connecting rod attached to crank arm. The small washer under the nut on the outside of the connecting rod was later replaced with a larger washer.

I decided to make the foot pedal out of common 2 x 4 pine lumber, because that was what I had on hand. I cut a section 16 inches long and drilled a hole completely through the board edgewise near one end to accommodate a 1/4- x 4-1/2-inch bolt that would attach to the connecting rod on one side. For the pedal's pivot, I drilled holes through the board 3 inches in from the other end to accept U

bolts that would hold a section of 1/2-inch nominal steel pipe under the board. I couldn't find any U bolts of the exact size I wanted, so I made my own by bending some threaded rod. I made use of two washer plates that came with a pair of shorter U bolts to secure the bolts to the pedal.

The pivot shaft is a 1/4- x 6-inch steel pipe nipple, fit loosely through the nominal half-inch pipe and capped at both ends to hold it in position. I modified a pair of 4-inch corner brackets to accommodate the pivot shaft and support the pedal. This assembly is screwed to a chunk of 2 x 6 pine that I attached to one of the legs of my small workbench with a single corner bracket.

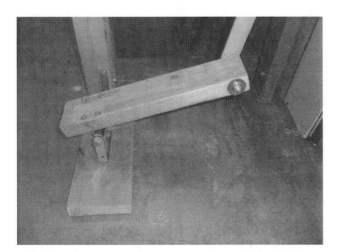

Close-ups of the foot pedal tilted up (left) and down (right).

The completed and fully operational treadle mechanism for the hand-crank bench grinder.

The connecting rod is a 1/4- x 1 1/2-inch oak board, which thus far seems to offer good strength and rigidity for its size and weight. I adjusted it to 32 inches in length between the centers of the holes for the bolts near each end. My workbench is 36 inches from the floor to the surface of its table.

I must admit that I initially had my doubts about how well a length of 2 x 4 framing stud would serve as a treadle foot pedal, but after applying a few drops of lubricating oil to the old grinder's shaft and gearbox, I found that this treadle adaptation works surprisingly well. It really doesn't take a great amount of effort to get the grinding wheel spinning fast and smoothly. I ultimately used fender washers under the nuts at most of the bolted connections to provide the smoothest and flattest surfaces possible where moving parts make contact.

The way I set this up, it would be very easy to disconnect and reconnect for operation at another workbench or location, as long as the new workbench table is 3 feet from the floor. This represents a uniquely portable and adaptable treadle apparatus.

SPRING-POLE MACHINES

Mike Abbot's intriguing craft book, *Green Woodwork—Working with Wood the Natural Way*, highlights an ingenuous ancient system for spinning a spindle using small-diameter rope, a foot treadle, and a spring pole. In his application, the spindle is used in a primitive wood lathe.

In my research, I discovered that spring-pole wood lathes are not as unusual as one might think. I found them featured on more websites than I ever would have imagined. They apparently were rather common in the 1300s and 1400s and probably much earlier, centuries before more advanced systems appeared. You'll sometimes find modern replicas demonstrated at medieval reenactment events.

The spring-pole mechanism is amazingly simple. It works on the same basic principle as a bow drill, having a small-diameter rope or cord wrapped one turn around a supported spindle just tight enough that a sawing back-and-forth motion on the cord produces rotation on the spindle. A foot pedal hinged at one end, somewhat similar to the foot treadle described above, is connected to one

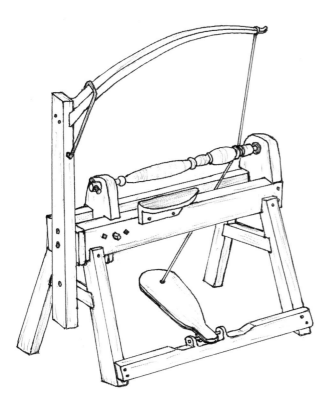

A medieval spring-pole lathe.

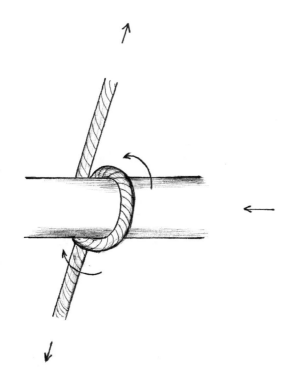

Rotation of a spindle facilitated by a taut cord pulled back and forth.

end of the cord; a sapling, springy stick, bow stave, or other type of pull spring is connected to the other end. (Some websites show a fantastic makeshift adaptation of the concept: using bungee cords in place of a spring pole.) Because this system serves well to turn a spindle, it is a fairly practical method for manually operating a lathe.

The spring-pole system was used to good effect in the Middle Ages and constitutes a simple, easy-to-build device in almost any primitive environment. It's biggest drawback, besides the possibility of the rope slipping and losing power and efficiency, is the fact that it produces its rotation in changing directions—a relatively short spin in one direction, then reversing direction for a relatively short spin in the other. By contrast, a simple treadle machine is able to keep a flywheel spinning in a continuous direction.

But that drawback can be an asset in other applications. Roy Underhill, in his book *The Woodwright's Shop: A Practical Guide to Traditional Woodcraft*, shows a reciprocating band saw powered by a spring pole. In that application, the reciprocating action provided by the spring pole directly powers the saw's up-and-down motion, as opposed to having the cord wrapped around a spindle to create rotation. The saw blade is mounted in a square frame set into a makeshift guide, and the spring-pole system moves the frame unit up and down.

MACHINES POWERED BY FOOT PEDALS OR HAND CRANKS

The modern bicycle is a highly developed manually powered machine, and this basic method for turning wheels can be used for many other applications, as we shall see.

Used bicycles are typically a dime a dozen at yard sales or online at places like Craigslist these days, and their pedal sprocket and chain mechanisms are particularly valuable to makeshift-it-yourselfers like me. This is because the technology is well developed, there are endless spare parts available, and the parts are perfectly suited and easily adapted to numerous other purposes besides their conventional function on a bicycle. In *Makeshift I*, we showed how an old bike could be converted into a manually powered blower

The pedal system removed from a bicycle might be considered a useful raw material.

Hand-cranked breast drill mounted to a small portable drill press to make it more controllable.

for a makeshift forge, but other possibilities include a pedal-powered bench grinder in the workshop, or a grain mill or blender in a "survival" kitchen.

Traditional eggbeater-style hand drills are still practical tools in remote areas where electrical power is not available. In the first book, we showed one way to rig an old eggbeater drill as a makeshift drill press. An inexpensive hand-cranked breast drill can also be mounted to a small portable drill press in a pinch and used to drill more precise holes than might be achieved easily by hand. While this wouldn't exactly be a homemade machine, it would constitute a practical makeshift adaptation of an existing manually powered machine to fill a unique purpose.

Pedal-Powered Wood Lathe

My dad became inspired to build his own foot-pedal-powered wood lathe after seeing a picture of an 1890s pedal-powered metal lathe in a book. Part of his inspiration was also this chapter as I was developing it—he fancied the idea of seeing his own

Gene Ballou tightening a nut on a bolt that secures a pulley mount on his lathe stand.

contraption featured in this section as an example of a functional, homemade, manually powered machine driven by a foot-pedal mechanism.

His initial thought about using foot pedals to power the spindle on a wood-cutting lathe was that if this type of system was sufficient to power a precision metal lathe, as was depicted in that book he saw, then it should work even easier for a wood lathe. So he went about designing and building his own lathe, mostly out of 2 x 4 and 2 x 6 framing lumber.

The stand, framework, or body of a machine like this can be made of lumber wherever wood is structurally sufficient, but the high wear or heaviest stress parts need to be of steel or other metal. By bolting wooden boards together rather than welding steel for the framework, it will be much easier to disassemble the lathe for moving, maintenance, or storage, should that ever become necessary. This is both an economical and quite practical approach to this type of project.

In conjunction with the pedal-power arrange-ment, Dad decided to use pulleys and belts to drive the spindle. Fortunately, he had an assortment of odd pulley wheels and V-belts and most of the necessary lumber in his supply of used hardware. I was able to provide him with a few shaft bearings from one of my junk boxes of yard sale treasures. He used a ball bearing unit to minimize friction on the spindle, set into a cavity cut into the face of the headstock he built for this lathe and then covered with a thin plate of steel to protect it from excessive exposure to sawdust.

A sprocket and pedal system from a bicycle could be adapted to power a lathe of this type, but Dad decided instead to build his own foot pedal mechanism the way he wanted it, welding together sections of steel rod and flat bar with his MIG welder. In order to maintain proper alignment of the pedal axle, he mounted it to its supporting bearings on both sides, attached his custom U-shaped pedals, and then, *after* everything was well supported and welded together, he cut the sections of the axle away for the foot spaces between the offset pedal bars.

Left side of lathe showing the pulleys and belts used to gain a speed advantage.

Underside view of the pulley and belt arrangement for the pulley drive train under the top rails.

The headstock. The steel plate covers a ball bearing unit inlet into the face for the spindle. Another option would have been to build in a bearing on each end of the shaft for additional support.

EXPLODED VIEW OF PEDAL-POWERED WOOD LATHE

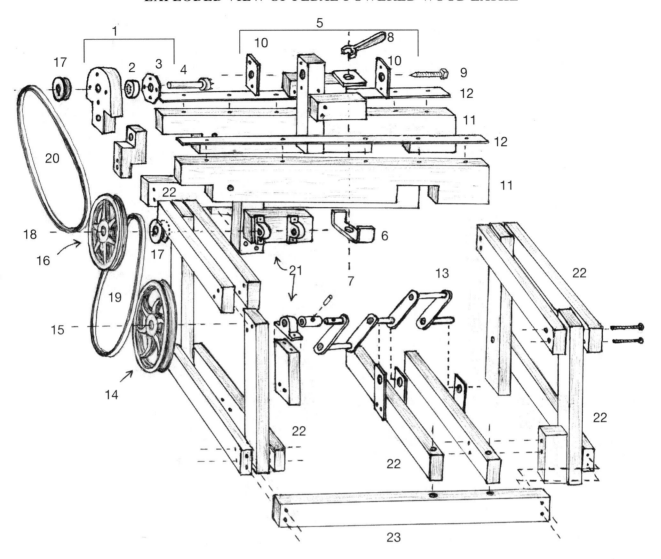

Parts 7, 15, and 18 are represented by dotted lines in the diagram.

1. Headstock assembly.
2. Ball bearing unit.
3. Steel plate—Holds ball bearing unit in position in headstock.
4. Spindle and live center.
5. Tailstock assembly.
6. Tailstock bottom bracket—Allows tightening of locking bolt.
7. Long vertical locking bolt (not shown)—For tightening the tailstock to the lathe bed.
8. Wrench for top nut (nut not shown) on tailstock locking bolt.
9. Dead center.
10. Steel plates (2)—Sandwich the tailstock post, each having a threaded center hole to secure the dead center piece.
11. Pine rails (2), 2 x 6—Form bed of lathe.

12. Lengths of strap iron (2), 1/8" thick x 1 1/2" wide—Cover rail tops to provide a solid surface for the moveable tailstock to rest upon.
13. Foot pedal assembly.
14. Large pulley wheel, 12" diameter—For the pedal drive shaft.
15. Pedal drive shaft (not shown), 5/8" diameter steel rod.
16. Large pulley wheel, 7" diameter—For the compound drive train.
17. Small pulleys (2), 2" diameter—One for headstock, one for pulley shaft.
18. Pulley shaft (not shown)—Upon which the middle 2" and 7" pulley wheels are stacked.
19. Drive belt—Links the 12" pulley with the middle 2" pulley.
20. Drive belt—Links the 7" pulley with the 2" headstock pulley at top.
21. Shaft bearings.
22. Frame pieces, 2 x 4.
23. Front brace, 2 x 4 x 33" long.

HEADSTOCK ASSEMBLY OF PEDAL-POWERED WOOD LATHE

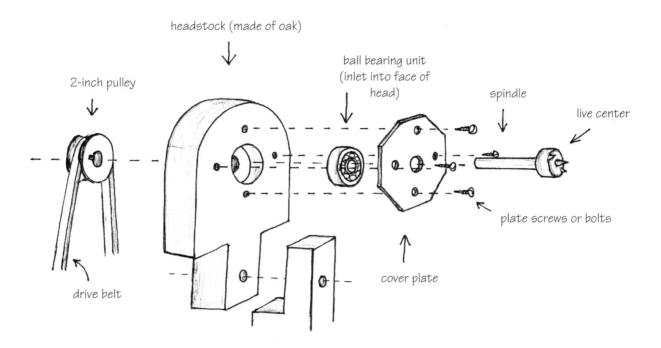

headstock (made of oak)

ball bearing unit
(inlet into face of
head)

spindle

live center

2-inch pulley

plate screws or bolts

drive belt

cover plate

OVERHEAD VIEW OF LATHE FOOT PEDALS

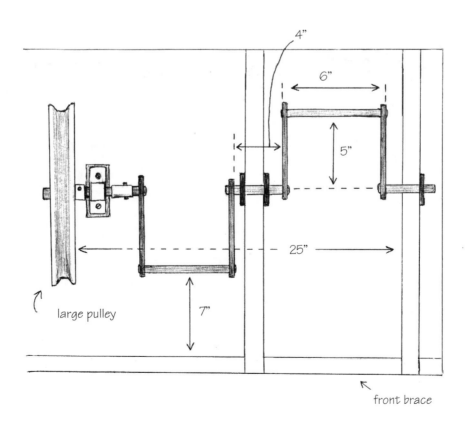

4"

6"

5"

25"

7"

large pulley

front brace

Looking down at the foot pedal system for the homemade wood lathe.

Operating the foot pedals.

Proper alignment of the headstock and tailstock of a lathe is critical so that the spindle and work will turn true. The headstock is a fixed piece that supports and houses the spindle; the tailstock must be a movable piece on the top rails, and it must be capable of being locked securely into whatever position is needed to center the workpiece. Dad achieved this with a 3/8-inch-diameter threaded rod running vertically through the top and bottom steel plates that sandwich the base of the tailstock, which can be tightened onto the rail wherever needed by turning the wrench that fits the top nut. To facilitate easier sliding and more solid, precise positioning of the tailstock, he covered the tops of the 2 x 6 rail boards with 1/8-inch steel plates.

A lathe also needs a tool rest to help the craftsman's hands support the cutting chisel while the workpiece is turning. In this case, Dad modified an existing lathe tool rest to create a movable, adjustable base that could be clamped to the rails wherever needed, as can be seen in the accompanying photos.

The pulley arrangement that Dad ultimately created for this lathe (after replacing one of the original pulleys with a larger wheel) employs a compound train of two pairs of large-to-small pulley wheels, which gives him an approximate 20:1 speed advantage ratio, according to our best count. In other words, for every full rotation of the pedal axle, the spindle (and the workpiece) rotates 20 times. This speed appears to be plenty adequate

End view of the top rails, which are 2 x 6 boards with 1/8-inch steel plates screwed to top edges.

Side view of tailstock.

Rear view of the tailstock showing tension bolt and wrench handles.

for a functional wood lathe.

The force required to spin the wheels of this machine, with the friction element included, is considerable. However, the beauty of a foot-pedal system is that the legs are generally much stronger than the arms, and the amount of effort required to

pedal this lathe is not perceptibly excessive.

I have only two criticisms about this particular lathe design. First, the way the pulleys and belts are arranged, the operator is forced to pedal backwards to make the spindle turn toward the operator for a suitable chisel cutting operation (although the backwards pedaling doesn't seem as awkward in practice as one might expect). Second, no provision was built into the design to allow adjustments to pulley shaft positioning, which would have made it much easier to adjust belt tension and remove and replace pulleys and belts.

I must emphasize that this was Dad's first attempt at building such a device. He and I both

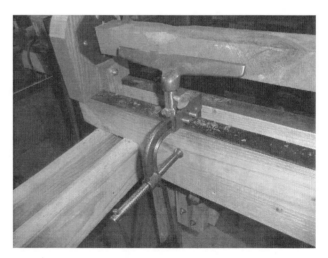

Close-up of left and right sides of customized lathe tool rest. To protect the sides of the 2 x 6 bed board, you can attach a thin steel plate or strip of sheet metal where the clamp digs in.

learned a lot from the project, and we would likely do some things differently in a second version. I include it here not necessarily as a recommended design for others to replicate but as an intriguing experiment in building a functional, manually powered machine. Overall, I am impressed with how effective the lathe turned out to be. It is a practical and fun-to-use tool for the woodshop, and that's what's important here.

The completed homemade wood lathe.

Gene Ballou testing his pedal-powered wood lathe.

Chapter 3

Useful Things from Discarded Plastic Products

Miscellaneous common plastic products that could be used as makeshift raw materials.

Disposable plastic products clutter our modern world. According to the Environmental Protection Agency, Americans generated more than 30 million tons of plastic waste in 2008 alone. But fortunately for us makeshifters, discarded plastic is easily adapted to seemingly endless useful purposes. Most types of common plastics are easy to cut and heat-form using inexpensive tools and are equally simple to join by gluing, duct taping, stitching, screwing, or riveting. The best thing for us, of course, is that these materials are almost everywhere. In this chapter, we will consider some practical ways to make good use of recycled plastic items.

READY-MADE PLASTIC CONTAINERS

The beauty of so many plastic containers that are often discarded without any thought is that they are usually 100 percent ready for other good uses without any modification whatsoever, or in some cases after only minor modification or cleaning. A good example that immediately comes to mind is the handy little plastic 35mm film canister. Most of us don't use regular film as often as we used to before the age of the digital camera, but those canisters are still pretty common, and they are great portable containers for storing things like fishhooks, split-shot fish sinkers, buttons, small screws, wooden matches, or other little items. They even have their own pressure-fitting lids to hold everything in and are normally watertight as well.

An often overlooked source for an inexpensive plastic container is the disposable ink pen. The body of a common disposable pen is a small plastic tube. When you open up either end and empty out the internal components, you end up with a neat plastic capsule, normally of 3/8-inch outside diameter. It is easy enough to cut the tube to whatever shorter length you want, and you can find tiny cork stoppers in most hardware stores that will perfectly fit the opening. A container like this might be just the thing for keeping a few sewing needles protected inside your field kit.

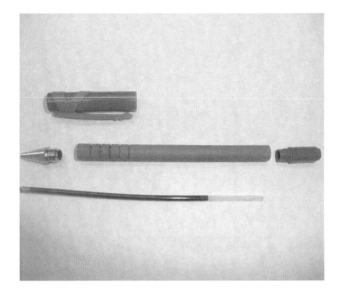

Disposable ink pen disassembled to salvage the tubular body.

Ink pen body with tiny cork stopper used as a small needle case.

I have found that the flat, round, plastic containers that chewing tobacco is commonly packaged in also make great little pocket containers for things like small first-aid kits. They are just the right size to stow in a pocket and have their own pressure-fitting lids. All you usually have to do to make them suitable for other purposes (besides keeping chewing tobacco) is to clean them out thoroughly. Avoid chew cans comprised of cardboard and metal, as it seems next to impossible to thoroughly clean the tobacco residue out of those, and the cardboard absorbs moisture. The all-plastic container is best for reuse in this case. I have assembled little pocket fishing kits to store in these cans, and this is a handy use for them. A strip of vinyl electrical or duct tape around the seam of the lid helps keep it securely in place.

In case you were wondering, no, I don't chew tobacco myself, but I've had friends who were

Small fishing kit housed in plastic pocket tobacco can.

First, secure a copper wire around the spout, with legs long enough to go through the coffee can and wrap together.

Thread wires through holes drilled through bottom of can, push up tight to the wall, and twist the wires tight to secure.

chewers. You may have friends who chew as well, and they should be able to provide you with plenty of empty cans.

Finally, don't overlook the utility of plastic food containers of all shapes and sizes. In chapter 7, there's a photo of large, empty pretzel jugs being used to store small pieces of scrap metal and wood. I use them, along with metal cans and glass jars, to store assorted hardware under my workbench (the

Wrap the hose bib with a generous wad of insulation, such as plastic grocery bags, rags, or fiberglass bat material. If the hose bib is small enough, you can use a small can inside a larger can with insulation stuffed between, as shown here.

plastic has the advantage here, as it doesn't break if you drop it). Our friend Don McLean described his nifty makeshift use of an empty plastic coffee container to protect an outdoor hose bib from freezing in the winter, as shown in the photos. There are too many handy applications for these sturdy containers to just throw them away.

PLASTIC BOTTLES

Bottled water, soft drinks, and certain liquid cleaning products are typically sold in disposable plastic containers. Many of these containers are worth saving and using for a multitude of other purposes rather than wastefully discarding them the way most of us routinely do.

Plastic containers for chemicals or cleaning products should be thoroughly cleaned out before using for other purposes. I normally avoid certain containers altogether—things like Drano, Liquid Plumber, or most any of the chemical bathroom cleaners—because getting them clean enough for reuse is not practical.

Plastic bottles that originally contained drinks are considered food safe and are easy to clean out for reuse. These are ideally suited as water canteens for

This plastic juice bottle has been cleaned out and attached to a cord to make a canteen for the field.

such outdoor enthusiasts as backpackers, treasure hunters, and fishermen. Sometimes the only thing needed to make one of these handy plastic bottles into a perfect canteen is simply adding a cord or carry strap. This might seem almost too obvious to mention, but it underscores the simplicity and convenience of adapting certain plastic products to a wide range of useful applications.

It's easy to make water carriers from common plastic bottles because they're so well suited for that, but you can modify these products to serve other purposes as well. The top section cut from almost any plastic bottle, for example, can serve as a simple funnel to help minimize spills when pouring liquids or other materials from one container to another.

I have used the screw-on caps from these throwaway bottles quite often as small cups in which to mix two-part epoxies for application. They are typically the ideal size for the amount of glue often needed for small jobs, and when you're done, you just throw the gummy cap in the garbage.

If you cut the top off a large plastic jug, such as a gallon milk jug, you end up with a handy open-top container like a little bucket. If you cut the top off at an angle such that you keep the handle attached to the lower part, your bucket will be much easier to use. A similarly configured but sturdier plastic juice jug could be so modified to serve as a handy little dirt scoop or watering can for gardening. Similarly, many of you have probably seen bleach jugs used as clothespin holders—cut a hand-size hole in the side and pass the clothesline through the handle.

I found a neat idea illustrated in *The SAS Survival Handbook* by John Wiseman. It showed the top half of a plastic bottle cut off and fit inverted into the open base of the same bottle to form a one-way fish trap. I haven't had the opportunity to try it myself, but it is an interesting application for a plastic bottle.

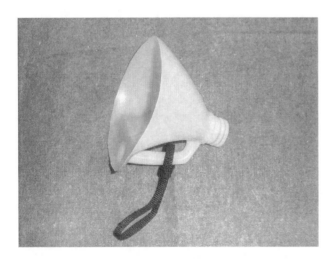

Handy plastic funnel made from the top of a plastic jug.

Plastic jug with handle retained makes a simple, practical scoop or watering can.

Cutting the neck off a wide-mouth plastic bottle with a pocketknife.

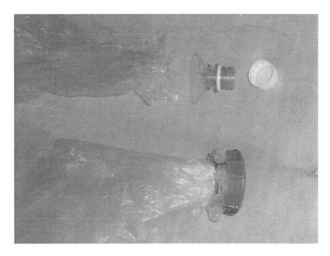

How the process works. At top, a small-neck plastic bottle ready to be stuffed with the bag to be closed. At bottom, a wide-mouth bottle with the bag inserted and the cap in place.

The bottle cap closes and seals the bag when it is screwed on.

Finally, an interesting idea was forwarded to me in an e-mail recently about how to securely close the opening of a plastic bag by using the neck cut from a plastic bottle, along with its screw-on cap. This merely entails cutting the neck portion off a disposable plastic bottle with a sharp knife or scissors and then stuffing the mouth of the plastic bag through the opening just enough to form a collar over which the cap will fit. Now just screw the cap onto the bottleneck to tightly seal the bag.

I found that the plastic bottles with larger mouths are easier to use than those with small necks, because the larger opening is much easier to feed the rim of the bag through, and the bag

bunches up less at the collar, making it easier to screw the cap on.

PLASTIC BUCKETS

It was noted in *Makeshift I* that the common 5-gallon plastic bucket or pail is made of thermoplastic, which is a particularly convenient material for the makeshift hobbyist because it can be heated to soften it up and then molded or shaped into a multitude of homemade products. When it cools, it becomes rigid again and retains the shape into which it was formed. Knife sheaths, belt clips, gun holsters, and various other things are commonly made of a type of thermoplastic called Kydex. You can make all of these things out of plastic buckets just the same.

The key to working with this material is understanding the appropriate heat application to soften it up. Heating the plastic too hot will damage it. Not enough heat will fail to make it malleable. I initially experimented with a little propane torch, but I quickly learned that it was extremely difficult, if not downright impossible, for me to warm the plastic sufficiently using an open flame without actually melting or burning the material.

The preferred tool for this job is an electric heat gun. A heat gun is a device frequently used in the painting industry that somewhat resembles a hair

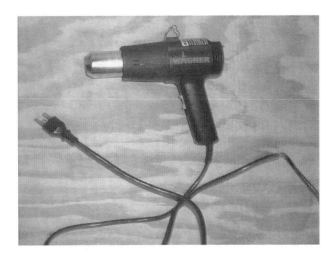

A heat gun can be a handy tool when working with thermoplastic.

Plastic bucket cut into workable pieces.

blow-dryer, except that it generates higher heat. There are industrial-grade heat guns on the market that cost well over $100. The one I bought at a local hardware store cost close to $20 and works perfectly for this kind of project.

The first thing you will need to do is cut your sacrificial plastic bucket into manageable pieces. I discovered this is not at all difficult using either a handsaw or tin snips. I reduced my bucket into pieces with a combination of a little crosscut handsaw to start the reduction process and the snips to finish up. Large tin snips or metal shears slice through this material quite easily, although you'd have to work pretty hard to cut it with regular household scissors, as the sides of the bucket are just thick and tough enough to make the use of such a lightweight tool a real chore. Not that it couldn't be done in a pinch with a sharp pair of sturdy steel scissors if that was the only tool available, but you'd have to work at it.

Before butchering your bucket, I recommend marking out a pattern for whatever you wish to fabricate, maybe with a permanent marker on newspaper or a large brown paper bag. Then cut that shape out of the paper with regular scissors and use it to determine the size of plastic you will need. You can then transpose the paper pattern directly onto your scrap of plastic with the marker before beginning the final stages of the material-reduction process.

Ax Head Cover

For my first plastic bucket project, I decided to build a protective cover for a large ax head, and I had plenty of raw material close at hand. The sand we normally buy for the cat's litter box comes in large, square plastic buckets. I just hate throwing them away—they have their own sturdy, tight-fitting lids, and they come in handy as storage containers occasionally. But in time we end up with more empty buckets than we could ever use.

My concept for the cover was a pretty simple affair that folded around the back of the head and fastened together in front, on the bit side. I created a simple fold-over pattern and marked it out on newspaper, gauging its size in relation to the ax head. (I made it slightly oversized to provide a margin for error.) Then I cut it out and used it to mark the pattern on the surface of the plastic as just described. Cutting the shape out of the plastic was an easy task with the tin snips.

Even with a heat gun, you have to be careful not to melt the plastic. It is best to go slow with the heat application and periodically test the softness of the plastic by trying to bend or fold it until it will give. This is a trial-and-error process at first, and you have to experiment with it. If you overheat and ruin your piece of plastic, just cut another hunk out of your bucket and try again.

I wore leather gloves because the plastic gets too hot to comfortably (or safely) handle with bare hands. I also recommend having a metal tray such as a baking pan on hand for a safe place to set down the heat gun while it's still hot. You wouldn't want to

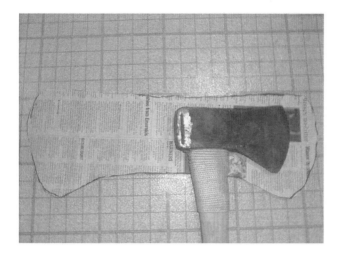
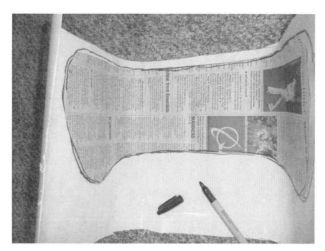

Creating a paper pattern and transposing it to the bucket plastic for the ax head cover.

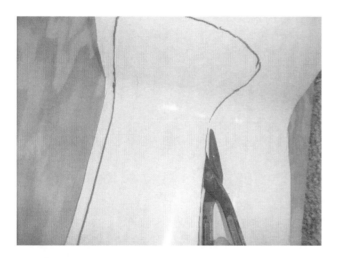

Cutting the shape of the cover out of the plastic using tin snips.

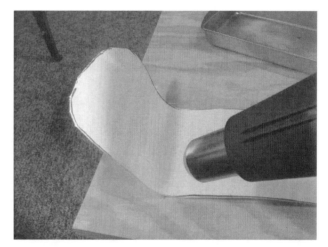

Heating the plastic with the heat gun so it will easily bend as needed.

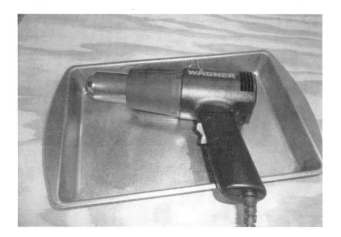

A metal tray is a safe place to set the heat gun until it cools.

place the hot gun directly on a nice wooden table or your carpet or flooring—it doesn't cool down instantly as soon as it is turned off. Think ahead and be safe.

After I had the cover basically shaped the way I wanted it, I drilled somewhat evenly spaced holes about an inch apart through both flaps where I wanted to join them, then used my pop riveter to set aluminum rivets. I used small flat washers under the rivets where they set on the opposite side to provide something more solid than plastic to support the expanding rivets. This may not be the prettiest method, but it is a very effective way to permanently join the plastic flaps.

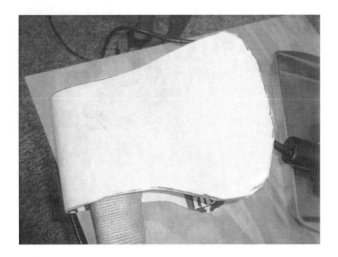

The plastic folds over the ax head.

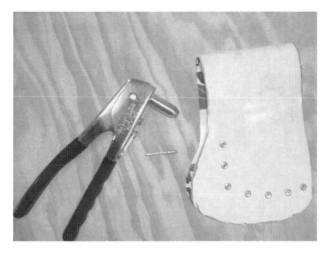

Joining the two flaps of the ax head cover with pop rivets.

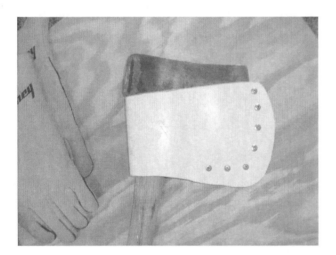

The ax slides into the cover through the top.

The resulting plastic cover slides up over the handle and fits snug over the ax head to protect both the bit and other tools and equipment from its sharp edge. This is just one practical way to use the plastic in an old, weathered, stained, or cracked bucket that may have lost most of its original usefulness. You could follow this same basic process to create sheaths for camp knives, machetes, and other bladed tools; arrow quivers and other equipment holders; and rugged gun holsters, as I will now explain.

The completed plastic bucket ax head cover.

Plastic Pistol Holster

A plastic pistol holster can easily be made using this exact same process. Again, you first create a paper pattern, then trace its outline onto a piece of thermoplastic, cut the shape in the plastic, and then heat it with a heat gun until it can be bent and formed over the pistol. I used a plastic bucket lid to create a small belt holster to hold a tiny Derringer.

I used my band saw to cut the shape out of the plastic this time, but as we saw with the previous project, metal shears or tin snips also work well for the task. I then heated the plastic with the heat gun exactly as described above and formed it to the Derringer. The belt loop was simply warmed where it needed to bend and then folded over against the back of the holster body.

Rather than attempting to rivet this tiny holster together with bulky pop rivets, I decided to stitch it instead. I aligned the separate parts and drilled small holes for attaching the belt loop as well as joining the main cover flap. I then stitched these parts together with strong braided polyester cord.

After the holster is sewn together, you can achieve a more perfect custom fit by additional warming with the heat gun and closer forming of the plastic to the gun, just as I did with this project.

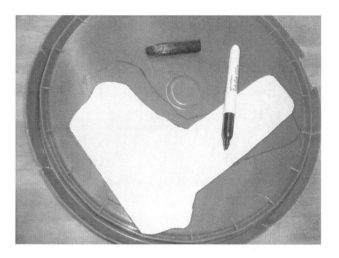

Transposing the paper pattern for the tiny holster onto the plastic bucket lid.

Cutting out the shape of the pattern with the band saw.

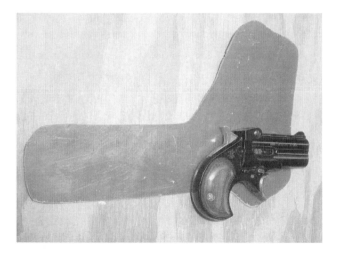

The plastic pattern ready to be heated and formed directly to the pistol.

In this photo you can see how the plastic holster was stitched together.

Wearing the gun in its plastic holster on the belt.

As can be seen in the photos, the resulting holster fits this gun like a glove.

If the gun fails to "click" firmly and securely into the holster as it should (some gun shapes are easier to conform warm plastic to than others), or if the gun tends to drop out of the holster whenever it is tilted upside down, a simple retainer cord can be attached. One way would be to punch two small holes through the plastic and add a loop of parachute cord or short length of boot lace, which could be drawn over the top of the hammer spur with your fingers to retain the gun and pushed up and off with your thumb to release it. Another, simpler retainer could be provided merely by tying a knot in the cord such that it's secured tight to the inside of the holster close to the gun, where it creates a bump over which the gun must slide when holstered and drawn. A third option would be to glue a small strip of material like cotton or nylon directly to the holster on one end; then add Velcro pieces to it and where it mates to the other side to create a functional hold-down strap that can loop over the frame or hammer of the gun.

Knife Sheath

If you do not have access to an electric heat gun, you're not out of luck. It just so happens that boiling the plastic in water is another way to heat it without burning it.

To test this method, I devised a plan to make a small knife sheath. First, I cut a piece of plastic from the lid of one of those cat sand pails. I then selected a large aluminum pot for the boiling task—

the plastic in its flat configuration was too wide to fit into a smaller pot or pan. I kept long-handled barbecue tongs on hand to grip the plastic in the boiling water.

While the boil method is clearly a viable option for softening thermoplastic, I have to admit that it was not as convenient or practical as using the heat gun, in my experience. I turned up the burner on the kitchen stove as high as it would go and kept the plastic in the boiling water for at least 20 minutes, yet the plastic reached only a certain semi-malleable state and would not seem to get any softer. Also, it was not as easy for me to handle and form the hot, drippy, wet plastic as it was to form plastic softened by the heat gun. Using the heat gun, you can form the plastic while it's on the knife or other object, whereas the same trick would be pretty awkward in a pot of boiling water—you have to pull the plastic out of the water for the actual form-to-fit stage, which we will talk about shortly. I did nevertheless manage to form the knife sheath somewhat as I had planned, and it turned out quite good in my estimation.

Ideally, a plastic sheath should be formed to closely fit the surface contours of the blade such that the knife will actually click into position and be firmly retained in place until deliberately removed (similar to what we achieved with the gun holster). The cooled plastic will be rigid and retain whatever shape it was formed into, but it will also possess a modest degree of elasticity so that a folded piece essentially acts like a spring clip.

This form-fitting of the warmed plastic to the

Keeping the plastic submerged in the boiling water to soften it up.

Plastic sheath in boiling water with clamp.

Plastic sheath with knife and additional clamps in place during the cooling process.

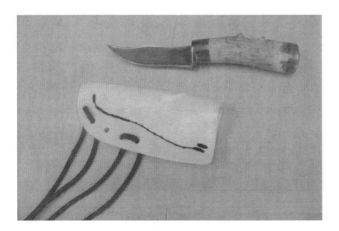

Sheath is sewn together to roughly match the contours of the knife blade.

object is done while the knife is *in* the sheath (or the handgun is in the holster). This is a fairly straightforward process when working with a heat gun, but accomplishing the same task while softening the plastic in a pot of boiling water would be awkward at best. I was able to do it by pulling the plastic out of the boiling water, quickly folding it around the knife and forcing the material to conform as much as I could by hand (while wearing leather gloves, of course). Then I strategically positioned a C-clamp to pinch the bent halves of the somewhat malleable plastic and gradually removed the knife while tightening the clamp to create a firmly fit sheath. (Leaving the knife in the plastic while tightening the clamp is another, perfectly valid option.) I soon learned that two clamps are better than one for this; in fact, the more clamps that space allows, the better.

I then plunked the whole works back into the boiling water for a while longer, with the clamp in place but without the knife. I wanted to "train" the material to the basic configuration while it was soft. After removing the clamped sheath from the hot water, I added two more clamps while the plastic was still warm and left them on for more than an hour, thus allowing it to completely cool before removing the clamps.

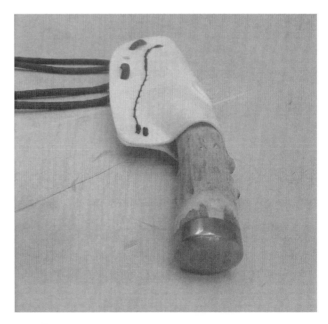

The finished plastic sheath holds the knife securely.

This trick worked moderately well, and I ended up with a kind of plastic shell that closely fit the main contours of my knife. The next order of business was to permanently join the folded halves together. Since this was a relatively small sheath to hold a small knife, I once again decided against riveting the seam. Instead, I drilled a string of tiny holes through both halves, just as I did with the holster for the Derringer, and then stitched the plastic parts together with the same strong, small-diameter braided polyester cord. It was not the prettiest stitch job I'd ever seen, but it served its purpose. A few drops of glue on each of the stitch knots on the backside help to prevent them from coming undone.

Finally, I drilled several larger holes through the flaps to accommodate bootlaces or parachute cord that I can use to tie or lace the sheath to something else, such as a belt, shoulder strap, or backpack. The only thing left to do after that was trim the outer edges of the plastic to the desired final dimensions, which was easy enough using tin snips, and then sanding all the edges smooth for a more finished look. In the end I had a very functional little knife sheath.

PLASTIC BAGS

Most of us routinely buy, use, and discard plastic bags of all kinds, so our discussion here would seem incomplete without mentioning at least some makeshift uses for them. Collectively, the vast assortment of plastic bags of all sizes comprises a sizable percentage of our most versatile makeshift materials.

Keeping several sturdy trash bags in your car or pack is always a good idea in my view, as they are not costly, and a few will not be too heavy or bulky to carry. I would also suggest finding the thickest and sturdiest bags available, as some are considerably stronger than others. I prefer bags of at least 3.0 or thicker mil, such as the durable, 42-gallon Ruffies Pro Contractor Clean-Up bags.

The majority of the heaviest large plastic trash bags are of a solid color like brown or black, but transparent bags and sheets of clear plastic are also available and have special uses, as sunlight can penetrate them while wind and water normally cannot, at least not until the plastic becomes

degraded by extended exposure to sun and wind, or if punctured. Hence, sheets of transparent plastic can be used for things like greenhouses, survival solar stills, or window insulation.

The polyethylene film sold under the brand name Visqueen is commonly used in construction as tarpaulins and drop cloths. The most popular is probably the transparent type, but solid-color Visqueen is also available, and it comes in sheets of from 4 to 10 mil thickness. If you can't get your hands on Visqueen, you could always spread out large trash bags as quickie drop cloths, as I have done when painting the walls inside my house.

Outdoor Applications

Extra heavy-duty 33- to 60-gallon plastic trash bags, like those used in lawn maintenance, have become popular in emergency survival literature, because in a pinch they can be used for so many different purposes, including things like expedient tarps, windbreaks, rain ponchos, emergency floatation devices, arm slings, kite material, gear bags, and other applications where a better material may not be readily available.

A bag can be opened up into a big square or rectangular shape and small cords tied to its corners such that it can be suspended overhead between tree branches or support poles to create a lightweight tent-like shelter that will shed rain or provide life-saving shade in the desert.

Several opened bags can be draped over a survival lean-to shelter or leaky tent to help it shed water. A windbreak or door flap on an expedient lean-to can be fabricated from a large trash bag, attaching the plastic wherever needed with small cord or duct tape.

An upside-down plastic trash bag pulled over your backpack or other gear could keep it dry overnight in camp, and you could store your food in another bag suspended from a high tree branch some distance from your tent to discourage bears from entering your camp at night.

By cutting a hole for your head into the bottom, a bag can be worn over your shoulders like a poncho to help protect you from wind and rain.

A large, thick plastic bag that's been opened up might be used as a quickie ground tarp where you can set your camp gear on a dry surface rather than on uncovered wet leaves or pine needles. Two or more such bags could also work as an expedient ground cloth on which to erect a one- or two-person tent, in cases where you forgot to pack the ground cloth, or you required its sturdier construction for something else, such as a makeshift roof over a camp kitchen.

A plastic bag with several tiny holes poked through the bottom and then filled with water can be suspended from an overhead tree branch or simple expedient framework to create a makeshift field shower.

If you had several plastic bags with a supply of cord and absolutely had to cross a river or other body of water without the help of a boat or bridge, you might be able to trap as much air as possible in a couple of bags and close their openings tightly with wrappings of cord to hold the air inside and create temporary floatation devices.

In Ron and Karen Hoods' *The Woodsmaster* video series #10, "Survival Camping," several members of the group constructed a makeshift forge bellows during a survival skills outing, using a plastic trash bag and a handful of other materials for the bellows bag. The contraption is shown being used for heating and forging small pieces of iron scavenged during their trip.

Plastic Bag Cordage

I learned an easy way to make a versatile string out of a plastic bag from several websites, and I also found a number of sites that discuss knitting, weaving, and crochet projects using strings made from plastic bags. And, of course, anything that can be made into cord can also be braided into ropes, belts, bands, straps, and slings, or woven into nets, clothing, mats, and so many other things.

According to the string-making instructions, you cut a 1-inch-wide strip from a bag, stretch it enough to substantially narrow and condense the material, and then simply twist it into a cord by rolling it between two fingers. I tried this with a tall kitchen bag having just 0.9-mil thickness and was surprised at how durable the resulting string actually was.

Cutting an even strip from a lightweight plastic trash bag with scissors is not nearly as easy for me as is cutting one from a bag of thicker plastic. I also discovered while using the lightweight bag that it is best to start with a strip considerably wider than an inch and roll it up as tightly as possible, and that

overstretching tends to break a strip from a thin bag fairly easily. However, after some trial and error I was able to produce a surprisingly strong cord of small diameter from even the lightweight bag.

Clothes

One or more expedient work aprons or dinner bibs could be easily fabricated from a single plastic trash bag. Not fancy, but they'll keep your clothes clean.

I have worn the gallon-size clear plastic zipper (Ziploc) bags on my hands as substitute mittens while working with wood stains, glues, and paints when I didn't happen to have any latex gloves handy. This expedient trick kept my hands mess free.

A poor man's substitute for temporary rain boots might be achieved by simply tying plastic bags over shoes.

Thankfully I haven't had to try this, but I've heard that plastic grocery bags make a good improvised insulation; just wad them up and stuff them into your pants and shirt. You can even make a surprisingly effective (though a little fragile) sleeping bag this way with two large leaf bags and enough wadded grocery bags to provide a thick layer of insulation.

Plastic bag secured over a shoe for a makeshift rain boot.

A PVC SCOOP FOR DIGGING IN SAND

Years ago, I needed a scoop to help me retrieve small metallic relics and treasures that I hoped to find with my metal detector at local lakes and rivers, and I wanted something impervious to moisture that could be used in the water. I also wanted to avoid using any type of metal for the scoop's construction, which would interfere with the search coil of the detector. The logical solution for me was to build the thing out of plastic.

Conveniently, a wonderful variety of PVC products for all sorts of water piping requirements is sold in hardware stores in just about every part of the country. I'm not sure if PVC pipe necessarily fits the "commonly discarded" class of plastic raw material we've been considering in this chapter, but it is very easy to find, and it is certainly easy and convenient to build things out of it. I collected the assorted components ready-made from a local hardware store, modified them as needed so they all

fit together properly, and then glued the main parts together with the PVC cement sold specifically for permanently bonding this kind of material.

A 4-inch PVC 22 1/2-degree bend served as the body of the scoop, while longer 3/4-inch pipe sections made up most of the handle in two main sections joined with couplings, as can be seen in the photos and sketch. I used a 1- x 3/4-inch T section to connect the scoop body to the handle, cutting a dip into the top (using a round file and a curved wood rasp) to make it conform to the curved contour of the scoop body before gluing it in place.

My original intent for the back of the scoop—where water, sand, and mud must pass through—was to glue a solid plastic disk into position after drilling a series of holes through it for venting, just like I drilled a number of 5/16-inch-diameter holes

Close-up side view of plastic scoop.

Digging scoop made of PVC pipe products.

Looking into the mouth of the scoop. Notice how the T section has been shaped to fit the round body of the scoop where the handle is glued to it.

through the outer wall of the scoop's body. However, I found a ready-made plastic drain unit that required very little shaping before I was able to fit it perfectly into the back of the scoop body, and I glued it into position. It had slotted openings that allowed water and mud to pass through, but this turned out not to be ideal for a treasure-hunting scoop, as these slots were also large enough to allow such treasures as coins on edge, small gold nuggets, and tiny items of jewelry to fall through. My solution was to install a second slotted drain vent flush up against the first, with its slots aligned perpendicular to the first to create much smaller crisscrossed vent openings that would hopefully trap the smaller items I wanted to retrieve with the scoop. As of this writing, I have not yet installed that second vent piece.

I filed a bevel on the inside of the lower rim of the scoop's mouth for a sharper edge along the lip in that area to create a kind of shovel blade shape, which helps it dig into sand and mud more easily. The 4-inch PVC bend component seems to be the

perfect basic configuration to start with for the body of this type of scoop.

The handle of my scoop, while completely functional, is not quite as rigid as I would prefer. Most of its length is comprised of two sections of schedule 80 3/4-inch pipe, one 12 inches and one 18, joined together with a 3/4-inch schedule 40 coupling. These parts of the handle come threaded, which makes joining them very simple, and you can disassemble them for storage if no glue is used in the threaded joints. The handle is connected to the neck by a 1-inch, 45-degree elbow with an adapter between it and the T and a coupling between it and the shorter handle pipe. This sets the scoop body at the desired angle to the handle for convenience while using the tool.

A schedule 80 PVC pipe having 3/4-inch nominal size designation actually has an outside diameter of 1 inch and an inside diameter of 11/16 inch—slightly smaller than 3/4 inch. If a more rigid handle is desired, one could easily fit a hardwood dowel of corresponding size inside the plastic pipe

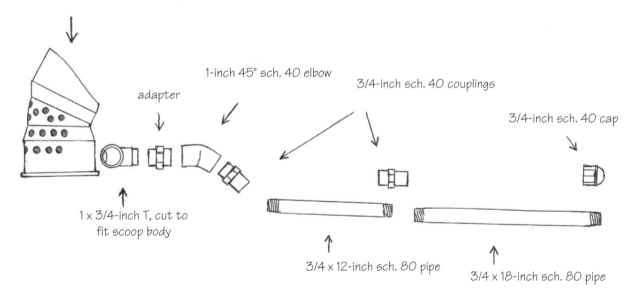

Scoop body is 4-inch PVC, 22 1/2° bend with vent holes drilled into belly.

1-inch 45° sch. 40 elbow

adapter

3/4-inch sch. 40 couplings

3/4-inch sch. 40 cap

1 x 3/4-inch T, cut to fit scoop body

3/4 x 12-inch sch. 80 pipe

3/4 x 18-inch sch. 80 pipe

PVC scoop parts (side view).

to reinforce it. A 3/4-inch PVC schedule 40 end cap screws onto the long end to close the tube.

MAKE USE OF THOSE FREE CREDIT CARD OFFERS

Who hasn't received an annoying number of credit card offers along with the rest of their junk mail, often including fancy plastic cards that are supposed to resemble credit cards? I used to chop them into small pieces whenever I saw my name and address imprinted on them, just to be on the safe side, and I considered them to be really nothing but a nuisance.

Then one day I examined one of these plastic cards more closely and wondered what useful purpose it might serve, besides opening locked doors without the aid of a key. People who know me well know how much I hate throwing away potentially useful things, so I considered the thickness and flexibility of the plastic.

As it turns out, the plastic cards are usually just the right thickness for making suitable flat guitar picks. The only tool required for this conversion is a pair of scissors, and the plastic is easy to cut. Simply snip out the teardrop or triangle shape of the pick, and the deed is done. I can usually get anywhere from three to five picks out of a single card, depending upon the size of the picks I want.

This is a great way to make good use of these little plastic items that we would merely dispose of otherwise. (By the way, the same goes for outdated credit cards that most people destroy by shredding

or cutting into small pieces with scissors.) I discovered that the credit card plastic guitar picks tend to work just as well for strumming chords or flat-picking riffs as any picks I have ever purchased at the music store. Now I will never again feel the need to spend money on factory-made picks!

Not all of those credit card offers come with sturdy plastic cards. Sometimes you'll find simulated credit cards made of thick laminated paper instead. I've tried those and, while they can be made to work as expedient guitar picks to some degree, they are not nearly as good as plastic, in my experience.

COMMONLY OVERLOOKED SOURCES OF PLASTIC RAW MATERIALS

As we've just seen with those junk mail credit cards, once you begin focusing on various ways to utilize plastic scraps, you will start to recognize sources that you never even dreamt of before. Every routinely discarded plastic jar lid, warped dustpan, mismatched Tupperware item, cracked poly trash

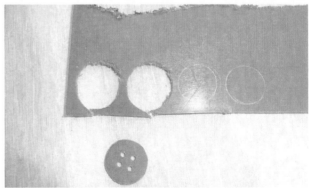

Cutting little disks out of a scrap of plastic with a coping saw for making shirt buttons. Smaller size hole saws would also work.

Guitar picks made out of credit cards.

barrel, old bucket or storage tub, broken kid's toy, electronic appliance casing, CD case or organizer, scratched vinyl record, dog-chewed Frisbee, or empty plastic jug will forever be seen as useful makeshift raw material. You merely have to open your mind and your eyes.

For example, I recently made some nice little shirt buttons out of a scrap of plastic from a ring notebook page divider. Another time, when a plastic propeller blade on my son's toy helicopter broke, I decided to make a hair comb out of the broken-off section, just to see how it would work. This was a quick and easy project using my band saw to cut slits into the plastic to separate the comb's teeth.

When you start cutting pieces of plastic for various homemade products, you will notice immediately that the saw blade produces rough, fuzzy edges. This is usually easily remedied by trimming away the rough spots with a razor blade or sharp knife, or in some instances smoothing edges with fine sandpaper. Thermoplastic is really quite soft and normally cuts and shapes very easily.

I should note here that my experience trying to cleanly cut an old, scratched, vinyl record album with my band saw turned out to be completely unsuccessful, because the record tended to chip and shatter along the edge being sawn. I am not sure if this was merely because it was a 30-year-old record that had become brittle with age, or if this is what we should expect when cutting into vinyl records— perhaps due to the groove in the plastic that might weaken it. I am not eager to saw up more of my record collection to find out.

A final note about working with plastics: the heavier materials, such as the buckets we discussed above, can be welded. Outlets such as Harbor Freight sell plastic welding kits for about 20 bucks that work like a hot-melt glue gun, only with thin sticks of plastic. Although I have yet to experiment with this, I'm told even dissimilar plastics can be welded to and even alloyed with one another. If done properly, the result can be as good as the base component. I can't wait to try it!

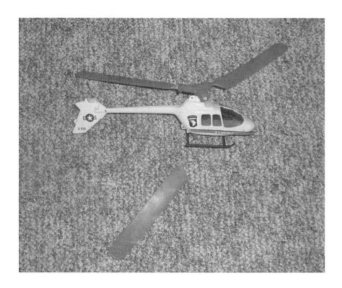

Toy helicopter with broken propeller blade.

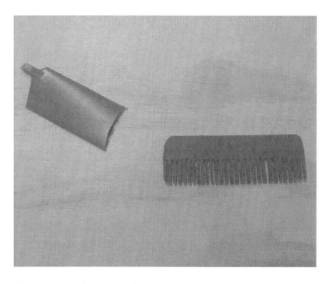

Plastic comb made from toy helicopter blade.

CHAPTER 4

More Odd Things Adapted from Common Household Items

Two beverage cans side by side. The thicker and sturdier of the two is on the left.

There really is no end to the types of expedient products or applications one might invent that make use of common materials found around the average house, a lot of which would merely be discarded otherwise. In this chapter we will consider some more new ideas (adding to the ones we explored in *Makeshift I*), and hopefully these will inspire you to find many others. Before you throw away cans, bottles, scraps of metal, or other odd things, stop to consider what you might make of some of these things, or how you might make them more useful. Ultimately, I believe we are only limited by our imagination.

THE VERSATILITY OF ORDINARY CANS

The metal cans in which products like juice, coffee, beverages, and various foods are packaged and sold are traditionally referred to as "tin cans," but these are not really made of tin at all. Most of the sturdier cans are actually composed of mild steel, but aluminum is also used for some of the lighter beverage containers like soda and beer cans. There was a time when steel food and beverage cans were coated with an alloy containing tin to inhibit rust, and this is apparently where the tin can reference originated.

Cans of every type of metal or metal alloy are quite versatile and lend themselves to innumerable makeshift projects. We considered some of the things we might make out of metal coffee cans in *Makeshift I*, and here we will broaden our source of raw materials to include all kinds and sizes of cans.

The neat thing about any metal can is that it is a lightweight, sturdy, inexpensive container that is easy to cut and bend and lends itself ideally to so many diverse purposes. For example, if you needed to quickly construct a handy water dipper, what better object is there to make it out of than a little metal can?

Beer and soda cans these days are most often composed of very thin, soft aluminum—thin enough that it is easy to cut with ordinary kitchen scissors. The shiny inside surface of a typical aluminum soda container could be saved and used as reflector material or for other applications where its smooth, flexible metallic surface may be needed for any number of special purposes. The bottom portion of the can might be cut free and used as a small disposable ashtray or a glue mix tray for those

A variety of makeshift applications for discarded metal cans.

inevitable quickie repair projects around the house.

Sturdier steel cans require different cutting methods, but they may be more versatile in their potential applications than super-thin aluminum because of their more rigid material. Tin snips are commonly used for cutting heavier can material, whereas a makeshift alternative is to fit a wooden post or log into the can opening for reinforcement, then secure it in the jaws of a vise (if they can be opened wide enough) and cut the can as needed with a hacksaw. But I find that a Dremel rotary tool with heavy cutoff disks works well for cutting thin steel or even the thicker aluminum in heavier

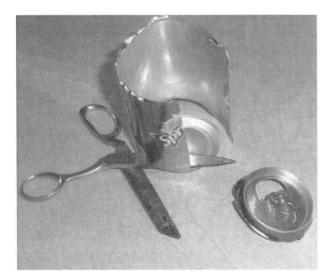

Cutting a pop can into pieces, using only scissors.

The bottom of a soda can cut off to use as a little mixing dish for two-part epoxy glue.

A heart-shaped cookie cutter made by my dad in his metal shop class in the 1940s.

Small upside-down steel can with a spring clamp soldered to its bottom to make a small vise.

containers. This tool makes the task so easy and produces a comparatively neat cut.

Thin steel from cans has been used in the fabrication of more hobby crafts than could be listed here, but a typical example worth mentioning is a homemade cookie cutter. The material can be taken from one or several cans, shaped with pliers or other tinsmith's tools, and then soldered together as needed to create the cookie cutter or some other decorative or useful product.

A makeshift stew-can cook stove. A bent section of coat hanger wire is fed through holes poked near the mouth of the can and formed into a combination handle/grate.

The thin metal in cans makes them conveniently suitable for endless soldering applications. I found that a small metal spring clamp soldered to the bottom of an upside-down fruit can makes a handy little fly-tying vise for around camp. It simply fits over a vertical tree branch or wooden post of slightly smaller diameter that is jammed into the ground to make a solid base.

Innumerable camp stove designs have been fabricated out of cans and used to cook and keep warm in the out of doors. "Tin can" stoves of all sorts can be heated by burning such materials as small twigs, wax-coated paper or cardboard, pinecones, charcoal, white gas, and even canned fuel. Metal cans of various sizes clearly allow for a wide range of innovation in this area.

The thin steel lid from a #10 metal can makes a pretty good base for a homemade candleholder. Simply solder a small, pointed tack or tiny wood screw to the surface of the lid in the center with its point facing up, where it can pierce the wax in the bottom of a candle to help hold it upright, and attach some type of handle to the edge to allow you to more conveniently pick it up if needed. I cut a section from a smaller steel tomato paste can and soldered it to one side of the flat lid to serve as a ring-shaped handle. Any burrs in the candleholder's rim or makeshift handle can be sanded smooth or simply folded over along the edge in some cases.

To attach a simple wooden handle to the side of

A #10 can lid serves as the base for this candleholder, with a ring handle cut from a smaller can and soldered to it.

A #10 can with short section of scrap 2 x 2 pine lumber nailed on to form a quickie handle.

a can, one quick and expedient approach is to cut a 6- or 7-inch section of 2 x 2 pine board and nail or screw it on from inside the can. I was in a hurry to get one of these made for a recent project that called for a small water bucket with a side handle, and I used two large nails to attach the handle to the rim of my #10 can (although screws would hold more securely). I predrilled the nail holes through the thin metal and partway into the wood with a slightly undersized drill bit to aid the process and to avoid splitting the wood.

One simple way to make a poor man's camp skillet is to cut the top half of a #10 can in such a way as to retain part of it to then shape around a wooden dowel that serves as a removable handle. The important thing is to allow enough metal between the upper half that wraps around the handle and the lower half that serves as the pan. If that part is cut too narrow, the handle connection won't be very strong, I discovered. Be sure to smooth up the resulting sharp edge on the can's lip with sandpaper, or you can simply fold over a narrow depth of the rim all the way around to cover the cut edge. A hose clamp can be used to tighten the thin metal around the handle.

Cans are ideal, of course, for holding all sorts of items in a workshop. Don McLean showed us how he adapted an old can as a handy tool holder for the shop. He uses a wet paintbrush as an example, but

the same concept can be applied to a hot soldering iron; just bend an additional trough on the other side and add some weight to the bottom so the can won't tip over so easily. Set the hot iron in the troughs to keep it off the workbench.

Once you grasp the potential for constructing

#10 can with top half cut and bent around a wooden dowel for a handle.

Starting to make a simple tool holder from a tin can with slip-joint pliers.

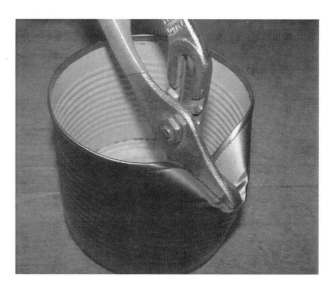

Finishing the bend for the trough.

Final product as used to hold a wet paintbrush. The same idea (and a bigger can) works for a hot soldering iron.

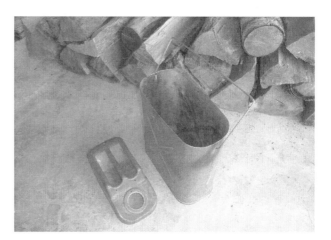

Charcoal bucket made out of the bottom portion of an old 5-gallon gas can.

things out of ordinary metal cans, you can extend your makeshift thinking to metal cans of any size or form. Take those 5-gallon steel gas cans (sometimes called jerry cans) that you can often find at yard sales and flea markets for around $5. I cut the top off an unused can with my Dremel tool and attached a bent steel rod for a bail to create a sturdy bucket. I use it in my blacksmith shop for charcoal. To avoid the potential danger from sparks, be sure to clean, rinse, and dry the inside of the can as much as possible, and leave the opening uncapped for awhile to allow any fumes to

dissipate. Then fill the can close to the cut line with water before you start cutting, just to be extra careful.

CUTTING AND BREAKING GLASS JARS AND BOTTLES

Have you ever wanted to lop off the top of a beverage bottle and make a drinking glass, or maybe reduce the height of a glass jar for any reason? I've always hated throwing away good bottles when it seemed like they should be converted into something useful. Making bottles into drinking glasses is one way to reuse something that is otherwise normally just thrown away.

For anyone lacking experience, attempting to neatly and reliably cut curved glass can be a challenge. Those little "pizza cutter" style window cutters that are available in every hardware store are inexpensive and easy to use for cutting flat windowpanes, but by themselves they don't work very well with bottles or jars, in my experience. It seems nearly impossible to keep them from sliding uncontrollably over the curved surface. Strips of tape around the bottle might be used to create an expedient track for the cutter, but I wanted to find a more reliable method.

I've learned a lot about this craft recently, and I am going to share all of it here. For those readers who tend to become bored with the details of lengthy experimentation, I suggest skipping ahead to the last part of this discussion. However, I do believe that interested readers can benefit from my own trials and errors with this, and some makeshift hobbyists will no doubt find it all totally fascinating, just as I do.

Some time ago, I learned an interesting trick from the book *Bushcraft: A Serious Guide to Survival and Camping* by Richard Graves. In it, the author describes heating a wire or, alternatively, igniting a grease-soaked string, tightening it around the circumference of a glass bottle where the break needs to be (in that book, to create a candleholder), and then submerging the bottle in water. The bottle separates along the line where the rapid temperature change shocks and cracks the glass.

I found that this does in fact work. My initial attempts involved cotton twine that I had saturated with kerosene and tied around a beer bottle as neatly as I could before lighting and dropping it in a pail of cold water. The glass broke instantly when it came in contact with the water, but the flames along the burning string heated a wider path around the bottle than I preferred, resulting in an uneven break. This required considerable effort sanding the rough edge smooth, and I never achieved a perfectly flat rim on that bottle.

Using the hot metal wire as opposed to a flaming string seemed to be a more precise method, as I expected the wire to concentrate the heat into a more restricted space along the intended break line. The challenge was to evenly constrict the hot wire to

Container for pens and pencils on the desktop made out of a beer bottle.

Beer bottle with top broken off using the burning string method.

the circumference of the bottle where the desired break was to be.

I did some additional research hoping to find a better way to do this and found that the dilemma I was having seemed to be the same basic problem for others—the awkward task of heating the wire and then quickly constricting it evenly around the entire circumference of the bottle before submerging.

Some people mentioned using an electrical current to heat the metal wire, but I have two concerns with this approach. First, the wire loop around the bottle would almost have to form a closed loop for maximum contact with the surface of the glass in order to break it completely and evenly, but if the ends of the loop make contact it would short the electrically active bare metal wire. Also, using an electric current to heat a wire around a bottle that must be quickly submerged in water presents safety complications that cannot be ignored.

I thought of another technique for heating the wire, quickly cinching it around the bottle, and then splashing water over everything to crack the glass where intended. Here's how I attempted to do it.

First, I secured one end of a short piece of thin steel wire (approximately 1 1/2-foot long) to an eye

screw that was screwed into a heavy log on my patio at the right height where the wire, when stretched horizontally, would align with the break line on the bottle standing upright on the patio roughly 8 inches away.

Next, I secured the other end of the wire to the middle of a dowel that I used as a toggle-style handle, and then I formed as round a loop as I could with a simple overhand knot in the center of the wire large enough to loosely slide over the bottle.

I set a pan full of cold water within easy reach, along with a little gas torch. I set the bottle in position where the wire loop would easily fit around it. I then put a leather glove on the hand that would grip the wire handle in case it got too hot to handle with bare hands.

When everything looked ready, I lit the torch, raised the wire handle to lift the loop off the bottle, and swept the flame around the loop. When the wire appeared hot enough all the way around, I lowered it over the bottle to the level of the intended break line and pulled the wire to close the loop as securely as possible around the bottle. While holding the hot wire taut with one hand, I quickly set the torch aside with its flame pointed in a safe direction and then picked up the pan of water and poured it over the bottle.

This neat little trick completely failed to cut or even crack the beer bottle.

The two biggest flaws in this approach appeared to be (1) the wire I used was of such small diameter that it failed to maintain and transmit sufficient heat to the surface of the glass, and (2) the overhand loop in the wire failed to adequately constrict around the bottle quickly and thoroughly while the wire was hot—it lacked the necessary tensile strength in the heated state, just as I suspected might be the case.

But I didn't give up on the metal wire idea just yet. I decided to try the same setup again, but this time heating the wire while it was already cinched firmly around the bottle. In this experiment, I filled the bottle with water up to the wire line in an attempt to

Everything I used in my first hot wire bottle-cutting experiment: thin steel wire in an overhand loop with handle and eye screw attached, leather glove, water can, gas torch, and bottles to be cut.

The broken beer bottle containing water up to the break line where the wire was heated by the torch flame on the glass.

Bottom half of broken beer bottle with jagged break line, especially in the area of the paper label.

prevent excessively heating the glass below the intended break line. This time the bottle did actually break more or less along the line when I poured the cold water over the top, as the wire did transfer the heat from the flame in a fairly concentrated area, but it was by no means a clean break. For one thing, I had carelessly neglected to remove the paper label from the bottle, and I soon discovered that the worst

of the cracks and jagged edges that resulted were in the area under the paper.

I then decided to try a thicker wire, twist its ends tighter to more firmly constrict the bottle than what was possible with the loose overhand knot, and once again apply the flame of the torch to the wire while it was already in position around the bottle. I selected a fairly thick coat hanger wire and this time

Getting things ready with thicker wire twisted around bottle.

Heating the wire on the partially water-filled bottle using the torch.

removed the paper label from the side of the bottle. This attempt yielded the best result yet, though definitely not as even or smooth a break as I was hoping for.

My last attempt with the hot and cold shock method involved submerging a bottle in a bucket of water up to the intended break line, with water also inside the bottle up to the same line. Again I removed the paper label first.

In this experiment I directed the torch flame to the entire neck and top portion of the bottle as it sat upright in the bucket, without any wire, and when it was hot (i.e., when the water began to boil due to the ambient heat), I poured cold water on the part above the surface.

The break that resulted was roughly the same as that in the previous experiment. I finally concluded to my own satisfaction that the hot/cold shock method was far from perfect on its own.

My next line of approach involved the window-cutting tool mentioned earlier with its tiny pizza cutter-style wheel for scoring glass. I thought I might employ one or more of these common, inexpensive tools in some kind of makeshift setup for neatly cutting the bottles—more successfully, I hoped, than my breaking experiments had proved thus far. Research on the Internet revealed several different products already available for cutting the

tops off beverage bottles. However, I find it so much more fun and interesting to try to create my own contraptions.

The key for this to work, I presumed, would be finding a reliable way to keep the little cutter pressing firmly against the glass and in proper alignment all the way around the circumference of the bottle in order to properly score the break line.

My first thought with this was to build something like a common pipe cutter, with maybe three of those window cutters mounted atop some kind of doughnut-shaped carriage that would encircle a bottle, just as a pipe cutter turns around a pipe. The cutters would be evenly spaced and directed inward, where they would score the line around the bottle. This concept would entail some method for gradually pushing the cutters' wheels toward the center while the entire unit would somehow be rotated around the bottle.

After considerable thought, I decided to abandon this pipe cutter concept, as it seemed like an awkward and complicated approach to the whole process. A much simpler idea suddenly came to me. Why not employ only a single cutter and, rather than rotate the tool around the bottle, instead just rotate the bottle in a fixed position while the cutter is kept on track and pressing against the glass? This method seemed to more closely follow at least one of the

Bottle in can of water before the top is heated

This bottle bottom (shown with its rim sanded smooth) had the cleanest break with any of my shock methods, but it still has an uneven break line.

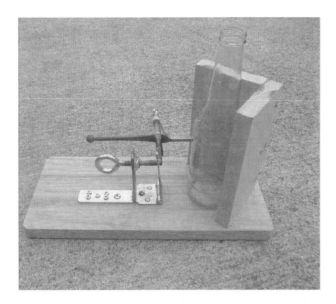

Right and left views of the bottle-cutting contraption I devised.

products I saw advertised on the Internet, so I proceeded with a degree of confidence that it would have a reasonable chance of actually working.

My contraption differs from any that I saw on the Internet in several respects. First, it keeps the bottle upright during the scoring process rather than having it lie horizontally. Also, it makes use of the commonly available (and inexpensive) little window cutters, and this simplifies a major component of the process. Two hardwood boards fastened together to form an inside corner support the upright bottle on its far side, while still allowing it to be rotated by its neck. The cutter is held in position by a small C-clamp brazed to the top of a tall latch hinge and is pressed against the side of the bottle by turning an eyebolt into a nut brazed onto a sturdy L-bracket screwed to the wooden base directly behind the hinge. (The setup is fairly self-explanatory from the accompanying photos.) As the cutter is pressing against the side of the bottle, the bottle is rotated by hand at the neck to score it all the way around its circumference.

My braze jobs appear rather hideous here, as I relied on my little MAPP gas torch for this project—out of convenience merely because one of the cylinders of my

oxyacetylene rig happened to be empty that day, and the smaller torch was just handier at the moment. The MAPP gas torch's flame doesn't get as hot as oxyacetylene, and it works better for things like soldering and brazing smaller pieces of metal, but nevertheless I was successful with this task, and the brazed connections are much stronger than they might look—perfectly suitable for this purpose.

The bottle is rotated by one hand; the cutter pressure is adjusted with the other.

Close-up of C-clamp brazed to top of hinge.

Close-up of nut brazed to L-bracket.

This device is fast and easy to use. The bottle to be scored is set upright against the angled boards. With the cutter properly secured by the C-clamp where its tiny wheel contacts the surface of the glass precisely on the break line, the eyebolt is turned until the cutter presses firmly against the bottle, and the bottle is rotated by hand at the neck until the score completely encircles it. Turning the eyebolt will increase the pressure slightly as the bottle is being rotated.

This makeshift contraption works even better than I had anticipated as a scoring tool for beer bottles. However, scoring a line is just part of what is required to cleanly break the bottle along the score line. One other step is required to complete the task, and I fabricated a nifty little tap hammer that fits down inside the mouth of the bottle, which I use to tap the glass on the inside all the way around along the score line to help the glass break free. This is merely a 3/16-inch-diameter steel rod with one end heated and snail-coiled up into a kind of bulb with just enough mass to serve as an effective little hammerhead. A tap hammer for this purpose has to be small enough to fit through the mouth of the bottle. The standard opening on a bottle of domestic beer is 3/4-inch inside diameter, but I found a Belgian beer bottle with a 5/8-inch opening.

Close-up of a beer bottle being scored by the cutter.

77

Even having progressed to this stage of experimentation, I still did not have the bottle-cutting process perfected to my satisfaction. Beer bottles, I had by now learned well, are surprisingly thin and fragile, especially those of the domestic beers. The clear, uncolored bottles also tended to be thinner and more fragile than the darker tinted bottles I experimented with. My contraption will accommodate the smallest wine bottles, which are heavier and more durable, but I really wanted to make drinking glasses out of beer bottles.

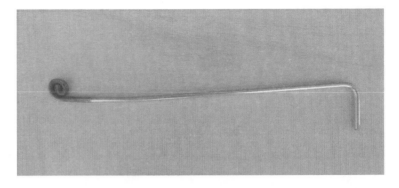

Small makeshift tap hammer for tapping the glass on the inside of the bottle along the score line.

My success rate up to this point yielded only one fairly decent drinking glass in about a dozen or so failed attempts. Time after time, the bottles would crack and break where I did not want them to—normally somewhere other than the score line. I was clearly doing something very wrong.

I decided to go talk to glass-cutting professionals at a local custom window glass shop to see what they had to say. This was the turning point in this endeavor. Perhaps I should have done this in the beginning and saved myself a lot of sleepless nights, but then if I had done that, I would not have had all these valuable experiences to share with you. Now, finally, I am going to tell you how to *properly* break a beer bottle.

Perhaps the most important thing to understand about this whole process is that you never want to score the surface of your glass more than once. In other words, you don't want to scratch over the same line again and again as I kept doing, naively hoping for the deepest possible cut into the glass along the line. Doing this only stresses the structure of the glass and leads to fractures outside the score line. One clean and not-too-deep scoring is all you need for the cleanest possible break. As soon as I applied this new wisdom, my success rate increased dramatically. When I obtained my first reasonably clean drinking glass from a beer bottle, I felt like a kid opening a big present on Christmas day!

Another helpful tip I learned is to lubricate the cutter. One little drop of oil on the cutting wheel works wonders in its ability to make the best possible cut in the glass. Coinciding with this new trick, I also learned about a more expensive ($22 for the product I bought), professional-quality cutter from the C. R. Laurence Company that has a self-

A larger foreign beer bottle, with thicker glass, also fits into this contraption.

lubricating head. A cap with a rubber O-ring seal screws off the end of the handle, where it will receive a small quantity of machine oil, and the cutter's wheel is then automatically lubricated during use.

The problem I initially had with this better quality cutter was that its head is not fixed into a rigid position on its handle but instead is designed

Finally, a fairly decent drinking glass made from a beer bottle!

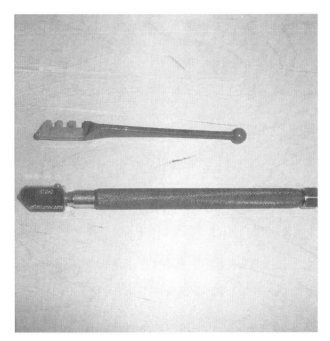

Two types of glass cutters: common hardware store variety at top, and the better self-lubricating cutter at bottom.

to partially swivel, which I assume aids in the more flexible freehand method of glass scoring. Its handle is also tubular and provides no flat surfaces like the more common, less expensive variety, which make them easier to lock into position with the C-clamp. I was not able to secure this new cutter properly into my scoring device as it was.

My solution to this problem was to mount the loose head of the new cutter into a block of wood to

stabilize it. I simply cut a corresponding space out of the top of a block of hardwood of appropriate dimensions, fit the head into the space, and trapped it in place with a small plate of steel screwed to the top of the block. Now I was able to secure the whole works as a fixed unit into my scoring device and use it that way. This arrangement worked well.

Once the new glass cutter with its wooden block base was operational, I was able to score bottles

The professional-quality glass cutter mounted into a block of wood for use in my scoring device.

with a dramatically higher success rate. I then applied all my newfound knowledge to the cheaper cutter (without any block and with a drop of oil), just to see if that would also work. I discovered that whenever I was able resist the temptation to overscore, or turn the eyebolt too far and thereby apply excessive pressure against the glass with the tool (which tends to shatter the bottle more often than not), even the cheaper cutter will sometimes accomplish the task successfully.

While this system will score small bottles as just described, it is not 100 percent reliable by any means. If the technique isn't executed correctly in every respect, the bottle will most likely crack or shatter. I have destroyed more bottles by far with my experiments than I have successfully converted into drinking glasses.

Another thing to watch out for is the undesirable situation of starting the score with the cutter wheel tilted on its leading edge, which tends to wrap the score line into a downward spiral that progresses under itself like the threads of a screw, where it never actually meets the starting end. The C-clamp holder on my contraption is, as I have explained and you can see in the photos, brazed to the top of a latch hinge. The problem with this is that the two parts of this hinge have loose tolerances, and the tool holder—the C-clamp on the hinge, in this case—has a degree of side-to-side wobble, allowing the cutter to easily "crawl" off the intended horizontal break line. I have to pay close attention to how the cutter is aligned at the start and also during the score so that it stays lined up properly and both ends of the score line meet at the end of one complete revolution.

A neatly cut bottle will still normally require final sanding to remove the resulting tiny burrs and to basically smooth up its lip in order to create a decent drinking glass. This was easy enough for me to do using fine grit sandpaper over the flat surface of a pine board. I later learned that a belt sander also works well. Emory cloth would work, too.

I would caution the readers about breathing in the glass dust. Microscopic glass slivers getting into your lungs would surely be dangerous. Also, during my earlier hot wire glass-breaking experiments, I attempted to trim up the surfaces along the uneven break line on some of the broken bottles using my bench grinder. The fast-spinning grinding wheel

Here is my first nearly perfect drinking glass from a beer bottle using this process.

Group of drinking glasses made out of beer bottles using homemade scoring contraption.

Note the burrs on the rim of this wine bottle bottom. Burrs must be removed for a finished glass.

Sanding the lip with a belt sander. Mask and goggles are essential to protect eyes, nose, and mouth from glass dust.

Cheers!!!!

merely crumbles away the edge of the glass, leaving a badly chipped lip that is very difficult, if not impossible, to ever sand completely smooth.

You can see that, in the end, this turned out to be a successful endeavor. Once I learned basically what *not* to do, the secret doorway to the magic world of bottle cutting had been unlocked forever.

MAKING THINGS OUT OF EMPTY AMMUNITION CARTRIDGE CASES

Just about everyone who owns firearms or enjoys the shooting sports will have a small supply of spent cartridge casings somewhere around the house. Some folks save their empty cases for reloading, but those cases can serve other purposes as well.

In *Makeshift I*, I described how an empty brass rifle casing squeezed flat at the mouth with pliers or in the jaws of a vise can be used to clean out the built-up crud from between the teeth of a file. The soft brass is grooved by the file teeth as it is pushed into them, allowing its edges to dive down into the low spaces of the file and basically scrape or push out the trapped material, kind of like tiny shovels. Even split or bulged cases that are no longer reloadable can be used for this purpose.

Another possibility for spent cases involves the fatter empty shotgun shells that have more volume capacity, which can be made into handy pocket containers for holding wooden matches, fishhooks, sewing needles, BB pellets, muzzleloader primers, or other small items. The little shotgun shell containers are easy to make by trimming away the opened, previously crimped end of the plastic shell near the mouth with an X-Acto knife or scissors to make a smooth, even rim, and then find a cork of the correct size to use as a stopper. The fired primer is kept in its pocket to fill the hole, and the inside of the shell can be cleaned out with an alcohol cloth to remove most of the powder residue. I've made several of these, and they work well for containing tiny items.

The brass casings of most modern rifle and pistol ammunition are ideally suited for making quickie powder measures for muzzleloaders, providing a fixed measure of black powder by volume. These can be modified for carrying more conveniently in your kit or "possibles bag" by soldering on a metal ring, loop of wire, or stud on which to attach a leather thong. Probably the easiest way to attach the looped rod or lanyard stud is to first remove the spent primer and firmly fit the added piece into the primer pocket before soldering it into position.

Similarly, a handy powder scoop is easy to make by simply affixing a metal wire handle

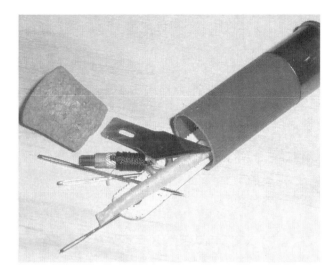

An empty 12-gauge shotgun shell and a cork are used to make a handy little container.

perpendicular to the base of an empty shell casing of the desired powder capacity. Loop the wire around and twist it to constrict the case and hold it firmly. When you no longer want to use the shell casing for this purpose, merely untwist the wire and free the case.

Years ago I adapted a pointed steel rod for probing into dirt and testing the hardness of the ground where I intended to dig, in an attempt to detect and hopefully avoid hitting any large rocks

with the blade of my shovel. I found that a foot-long spike of 3/8-inch diameter was perfect for such a probing rod, and I ground a nice point on its tapered end. To protect the spike's point (and protect myself and my gear from being pierced by the point), I fit a .38 Special casing firmly over it. I drilled a tiny hole through the side of the cartridge and attached a thin, strong pull cord, which facilitated removing the casing when I was ready to probe.

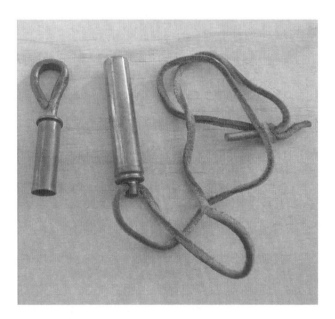

The powder measure on the left is made from a shortened .30-30 casing; the other is from a .300 Weatherby Magnum case.

The shell casing powder scoop with wire handle.

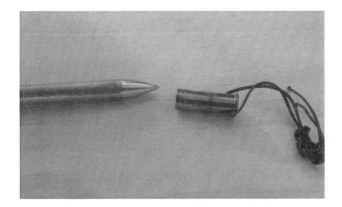 

Point on 3/8-inch-diameter spike and .38 shell casing. Casing fits firmly over point.

My dad made an interesting nozzle for one of his powder horns, mostly from a .348 Winchester rifle casing. As can be seen in the photo below, he soldered the bottlenecked case body to a brass plumbing fixture into which he had devised a button-activated spring valve to open or cut off the flow of powder through the nozzle. The sturdy rifle case makes an attractive and functional powder horn nozzle in this example.

Rimfire .22-caliber ammunition is extremely common and inexpensive compared to centerfire ammunition, and the thin brass cases are normally discarded because they aren't reloadable with conventional methods. This is when saving them for other purposes could be especially practical.

The little empty .22 cartridge casing is perfectly suited as a collar to hold the bristles on the handle of an artist's paintbrush. First, drill out the back of the case so it will accommodate a slightly tapered end of a small wooden dowel of similar diameter, and then fit the handle into the case only partway to allow plenty of unused case length to house the bristles. Glue or epoxy could be added to help hold the brass case onto the handle.

Next, insert the bristles (horse hairs, human hairs, squirrel tail fur, feather vanes, or other bristle fibers grouped into a small bundle) into the mouth of the case, perhaps with a small amount of glue, and then crimp the mouth closed over the bristles with pliers to keep them from falling out.

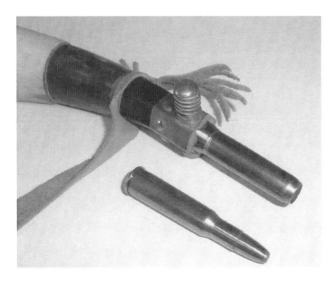 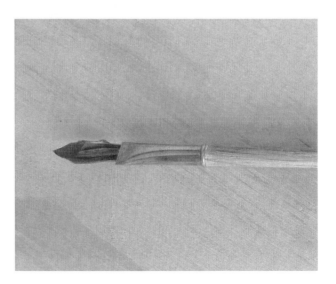

Powder horn nozzle made from .348 Winchester rifle case, shown next to a loaded cartridge for comparison.

Artist's paintbrush that uses a .22 Magnum casing as a collar to hold feather bristles to handle.

I used an empty .22 Magnum casing for my experimental brush collar. I like the extra length of the .22 Magnum for this compared with the shorter .22 LR cases, although I am confident the shorter cases would also work just fine. For the bristles, I used part of a feather I had left over from an earlier arrow-fletching project. This made a nice, delicate artist's paintbrush, as you can see in the accompanying photos.

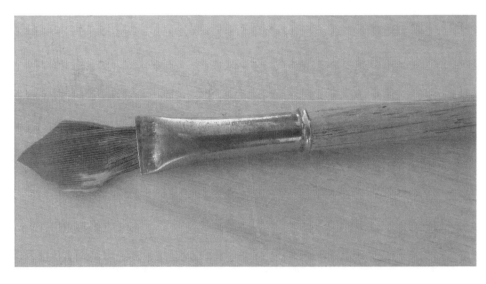

Close-up of the makeshift collar on the feather paintbrush.

One of the neat things about brass ammunition cases is that the brass is soft and very easy to cut, file, grind, drill, bend, sand, or heat for soldering as needed for any particular project. (That's another point worth emphasizing: brass solders very well.) Also, tarnished or dirty cases could always be cleaned and polished in a case tumbler or rock tumbler, just as hand loaders often do with their used brass.

I'll close this section with one of the most memorable makeshift uses for empty brass I've ever heard: a plumb bob made from a .50 BMG case and

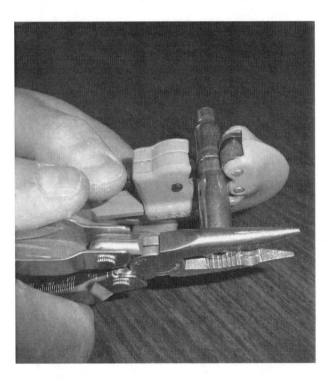

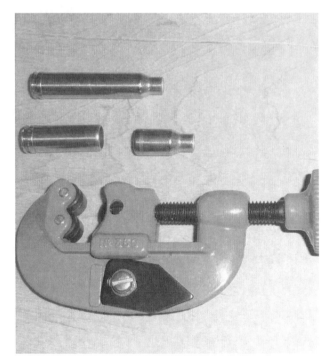

Using a tube cutter to cut a .300 Win Mag case. The Leatherman tool provides a better purchase on the base of the case for turning in the cutter.

bullet. The guy knocked out the primer and ran the string in through the primer hole, knotted it, and then reseated a bullet. The bullet point hung dead on and made a great plumb bob!

ALTERNATE USES FOR ORDINARY BOOKS

Something as seemingly singular in purpose and commonplace in most American households as books can provide the creative hobbyist with a number of makeshift possibilities. Alternate functions for books include using them as props to adjust the height of various items, or tearing out pages for things like emergency toilet paper, wadding for muzzleloading shotguns, or fire starter tinder. You can use the dimensions of a book as a reference gauge for measuring other things (the book in your hands is approximately 8 1/2 x 11 inches). A hardcover makes a rigid support table for writing letters on, and the side of a hardcover makes a crude straight edge for drawing lines. Need quickie hot pot lifters? Grab two paperback books, open them in the middle, and grasp the hot handles.

A more elaborate project involves cutting enough same-size windows in the center pages of a thick book to make a cavity. Glue those pages together to form inside walls for the space, and presto—an instant hiding spot! Hide your goodies on your bookshelf, where very few people would think to look, especially if you used some unknown book with a boring title.

A hollowed-out book makes a great hideaway for small valuables.

CHAPTER 5

Additional Uses for Duct Tape

A variety of functional makeshift products can be fabricated from duct tape, including moccasins, arrow fins, pistol holsters, knife sheaths, small bag pouches, laces and ropes, waist belts, and God only knows what else!

As if there aren't already enough books, videos, and websites about the endless uses for duct tape, we will explore yet several more ideas in this chapter. In *Makeshift I*, we discussed what duct tape is and some examples of how it might be used for making expedient repairs, but we will revisit this amazingly utilitarian product for those who missed the first discussion and also to shed more light on the subject.

WHICH BRAND TO USE?

There are quite a few makers of duct tape these days, and the various brands can have somewhat different characteristics. Products referred to as "duct tape" come in a wide variety of colors and patterns—there is even a transparent duct tape on the market by Scotch Brand. Most of us, however, tend to automatically think of the silvery gray version when we think of duct tape. The most common large-size roll typically contains 60 yards (180 feet) of tape, most often about 2 inches wide (although other widths and lengths are available). Of the brands I experimented with, I found some were obviously stickier and tougher than others, but most seemed usable for my purposes.

In the March 2009 issue of *Popular Mechanics* magazine, Harry Sawyers provides a product test of four different duct tape brands. The easy winner of that test, for sturdiness, stickiness, and water resistance, turned out to be Gorilla Tape. It is advertised to be "for the toughest jobs on planet Earth."

Naturally, I had to buy a roll of Gorilla Tape to experiment with. In my own limited experience with this product, it does appear amazingly sticky and tough, yet it is still easy enough to tear by hand. It also seems to weather better than ordinary duct tape in outdoor applications, which is one of the biggest drawbacks of the regular stuff. For all these reasons, Gorilla Tape would probably be my first choice for general heavy-duty outdoor tasks. As of this writing, I have only found it in one color—black—and this gives it a kind of nongeneric look compared with more common versions of silvery duct tape, at least in my view. The projects in this chapter were created from miscellaneous versions of silvery duct tape, as the more "traditional" lighter gray color seems to show the details of construction better in the photos.

One of the biggest challenges I've encountered while working with any brand of duct tape, especially with long strips, is keeping the pieces from unintentionally folding on themselves, or preventing separate strips from sticking to each other. Whenever one part flops over onto another sticky part, it can be a hassle to separate them cleanly. In that sense, duct tape can be aggravating to work with. And being sticky, it can also be rather messy to work with. It takes some getting used to, but after a while this becomes less of a challenge. I'll give you some tips as we discuss the projects to follow.

A few examples of the different duct tape brands currently available.

DUCT TAPE CORDAGE

I discovered that it is easy and quick to make a functional cord from strips of duct tape. The single-ply cords that I created in my experiments were all strong enough to lift a 25-lb. object (my son when he was four years old) without breaking. That seems to be pretty close to the limit of tensile strength of the first type of duct tape cord I will describe; afterward, I'll explain how to create a substantially stronger version.

First, tear off a length of tape from the roll about 1 or 2 feet long. Then, split this section down the middle (i.e., tear it in half lengthwise). If you don't already know, you will learn that duct tape tears quite easily by using only your fingers. I think that's part of the beauty of working with the stuff— it tears so easily. I would recommend using scissors only for trimming up finished pieces, but do most of your tearing by hand. Besides, cutting long sections with scissors doesn't work very well, as it tends to gum up the blades. Ripping the tape in half lengthwise gives you two strips, roughly an inch wide each.

Now, roll one of the corners of an end of one of the strips. Once the end is rolled into something like

A chair suspended by a single strand of twisted duct tape.

Twisting a half-wide strip of duct tape into a usable cord.

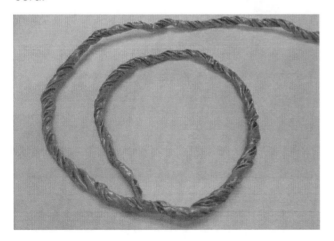

Single strand of twisted duct tape cord.

Splitting a strip of duct tape in half to obtain two narrower strips for twisting into cord.

a narrow tube or funnel, it becomes easy to start twisting the flat strip into a more rounded cord. If you keep the rolling edge constantly curled inward (toward the sticky side) before the tighter twisting, you can avoid having sticky areas on the *outside* of the final twisted cord to some degree. It can take a bit of experimentation to get the twisting technique exactly the way you want it, but it really is fast and easy once you do.

Holding the untwisted part of the strip in one hand with its sticky side facing up, roll (twist) the strand with the fingers of your other hand. The trick, remember, is to end up with a fairly round cord with as much of the sticky part on the *inside* as possible.

When the twisting process nearly approaches the end of the strip, it is a simple matter to add (splice in) a new strip by overlapping the second flat strip directly on top of (and aligned with) the ending strip, with maybe an inch or so of overlap. Remember to keep both strips sticky-side up when overlapping with the new strip (as opposed to having the sticky sides facing each other, which you don't want) and evenly aligned such that it results in one long, continuing strip exactly the same as the original section. Uniformity is one of the main objectives with this process. It is hard to avoid bulges where the two strips are joined, but I generally don't worry about a subtle bulge in the cord.

Once you've got at least three long twisted

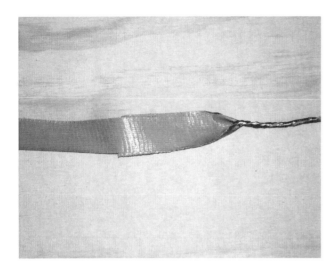

Adding the new strip to the ending strip in order to continue twisting cordage.

Braiding three individual cords of twisted duct tape.

cords to work with, it is a simple matter to braid them to create a three-plait braided rope. The final braided cord will be much stronger than any of the individual twisted cords by themselves.

To start the braid, you need to somehow attach the three cords at one end. One way is to simply wrap them together at one end with more pieces of duct tape. From there it is just a matter of laying the individual cords over each other in alternating fashion, starting with an outside cord over the middle cord, and then the opposite outside cord over that cord (which becomes the new middle cord) and so on, such that they will be more or less interwoven (technically, braided) when you're done. The process is very easy to learn by following a visual guide. In the accompanying photos, you can see what a three-plait braid looks like and which strands cross over which to create the braid.

Braided duct tape rope.

AN ALL DUCT TAPE BAG

Making a small bag or pouch entirely from duct tape is a fast and fun project, and the resulting product can be useful for keeping small items together. I created a handy little bag that closes with a drawstring, which was also made from duct tape as described above.

First you need to find a form to provide the desired shape around which to construct the bag. I used a tall, empty pickle jar, as it was just the size I wanted and the glass surface was smooth, making it easier to slide the final bag off the form when the time came.

Next, tear off a dozen or so 8- to 12-inch-long

The all duct tape bag.

working strips from the roll of tape to make them conveniently ready for quick use. I gently stick a small corner of each to the edge of a tabletop where I can reach them easily while working. Keep in mind that if you suspend long strips of tape closer than about 8 inches apart, static electricity will make them attract each other, and if they happen to stick together, they're usually beyond salvaging.

The first layer of tape—and I used the full width of the tape for this project—wrapped around the outside and over the bottom of the upside-down jar (as it stands on the table in front of you) should be sticky side *out*. The side touching the glass will end up being the inside surface of your bag, and you don't want the inside of your final bag to be at all sticky. Wrap slightly overlapping rings of tape around the outside to form a kind of cylinder shape, and form Xs over the jar's bottom with your ready strips until you've got a complete "skin" of tape. Add strips until all the spaces and holes are covered, but try not to make the skin too tight on the jar, because you will have to slide it off when you're done. Remember, the sticky side of the strips should be facing *out* at this stage.

The second layer that covers the first layer should be sticky side *in*, because it will be the outside skin of the final product. Cover over all the sticky parts. Once this is accomplished and only the smooth sides of the tape strips are exposed, you should be able to slide the bag off the jar without too much trouble—if you didn't wrap the pieces on too tight. Your bag is now almost done.

When you get the bag pulled free from the jar, you can now form a rim or collar for the mouth.

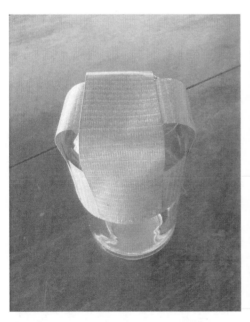

Starting the first layer for the bottom of the bag by forming an X of crossing strips of tape over the base of the jar, sticky side facing out.

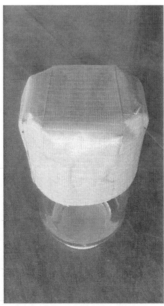

Base of jar completely covered with first layer.

Body of bag built up with second layer of tape strips.

This will cover over the exposed sticky edge on that end and provide a more durable opening. For this, it helps to first estimate the circumference of the bag's mouth, which will be roughly the same as that of the jar. Circumference is easy to determine by wrapping a piece of string or any cord around the object until one end meets the other, marking or simply noting the point where they meet, and straightening out the string to gauge the length. Another way to quickly find circumference is to measure the diameter and then multiply that number by 3.1416. Either way, take your best estimate and then add a couple of inches to ensure adequate length—it is much better to be too long with this than too short. This is the length of tape you will want to tear off the roll.

Tear off two strips of approximately the same length. Fold one strip in half lengthwise over the other to create a kind of reinforced collar. After having done this, you should still have a sticky strip on approximately half the width of the resulting collar piece. You may wish to trim both ends of this collar strip with scissors to make it neater, but keep in mind that these ends ultimately will be covered over with a short strip where they meet or overlap at the mouth of the bag.

Now, with the collar strip's sticky portion facing inward toward the bag, begin attaching it to the outside of the bag around the opening, with only the reinforced smooth half hanging over the open edge. It is important to keep it as evenly aligned as

Forming the collar piece for the bag by folding one strip over one edge of another.

possible as you continue applying this sticky section all the way around the mouth of the bag. You can cover over any seams or overlapped pieces with additional pieces of tape when all of this is done to more or less seal everything up. The resulting bag should be completely smooth on all surfaces inside and out, with a minimal amount of sticky edges of tape exposed. It should resemble a kind of small vinyl pail.

The only thing left to do at this point is to poke or punch the holes around the mouth of the bag (I used my rotary leather punch for this), and then lace

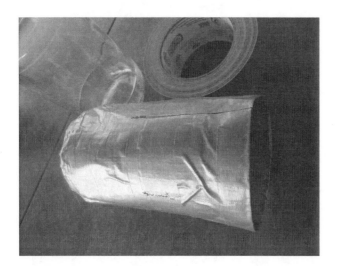

Here is what the bag should basically look like with the collar attached at the opening.

Completed bag with duct tape drawstring.

in the drawstring cord. As mentioned, I made my drawstring out of duct tape as well, using the single-ply twisting method on a half strip. But really, any bootlace or string would serve the same purpose.

This little bag is ideally suited for conveniently containing tiny kid's toys, marbles, coins, nails, screws, fishing lures, musket balls, pebbles for a slingshot, or even a little emergency survival kit.

A DUCT TAPE HANDGUN HOLSTER

Leather and plastic need not be the only materials with which we might craft functional holsters for our sidearms. Duct tape, while decidedly not most peoples' first choice, can nevertheless be used in a pinch to fabricate a fast and easy, very inexpensive, temporary handgun carrier. You may be surprised just how functional such a holster can actually be.

I used a rugged Glock Model 19 semiauto pistol for the willing subject of my experiment. The same basic procedures would apply to making a duct tape holster for any other model of handgun.

Start with the same methodology we followed when making the bag just described. Wrap the first layer of tape over the forward portion of the gun's slide and frame *sticky side out* to maintain a smooth inner surface in contact with the gun. Again, be careful to wrap the tape rather loosely in this stage; you want to avoid forming a covering on the gun

with too tight a fit, and you'll need adequate clearance for such protruding things as sights and slide release buttons.

Adding the outside layer, now *sticky side in* for a smooth outside surface on the holster, is quick and easy. I discovered that shorter strips of tape no longer than 5 or 6 inches were much easier to apply over the contours of the pistol than strips of 8 to 12 inches, even though more pieces are needed. This process made me recall making papier-mâché sculptures in kindergarten, when we would apply strips of newspapers saturated with water and flour over balloons.

You might want to flare the opening of the holster slightly to more easily accommodate the gun sliding in and out. This is easily accomplished by making several short cuts along the opening rim and then folding these pieces back over the outside, almost like the petals of a flower, before taping them down to the holster. This also provides a thicker and smoother rim at the opening, as opposed to the sticky edges of tape strips.

Once you've completed the basic shell of the holster and made whatever adjustments for the desired fit, other things can be attached, such as a belt loop or an overstrap or flap to keep the gun from falling out.

The belt loop is easy to construct simply by attaching two strips to a base strip, sticky side to sticky side, and folding them in half lengthwise so

Starting the first layer of tape over the front of the gun with the sticky side facing out.

The basic shell of the holster is formed.

The opening is cut at intervals to allow that portion to be folded back before being taped over.

The first step to creating the belt loop: attach two strips to a base strip.

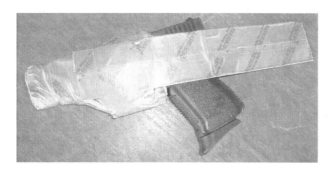

Fold the sticky sides over and attach the thick strip to the holster with more tape.

Form the loop and secure with tape.

you end up with a double-thickness strip with no sticky edges. Then simply fold this as needed to form the belt loop and attach it where it needs to go on the shell of the holster with other strips of tape.

I considered various options for an overstrap to secure the gun, including rubber bands, cords with quick-release slipknots, various button-type closures, and finally strips of Velcro. This holster was quite functional as it was, even without a strap, because my gun fit snuggly inside with no tendency at all to drop out if tipped upside down. However, just to be on the safe side, I attached a strap of doubled tape where it could wrap over the gun, and then I secured short strips of Velcro with duct tape where they needed to go for an effective hold-down.

The finished loop slipped over a belt.

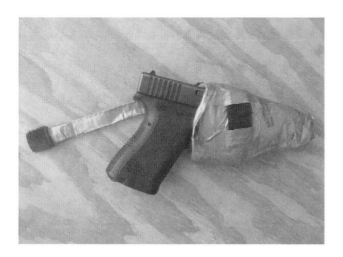

The holster with an overstrap added to help hold the gun securely.

A DUCT TAPE KNIFE SHEATH

Making a functional sheath out of duct tape is incredibly easy if you combine the tape with stiff cardboard. The cardboard provides better protection for the sharp blade than just layers of tape could by themselves.

Creating one of these quickie sheaths is as simple as folding a piece of stiff cardboard over the blade of your knife to the shape you want, and then wrapping strips of duct tape over the outside to hold everything in place. That's really all there is to it. You could add a belt loop to the sheath exactly as just described with the gun holster.

I acquired a dagger-style knife that was particularly difficult to find a suitable leather or Kydex sheath for, so I constructed a functional sheath out of duct tape and cardboard mainly as a temporary measure, just to have something to protect the blade until I found a more permanent sheath. As it turned out, the homemade duct tape sheath does a great job of holding and protecting the blade. As can be seen in the photos, I made flaps that wrap over the knife's handle and then attached a bootlace in such a way that the flaps can be tied down to hold the knife securely in the sheath.

Done methodically, one of these duct tape and cardboard sheaths will work quite well for its

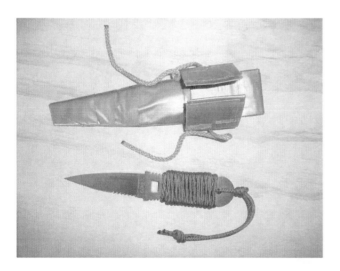

To make this sheath, I folded a cardboard pattern with cover flaps to fit the dagger and then sealed it up with strips of duct tape.

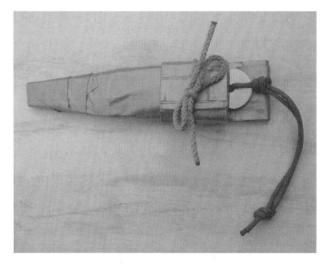

The dagger secured in its cardboard and duct tape sheath.

intended purpose and I'm guessing should survive a surprisingly long time if not abused too severely. However, its biggest disadvantage is its inability to handle dampness or rainy weather very well. It should be used where it can be kept dry; otherwise the cardboard will surely get soggy and the tape will eventually lose some of its stickiness.

A DUCT TAPE BELT

Strips of tape are conveniently suited for fabricating belts to hold up your pants, as they come from a long, continuous, flat strip on their roll. The primary objectives are to keep the pieces even while marrying them for multiple plies, attach enough plies together to provide the required thickness and tensile strength, and make the belt the necessary length.

The duct tape belt can be expected to be comparatively stretchy, given the nature of the material from which duct tape is made. For the purpose of a waist belt, it should work just fine because we're not going to be suspending our body weight from a tree with it—this belt will only be used to hold up trousers.

There are a lot of ways you could go about creating a serviceable duct tape belt, but my method produced a pretty good one, and I think it looks pretty good, too, but I'll let you be the judge of that.

My prototype duct tape belt measured slightly over an inch wide, which seems almost too narrow for the belt buckle size that I had available for this project. To make it, take two full, wide strips of tape about 3 feet long and overlap them along their full length, with half of one strip's sticky side facing an equal amount of sticky side on the other. Fold the overhanging sticky parts on each so they stick down to the smooth back portion of the marrying strip. The resulting strap is a double-thickness of tape having only smooth sides exposed, which can be cut to any shorter length necessary. Punch holes wherever needed, following the (almost) center seam on either side as a guide for alignment. Again, I used my rotary leather punch for this task, but nearly any pointed instrument could be used to make holes in soft duct tape, including the point of a sharp knife, a nail, or an awl. The holes don't have to be perfect or pretty.

The standard-size strip of duct tape as it comes off the roll measures roughly 2 inches wide. If you want to create a thicker, stronger, and wider belt than the one shown in the photos (in other words, if you want a belt that is 2 inches wide), simply stick two full-sized strips together as evenly as possible, sticky side to sticky side, along their entire length. (A 3-foot length is usually a good working length to start with for making a belt for the average adult waist size.) Then fit folded strips over each edge, exactly like we did with the belt loop for the holster, to cover the sticky edges.

You could follow this same basic procedure to create a variety of useful carry straps and slings for things like duffel bags, rifles, arrow quivers, canteens, purses, and so on. Just remember that the

Duct tape belt before adding the keeper loop.

Details of my stylish duct tape belt.

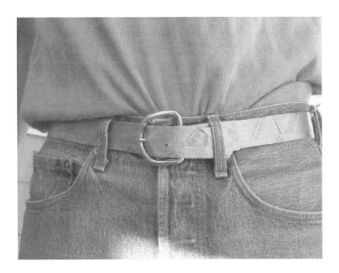

Wearing a duct tape belt. Kind of retro 1960s sci-fi look, don't you think?

more strips (or plies) your strap is composed of, the more tensile strength it can be expected to possess. I think that a temporary rifle sling out of duct tape, for example, should be pretty thick.

Perhaps the key word with most or all of these duct tape projects is "temporary." As long as you keep it in that perspective, duct tape should serve you well. Not that I would be particularly eager to trust my life to this stuff or anything made of duct tape (such as if substituted in place of a regulation seat belt, for example, which I wouldn't recommend), but it might actually be tougher than most people realize, especially with multiple strips married together.

In the future, Gorilla Tape will be my first choice of duct tape for a belt, being heavier and stronger than the average tape, but also because the black color looks better than the silvery gray I used for my first duct tape belt.

Again, neatly sticking together long strips of tape can be awkward and tricky at first, but after a bit of practice it does get easier. I read online about covering a tabletop with waxed paper when working with duct tape, since the tape supposedly won't readily adhere to the surface of the waxed paper. That might be worth a try, although I have not personally done so. So far I have not experienced *too* many frustrations with strips of tape sticking to everything during my projects. I will say, though, that a clean, smooth work surface sure helps make the working conditions manageable.

DUCT TAPE MOCCASINS

Multiple overlapped strips of vinyl tape create a kind of leathery material, as we have seen, and to not attempt to make footgear out of this amazing resource would seem almost a sacrilegious omission for someone writing a book about makeshift projects. So I *had* to try it.

I've constructed moccasins by hand before, using tanned animal hides and needles and thread, and I can tell you that making this same basic kind of shoe out of duct tape is much easier and faster. I will admit, however, that a traditional hide moccasin will be superior in almost every respect to a duct tape version. Even so, I can envision a scenario in which a survivor needs expedient footgear, and while a supply of animal hide may not be immediately available, a roll of duct tape just might be on hand. So let's do it!

Start this project much the same way we did with the duct tape bag and pistol holster: begin looping strips of tape around the form (in this case, your bare foot) with the sticky side facing out. Once again, you want that first layer, which will ultimately be the inside surface of the final product, to be smooth rather than sticky, since the inside surface of your moccasin will obviously be in direct contact with your foot.

Once you've mummified most of the lower half of your foot, apply a fresh layer of tape strips over that with their sticky sides facing

Building the basic shell of the duct tape moccasin while it's on the foot.

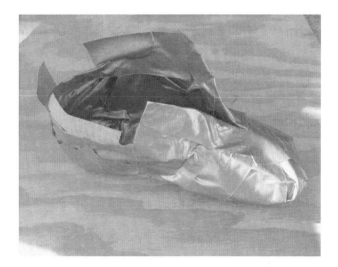 

Forming the "petals" and folding them over to create the collar around the opening.

inward to form the outside surface of the moccasin. You want to completely cover all the sticky spots with this outer layer.

Now here again we have this important consideration before we get too far along with things. You want to apply the tape strips fairly loosely over your foot, just like we did with the bag that we started on the jar form and the holster on the gun. If you wrap your foot too tight with the tape, you will end up with a moccasin that will be very difficult to put on and wear.

The next thing to do is create a collar for the rim around the shoe's opening, kind of like what we did for the mouth of the bag, to cover over and reinforce the rough, thin edge of the tape strips that form the shell of the shoe. Simply fit a strip into the inside of the shoe's opening around the back and sides, with its sticky side facing out and with roughly half the strip showing above the top line. Then make vertical cuts at intervals in the exposed sticky top portion of this collar strip (like those petals described in the holster project) so you can neatly fold each piece over around the curve of the moccasin opening.

With the shell of the moccasin basically complete, it is time to create a seam where the top of the shoe can be opened to facilitate removing it from the foot, or closed with lacing to help tighten it on the foot. Slowly snip a center seam in the duct tape over the top of your foot while you are wearing the shoe. (I couldn't easily remove it until I cut this seam.) Needless to say, go about this very carefully to avoid stabbing the top of your foot with the scissors.

Once you have the shoe off your foot, it is a simple task to fold and fit additional pieces of tape to cover the rough edges on both sides of the seam and then punch the lace holes where you want them. My design lacks a tongue piece under the laces, but I'm confident that something like that could be made of duct tape easily enough and then attached inside, if desired.

I made my shoelace out of duct tape as well (as you can see in the photos), exactly as I made the drawstring for the duct tape bag and, as we discussed earlier, in making duct tape cord.

Moccasin with duct tape shoelace added.

Wearing the finished duct tape moccasin.

Strips of tape could be added to the bottom of the moccasin to build up the sole. To keep these additional layers relatively flat, you could create a separate foot-shaped mat of even thickness before attaching it to the bottom of the shoe. I might even glue the individual layers together and then glue the finished mat onto the sole, if barge cement happened to be available, as I believe this would wear better than the duct tape alone. (Come to think of it, these flat, foot-shaped mats might make excellent bases for duct tape sandals.) Another, even sturdier option would be to cut a sole shape out of a plastic bucket and build it into the bottom of the moccasin.

While this moccasin would clearly never be my first choice of footgear, I am confident that it would provide some degree of protection for the bottom and sides of the foot—certainly better than having no footgear at all under certain conditions.

Another possibility for a duct tape moccasin is to first put socks on the feet, preferably thick boot socks, and then build the footgear over them. In fact, I might go as far as to put on a pair of socks for proper sizing and then an outer pair over that and actually apply the first layer of duct tape strips sticky-side *in*, so that they adhere directly to the outer pair of socks. This would form a soft interior liner for a much more comfortable feel on the feet, and the moccasins would have better insulation in

cold weather. You could even build high boot-type moccasins this way.

FUNCTIONAL DUCT TAPE ARROW FLETCHING

We saw an example of duct tape arrow fletching in *Makeshift I*, but in this book I will explain exactly how to make them. Although duct tape fins are admittedly not as lightweight, rigid, or durable as either plastic vanes or real bird feathers, I have found that they will indeed perform their intended function of stabilizing an arrow in flight. Not only that, but such makeshift arrows are inexpensive and very easy to fabricate in a hurry. I have launched the same duct tape-finned arrow a number of times, from several recurve bows, and it is still perfectly serviceable.

An important consideration with this application is the weight of the tape. Ideally, you want to use one of the thinnest, lightest duct tape brands you can find, as some are thicker and heavier than others, and arrow fins need not be heavy. A very strong duct tape, in my observation, is one marketed by the Berry Plastics Corporation called Nashua 357 Premium Grade Duct Tape, but at 13 mils thickness (according to the specs offered on FindTape.com), this particular product is a bit too thick and heavy for the optimum in arrow fins. This would be the case with Gorilla Tape as well, which is even thicker (17 mils, according to Grainger's duct tape comparison page). For sturdy, yet thin and lightweight arrow fletching, I prefer using something like Duck Brand Duck Tape, marketed by the Henkel Corporation. It is visibly thinner than other brands, yet it is sturdy enough for the task. Keep in mind that with this project we are trying our best to simulate real bird feathers, which happen to be, as they say, "as *light* as a feather."

The first step is to look at the back of your arrow shaft and envision the triangular pattern of the three arrow fins from that end and where they should be positioned in relation to the notch for the string in the nock. When pulling back the bowstring to launch the arrow, it is generally considered best to have one feather—usually the odd-colored one—aligned directly opposite from the bow to facilitate

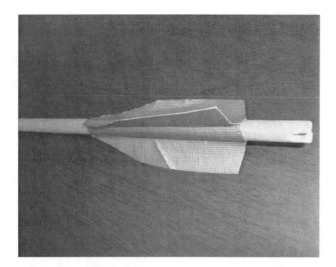

A quick and easy expedient arrow with duct tape fletching.

Looking at the back, or nock end of the arrow shaft. Note the position of the tape strips that form the three fins.

the optimum arrangement for clearance between the fletching and the arrow shelf during the launch. I recommend following this same methodology with the duct tape fins and arrange them with one fin facing away from the bow when readying the arrow for a shot. You could always mark the odd fin with a pen for quick visual identification during target practice, or you could even make two fins out of gray tape and one out of some other color. (Duck Brand, for one, offers several colors of duct tape.)

Now, tear three strips of tape from the roll roughly 3 to 5 inches in length, and position the first strip where you want it on the shaft, considering what was just mentioned and ideally 1 1/2 to 2 inches forward of the nock. Stick it so it adheres to the side of the shaft along its center lengthwise, with equal portions of its sticky side hanging over the shaft on both sides.

Next, align the second tape strip so it adheres (along its center) to its own portion of the shaft in the same way as with the first strip, but where its sticky part closest to the first strip marries to the closest sticky overhanging part of the first strip along their full length.

The third strip must then be added to adhere equally to the remaining sticky overhanging parts of the first two strips and to the last exposed portion of the arrow shaft to complete the triad. In this way, all of the tape strips' sticky portions are facing each other (and to the shaft in their middle sections), and

the resulting three fins are each a fairly rigid double thickness of duct tape.

You can trim and shape these fins to your liking with scissors to finish the process. The resulting duct tape fletching should look something like what you see in the photos, if you followed my tedious instructions correctly. There may be other practical techniques for applying duct tape fletching to an arrow shaft, but I found that this approach is very fast and produces a neatly fletched arrow.

OTHER USEFUL MAKESHIFT APPLICATIONS FOR DUCT TAPE

Several years ago, I acquired a used .357 Magnum double-action revolver that wore a set of grips I detested—they were too small for my hand and were not at all comfortable for me—so I immediately sent away for a good set from Hogue. While I waited for the new grips to arrive in the mail, an opportunity presented itself for a trip to the woods to try out the gun.

The grips from Hogue weren't expected to arrive for another week or two, so for a temporary expedient, I decided to form my own quickie handles on the revolver's grip frame—just something to use for one day. The notion to build up the handle with duct tape came to me, and I got busy with it before heading out for a Sunday morning of target practice.

Expedient duct tape handgun grip.

The duct tape luggage nametag.

The first thing I did was tightly wrap the grip frame with a sheet of paper so that the tape wouldn't stick directly to the steel and gum it up, making it a chore to remove later. (Aluminum foil could also be used as an underlayer like this, or whatever will prevent the tape from sticking directly to the gun.) I then proceeded to wrap layer after layer of duct tape over that until the handle was large enough to hold onto. This only took a few minutes. Not only was I pleasantly surprised at how comfortable this cushiony handle felt during the entire plinking session, but I was able to shoot consistent groups with it.

I can envision another practical application for duct tape at the firing range. How many times have you taken your big-bore high-powered rifles to the range before hunting season to sight them in, and after a series of shots, especially fired from a bench-rested position, started to really feel the punishing recoil against your shoulder? Or how about the way your shoulder feels after a day of trap shooting with your 12-gauge?

Some shooters are naturally more sensitive to recoil than others, and there are a number of methods for managing stiff recoil. Some long guns are custom-equipped with recoil-reducer devices inserted into their butt stocks, utilizing things like inertia weights and springs. Some guns have thicker than usual butt pads, and some even have specially vented barrels or muzzle brakes that redirect the combustion gases to minimize the backward thrust of the weapon when fired. And then, of course,

some shooters simply wear a shooting vest with padded shoulders or a heavy jacket to absorb a percentage of their rifle's kick.

The shooting vest or jacket with a padded shoulder is a simple enough solution, to the degree that it works. They can be purchased in sporting goods and shooter's supply stores; Brownells, for example, currently lists in its catalog two different shoulder pad products to absorb heavy recoil.

But why shell out the money for a new item when you can create your own shooting jacket or shirt? Take an old, faded shirt, jacket, or vest and use duct tape to build up the shoulder area where you seat the butt of your rifle or shotgun. Enough strips of tape adhered to that area would create a kind of buffer pad that would surely reduce the amount of punishing recoil you would otherwise feel while shooting your big guns. This is just a quick and easy way to possibly save you from shoulder bruises, not to mention a few bucks. If you're concerned about the sort of fashion statement you'd be making with such duct tape tailoring, you could always throw a sweater, shirt, or jacket over your new shooting garment.

Finally, I recently resorted to using duct tape when my wife and son traveled by air to visit my sister and her family in another state. (I would have gone with them, but I simply couldn't take the vacation time away from my work on this book. This is my best excuse, anyway, and I'm sticking to it!) My wife asked me to make luggage identification tags just before we headed out to the airport, and my quick idea was to fold a strip of gray duct tape back onto itself, write her name and contact info on the smooth side with a permanent black marker, and then cover it over with clear tape so the ink wouldn't smear. The final step was to punch a hole and connect a rubber band to attach it to the suitcase handle. (A piece of cord would work as well.)

We discovered that the duct tape does indeed make a suitable and surprisingly durable nametag, and it only took a few seconds to create. This shows just one more example of how duct tape can save the day, especially when you're in a hurry.

CHAPTER 6

Handy Little Makeshift Tricks

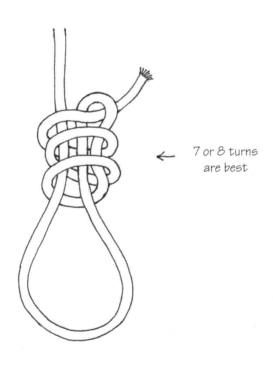

← *7 or 8 turns are best*

Forming a hangman's knot.

Some of the miscellaneous little tricks or repairs we find ourselves implementing in unique situations might be correctly described as makeshift or expedient. While a few of the ideas presented here admittedly are somewhat elaborate, most of them are probably too simple to devote much explanation to. But because they can be so useful, I think it's a good idea to review how and when to use them. In this chapter, we will take a look at some more of my favorite handy little makeshift tricks.

ATTACH ROPES TO A SHEET OR TARP WITH NO GROMMETS

Any blanket, sheet, tarp, sailboat's sail, or animal hide that needs to be connected by ropes or cords but lacks any grommets to tie into can normally still be attached to cords simply and securely without cutting holes in the material or sewing in eyes or loops. It's an easy little trick that can be really handy to know when you need it.

The first thing to do is to put a hangman's slipknot in the end of the rope that will attach to the sheet. The hangman's knot is ideal for this purpose

A cord with a hangman's knot and a small stone are all you need to attach the cord to a sheet or tarp.

Cord successfully attached to the sheet.

because it provides a constricting loop that doesn't loosen easily. It will tend to hold its choke grip, and that is what it needs to do in this case.

The next thing to do is to find a little round stone, musket ball, steel ball bearing, glass marble, or even a hard-shelled nut or acorn of the appropriate size. Now, cup a small area of the tarp, typically a corner section, over the little object such that the material can be tightened around behind it. Finally, cinch the rope's noose tight around the material behind the object and the connection is thus made.

One example of a makeshift application for this trick is when using a heavy trash bag or other plastic sheet for an expedient shelter system. Cutting tie-in holes into the plastic would cause it to rip, whereas this method is a quick, convenient way to attach small ropes to the corners of the plastic sheet.

INFLATE TUBELESS TIRES

The flat tubeless tire dilemma was one that plagued me for years until a friend of mine recently offered his help. After some experimentation, he figured out the problem.

The pneumatic tire on my wheelbarrow kept losing air, and every time I attempted to pump it back up, the air would merely escape between the rubber tire and the steel wheel. An inner tube to contain the air would have been nice, but tires on wheelbarrow wheels often lack inner tubes for some

reason—my guess is to save production costs, because I cannot see any other advantage.

For the tubeless tire to hold air, the rubber-to-metal contact obviously has to be airtight. This can be accomplished in one of several ways. A method commonly mentioned on the Internet describes tightening a rope around the entire circumference of the tire so that it tightly presses the inside edges of the rubber against the inside rim of the wheel equally at every spot along the seams. The rope is then tightened by tourniquet action, using a steel bar or sturdy wooden stick to twist it up, and air is

Attempting to inflate a flat tubeless wheelbarrow tire using a rope and steel rod for a tourniquet stick and a bicycle tire pump. This was not successful.

The better method of inflating the tire, with a ratchet strap and air compressor.

pumped in while the rubber is (hopefully) compressed firmly and evenly against the steel rim all the way around. If you're lucky, the tire should begin to hold air and allow you to inflate it while you slowly loosen the tourniquet stick to allow complete inflation. The rope can be removed as soon as it becomes clear that the tire is holding air. This turned out to be an awkward and unreliable method for us, so we went to plan B.

We found that a ratchet tie-down strap works a lot better than the rope-and-stick tourniquet approach, as it more evenly constricts the circumference of the tire. We also found that wiping the inside edges of the rubber with a wet, soapy swab first will remove much of the dirt and cobwebs that tend to accumulate in there, which can interfere with a clean, tight, rubber-to-metal seal.

Even using the ratchet strap, I discovered that attempting to inflate a tubeless tire with a bicycle tire pump can be quite a challenge. I was simply not able to make it work. This is where an air compressor is particularly useful. The fast, powerful, steady blast of air seems to be the key to more or less blow the edges of the rubber outward against the steel rim to create the proper seal. You could be there all day trying it with a hand pump in vain. The air compressor makes all the difference.

I've heard of people filling tubeless tires with expanding foam, which is the stuff you normally use for weatherization chores. With the tire inflated and the bead well sealed, you pull the valve stem up and fill the tire until foam comes out the hole. Make sure to use plenty to fill the entire cavity, as you'll only get one shot at it. Don't put a load on the tire for a couple days to allow the foam to set up fully. Simply trim the extra with a utility blade after it's dry.

NEAT WAYS TO USE SECTIONS OF GARDEN HOSE

This one might be considered almost common knowledge these days, but it's a neat little trick and definitely a good way to bring new life to those leaky old garden hoses instead of merely sending them to the landfill.

Some new handsaws are sold with blade covers to protect the sharp saw teeth, but not always, and those covers that do come with new saws, usually made of cardboard or soft plastic, have a way of getting lost eventually. Most of the crosscut handsaws, bow saws, bucksaws, or pruning saws that I've ever seen hanging on someone's garage wall were without blade covers. This is usually not a problem—until the tool is stuffed into a plastic barrel with other garden supplies and hauled out to the backyard for use. That's when the exposed saw teeth can jam against other tools and become dulled or bent, or puncture bags of fertilizer or plastic trash bags, or cause nasty cuts to good garden hoses, work gloves, or human flesh.

The simple solution is to split a section of rubber garden hose along one side so it can slide firmly over the edge of the saw blade. This makeshift cover provides a pretty good protective barrier over the teeth, being fairly thick and tough. It works a lot better if the hose section is straight, so before you cut the slit, first cut the length you need, blast your heat gun through it until it gets soft, then straighten it, squash it slightly flat, and let it cool.

I've been told an even better material for a blade guard is fire hose. It's got a sturdy rubber lining, has a heavy woven canvas exterior, and is made to lie flat. See if you can talk your local fire station out of a supply of hose that will no longer pass their test.

Protecting the teeth of a saw blade with a section of garden hose.

A one-man crosscut saw with fire-hose protector.

Another practical use for a section of garden hose is as a tubular sheath slid over a rope and positioned wherever the rope wraps over a sharp or jagged rock, or maybe over a sharp, narrow edge of sheet metal or plate steel. The hose will provide a degree of protection in that section of the rope.

Here's a twist on the leather tubes for holding tools that we showed in *Makeshift I*. Cut a 3-inch piece out of an old garden hose; then cut that in half in the middle but at a diagonal, which gives you a tab to drive a nail through. Attach to a tool shelf for holding screwdrivers, chisels, and other shafted hand tools.

Finally—and this is *not* to code—I've heard of someone sheathing garden hose over bare copper wires leading to a barn!

Section of garden hose used as a protective sheath for rope.

DRILL BIT DEPTH GAUGE

Most craftsmen know about this one already, but I find that wrapping a strip of masking tape around a drill bit to serve as an expedient reference marker for drilling depth works fine, as long as absolute precision isn't called for. This little trick demands some careful visual attention while manually gauging the depth to avoid drilling deeper than the tape line on the bit, but executed carefully, it will facilitate a degree of consistency with a series of holes.

A more precise and controlled technique to ensure consistent drilling depth for a series of holes is to simply set the depth stop on your drill press so it won't allow the turning chuck to descend beyond

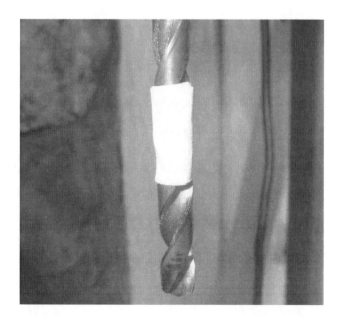

Makeshift depth gauge on a drill bit with masking tape.

Most drill presses have a depth stop as shown here, which can be set to prevent drilling too deep.

Positioning an unsecured workpiece in your drill press in this way will prevent it from being wrenched from your hands.

a specific point. This will prevent any chance of accidentally drilling too deep, assuming the depth setting is correct. However, the tape trick could still be useful when using any type of hand drill that would lack a depth-control feature.

Another possibility for an effective makeshift depth stop is to fit a precision collar onto the shank of a drill bit that could be tightened at the required position with a setscrew to prevent it from sliding up and down. Such a collar can be created from most any short tube that will slide perfectly over the shaft of the bit and is thick enough to accommodate a threaded hole into one side for the setscrew. Possibilities include steel, aluminum, brass, and perhaps even hard plastic.

DRILL PRESS SAFETY TIP

Sometimes you may have to use your drill press to quickly drill a hole near one end of a wooden

board, dowel, ax handle, metal bar, or other lengthy workpiece that is too awkwardly shaped to properly secure in the drill press vise or with hold-down clamps. Like many people, you might plan to simply hold it in position by hand while you drill the hole. If so, think about what would happen if the bit grabbed the work out of your hand and twirled it around. This has happened to me on a few occasions when I've been careless, and it's a scary, dangerous experience.

Drill bits turn clockwise when cutting, so if you position your work such that any potentially uncontrolled rotation of the work is blocked by the column of your drill press (in other words, the long end of the work is resting up against the left side of your drill press as you look at it), your drilling operation will be safer and more successful. Even still, it is also a good idea to wear protective goggles while working at the drill press, and always mind long hair, loose shirts, shirtsleeves, necklaces, or anything dangling loose about the body so it doesn't get grabbed by the spinning drill bit or chuck. Some people won't even wear gloves at the drill press for this reason.

PRACTICAL SOLDERING TECHNIQUES

Instructional resources on soldering typically describe techniques for tinning, but there is one handy little variation to this trick that isn't always explained clearly enough in my view, yet experience has shown that it can be very effective.

In soldering, tinning the metal means to add a thin coating of solder to both pieces before joining them. In this preparatory tinning process, you typically clean and flux the pieces before applying a thin layer of solder to each. The well-illustrated book *Working With Metal* from Time-Life Books describes coating the tip of the soldering iron with a thin layer of solder and then lightly rubbing the tip on a dampened sponge to remove excess solder and flux. With the iron tip tinned, and both items to be soldered tinned, the actual soldering process will usually be much easier and more effective than without these initial steps.

It can be tricky to solder or braze together separate parts of different thicknesses, because each will reach the point of being hot enough for best adhesion at different temperatures. This problem can be sidestepped to a degree by first tinning both surfaces as just described so that solder is prestuck to each surface, so to speak. This way the solder will be able to stick to solder in the final process, as opposed to having to stick to the original surfaces.

REPAIRS WITH A NATURAL ADHESIVE

We talked about a variety of glues and how to best use them in *Makeshift I*, and we even explored several kinds of home-mixed adhesives, but I recently saw a neat trick involving a completely primitive (though very effective) makeshift glue while watching the television program *Man vs. Wild* with wilderness survival expert Bear Grylls. In the episode, Bear needed to travel down a raging river, but he lacked a raft or boat. He eventually found an abandoned plastic canoe trapped by branches along the side of the river. After he managed to free the vessel and examine it closely, he discovered that it

had a hole torn in the bottom of the hull and somewhat buckled sides.

He was able to restore much of the canoe's original shape by bracing it up inside with tree branch reinforcements. He also fashioned an interesting functional paddle by fitting a stuff sack over a Y-shaped tree branch. I thought these were quite creative and fascinating little makeshift adaptations, but my favorite part was the way he patched the hole in the bottom.

Bear collected a supply of tree pitch, or sap, and plopped it into his metal canteen cup. He then added some ashes from his campfire and warmed the mixture over the hot coals, occasionally stirring it with a stick until he had a considerably gooey, sticky batch of "tar." He cut a scrap from the canoe's seat—a mesh of fiber-woven material—to create an expedient patch to place over the hole in the canoe, which provided a grid structure for the tar to adhere to over the hole. He then allowed this glob to more or less dry and harden.

Even though Bear eventually capsized and lost the canoe in the river's rapids, he did note that the hole he had sealed with the tar was not leaking at all.

I remember reading about Native Americans using this pitch-based type of glue to good effect, especially in their primitive manufacturing of archery tackle, birch bark canoes, and other tools and weapons, but I had forgotten about adding the ash. It serves as an expedient filler ingredient to provide more substance to the pitch, making it easier to apply.

This is a very good trick to remember for all sorts of outdoor survival and primitive construction applications. I did wonder, though, how Bear ever managed to clean out that canteen cup for reuse!

DOVETAILED JOINTS, WEDGE KEYS, AND PLUGS

Wooden drawers, boxes, furniture, and cabinets of above-average quality and even some squared log structures have been assembled with dovetailed corner joints for generations. Such connections are very strong and have the appearance of superior craftsmanship compared to simpler connections that are either nailed or screwed together on butted ends. Dovetailed connections have interlocking fingers

The ends of these boards are cut for a dovetailed joint.

Here we see a tight dovetailed corner joint in a side view of a cabinet drawer.

shaped like doves' tails that fit into corresponding wedge-shaped sockets and tend to lock the parts together amazingly well.

A skilled craftsman can saw or chisel out dovetailed cutouts in wooden boards by hand. If you don't feel comfortable attempting that, you can always use a special jig for dovetailing in conjunction with a router and dovetailing router bit.

To mark the angles of dovetails, it is easy to devise a simple marking gauge out of small pieces of hardwood, sheet metal, or hard plastic, as can be seen in the photo on the next page. Alternatively, you

could create a full-length dovetailing template to mark an entire side in the wood for the dovetail cuts.

The joining of wooden boards is certainly not the only application where dovetailing can be beneficial. If you wish to fill a small hole in a steel bar or otherwise restore a damaged spot in the outside surface of something, a tight-fitting dovetailed plug might be the way to go. The neat thing about this process is that it doesn't normally require gluing, welding, soldering, heating, nailing, or screwing parts together at all.

The first thing you do is cut away the damaged section completely, making the cutout in the shape of the dovetail. In other words, you will be sawing, grinding, or filing out the space in the workpiece at an angle on each end that undercuts the surface opening at both ends so that a wedge-shaped filler

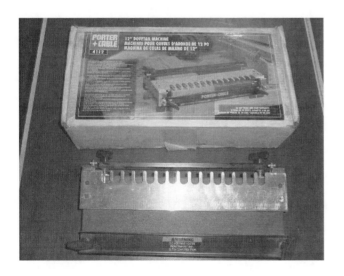

Dovetailing jig by Porter Cable.

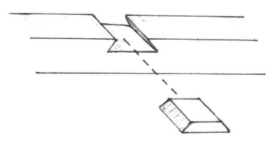

Dovetailed slot and hole plug in an octagonal rifle barrel.

Simple homemade wooden dovetail marking gauge used to accurately mark the angles. A piece shaped in the form of the needed dovetail is fastened to the top edge of the block of wood at left, which is slid along the edge of the board to make the marks for cutting.

piece will only fit in sideways, which won't have any tendency to fall out. Small triangular files are the preferred tools for cutting such dovetailed slots by hand.

Iron rear sights on rifles, and even some front sights, have occasionally been secured into position with this same basic dovetail method for over 200 years. These sights are typically drift adjustable for windage, which means they can be moved sideways in their wedge-shaped slot in the barrel, usually using a light hammer and small drift punch.

Naturally, the tolerances will be closer in a filler plug than on an adjustable sight base. The tighter the plug fits into the slot on all contact surfaces, the more subtle the line between the plug and the workpiece, and the less obvious the fill. Precise sawing or filing and fitting is required with this process.

An example of a rifle rear sight base dovetailed into the top of the barrel.

The end of a round gun barrel with a dovetailed slot cut into the top for a front sight base.

A carefully fitted plug will be difficult to detect at a glance, as is this one in a rifle barrel.

A filler plug that fits tightly into a dovetailed slot with part of its center section protruding above the surface of the workpiece can be carefully peened down with a hammer. This will push (i.e., upset) its sides outward against the inside walls of the slot for a tighter, more secure fit. This is the same process as a rivet upsetting within a hole that locks separate parts together.

Another useful way to use dovetail plugs is as keys to hold two parts together, such as a lug or rib to a gun barrel or even two thick barrels together,

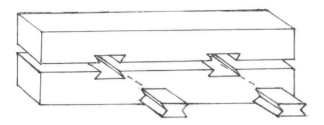

Angle view of slots and wedge keys.

End view, with pieces locked together.

Locking two parts together with wedge keys.

In this photo, the damage to a splitter maul's handle can be seen, the result of swinging long at a chunk of firewood. This kind of damage could have been prevented with wraps of cord to protect that area of the handle.

wherever welding, riveting, or screwing might be less practical for whatever reason. In this application, an hourglass-shaped wedge key is fitted into dovetail slots in each piece to be joined, thus locking them together.

PROTECT WOODEN AX HANDLES WITH CORD

I've described the fundamentals of this neat little cord trick more than a few times in my past writings, but it is one of those things that cannot be mentioned enough in my view, given its utilitarian value and versatility. I have found that it can be used to hold something firmly in position, join things together, or create a covering over something to help insulate it from surface damage or provide a better grip. Specific applications include whipping the ends of rope to prevent unraveling, hafting primitive arrow or spear points onto the ends of shafts, wrapping the line eyes onto fishing rods, creating a kind of expedient gasket seal on an undersized peg that must fit tightly into a socket, securing cracked wooden handles to prevent further damage, and binding multiple shafts or other items, among plenty of other uses.

Regardless of the application, the technique for securing windings of thread, rope, strips of hide, or other cord into a fixed wrap that girds something is the same. The result, when done properly, is a fairly permanent, tightly wrapped covering of cord that holds itself in place and lacks any bulky knots. Here we will look at creating a protective collar on a handle just below the head of a splitter maul or ax.

The handle of a chopping tool near the head tends to receive a lot of abuse when the splitter miscalculates the radius of his swing and clobbers the log with the handle rather than the head (it happens), or when the handle catches on knots in a partially split stubborn log. A bare wooden handle is easily cracked or broken this way.

You could always buy one of those thick rubber collars for ax and maul handles, and they're great for preventing damage to a wooden handle. Lacking one of those, however, you could instead bind that area with cord, preferably several layers of small rope such as parachute cord, to create a shock-absorbing collar that will provide some degree of protection. I suppose layers of duct tape would likely also work to some degree, but cord is much stronger. In any case, two or three wrappings of small rope on the handle just below the head will make it more resistant to shock than would be a bare handle. While you're at it, you could also wrap the lower portion of the handle to create a more secure handhold.

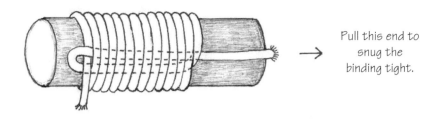

Pull this end to snug the binding tight.

Binding with cord.

Here's how to do it. Align a bight of cord on the section to be wrapped, and then begin winding the cord around and around the item and over the bight, keeping the windings close and tight to one another as you progress, until you have covered over most of the bight. You want to move your wrappings toward the closed loop in the bight. When only a small loop or "eye" of the original bight is exposed at the far end of the wrapping, pass the running end of the cord through it and pull the standing end to draw the loop and the running end securely under the wraps, where they will remain mostly hidden and protected from coming undone. The result is a tight, neat wrapping of cord that uses no knots at all.

A useful tip here is to keep a pair of pliers handy for gripping the standing end of the cord during the final step in the process, because typically you have to pull pretty hard to draw the running end under a tight wrap. You can see why this only works well with cord of high tensile strength. Parachute cord is my favorite wherever its size is appropriate for the application.

This same technique is also popular for decorative wraps with colorful cords. I have even wrapped knife handles and gunstocks in this way to ensure that I always have a supply of cord with me whenever I carry these items. The knife or gun serves as a kind of storage spool for the cord.

CLAMPS AND VISES FROM SECTIONS OF PVC PIPE

A fairly common little trick that is simple and easy is to cut short lengths of PVC or ABS plastic pipe, saw through one side to create a kind of plastic split ring, and use it as a small clamp or vise.

I have found several useful applications for this. A small utility blade or single-edged razor blade can be awkward and even dangerous to use without

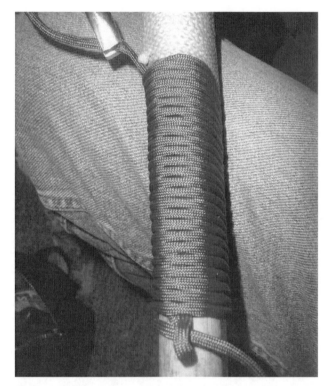

Pulling the standing part of the cord with pliers to draw the running end under the wrap.

Ax handle wrapped with parachute cord—two layers for added protection.

Sometimes you have to make the most of whatever is available.

Additionally, I discovered that two or three of these modified sections of pipe make excellent quick-and-simple paper clamps for holding bunches of pages together. Gluing thin materials, holding leather seams together for stitching—there really are endless light-duty uses for this simple makeshift clamp.

HANDY TRICKS FOR JOINING LEATHER

If you don't have a lot of experience stitching leather but nevertheless wish to construct a gun holster, knife sheath, utility bag, or some other item from cowhide, there are some useful common tricks that can make the project easier.

Your first order of business is to make a pattern that can be traced onto the leather to ensure that your dimensions will be roughly correct. Newspaper usually serves well for projects that aren't particularly large, but any kind of paper that is big enough will do. You can make any necessary adjustments to your pattern before tracing its shape onto the leather.

Before joining the flaps or parts of leather together, it is sometimes practical to wet the leather to help it better conform to the gun, knife, or other form for your project. The downside is that the moisture may not be too good for the surface of the steel in the gun or knife blade, especially if left overnight until the leather dries (which would be ideal for a custom fit), because the steel might rust. The ideal solution is to fabricate a wooden or plastic form with the exact same contours and dimensions as your gun or knife to use as a substitute during the wet form-to-fit stage. It would certainly be something practical to construct if you intend to produce a number of like leather products.

The next step is to join the flaps or parts of leather wherever required for your particular project. A common trick is to first glue the parts together and *then* sew or lace them along their edges after the glue dries. The sewn/stitched edges are more durable and have a more traditional appearance than parts merely glued together, but the glue alone would actually be sufficient for a good connection in many cases, assuming the task was done properly.

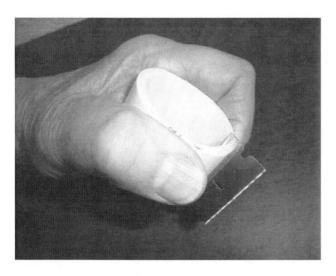

Gripping a single-edged razor blade with a section of split pipe.

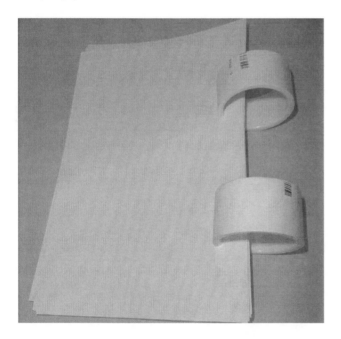

Papers held together with two short sections of PVC pipe. Run a horizontal string or dowel through the PVC clamps and use it as an upright holder for work plans for easy, eye-level viewing.

some type of handle. My dad showed me how conveniently a piece of plastic pipe, cut as described, can be used to comfortably handle a single-edged razor blade. It may not be quite as secure as a retractable scraper/razor blade holder, but held firmly, it will provide an expedient yet comfortable way to grip and use the blade.

I sometimes use liquid hide glue for this because it bonds leather well and is very easy to use, though it usually takes about eight hours or longer to set up properly, and it isn't waterproof. Alternatively, I have found that a good rubber adhesive like Shoe Goo can be used, and it sets up enough to hold the leather together in considerably less time, like in a half hour. For best results, make sure your leather is dry and free of oils or surface finishes like lacquer or paint before gluing.

Gluing is easier than sewing, but the obvious advantage of using glue in addition to sewing is that by gluing first, the sewing is easier, since the parts will already be joined and thus be easier to handle during the sewing operation. This will allow you to focus on your needle and thread work as opposed to keeping separate parts aligned and clamped.

Stitch holes should be spaced as evenly as possible along the stitch line. I usually just try to visually estimate intervals of about an eighth of an inch or longer and say close is good enough, but this is mainly because I tend to prefer a rustic appearance with a lot of my own leather products. My stitching isn't often pretty, and there are clearly more precise methods for keeping the stitches more uniform and neat. Experienced leather workers use various tools for marking their stitch holes.

In the chapter on improvised tools, we considered how to make an effective little tool called a pricking wheel that marks evenly spaced intervals in leather for the stitch holes. Another kind of tool, sometimes called a pricking iron, is essentially a punch with multiple tines in a row that is aligned on the stitch line and then struck with a

The flaps of this leather knife sheath are glued and clamped together until the glue dries.

Drilling the stitch holes in the glue-joined leather seam before sewing.

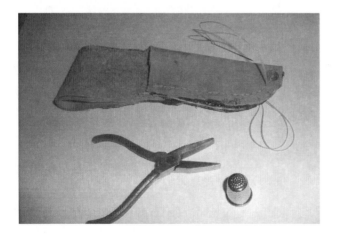

Stitching the seam in the leather sheath.

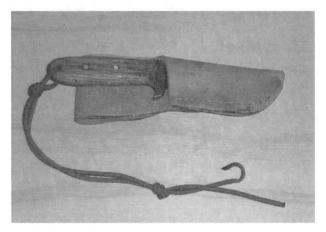

The finished product.

mallet to mark evenly spaced stitch hole positions. Marking positions beyond the length of the pricking iron's row of tines is easily accomplished by overlapping a few of the previously marked holes with maybe two tines and continuing the process.

Another useful trick employed by a lot of leather workers is to drill the stitch holes before sewing or lacing. Drilling is usually a lot easier than punching the holes with an awl, especially with thick cowhide. With the leather parts glued together, it is usually easy to drill the holes in proper alignment, using a hand drill or drill press and an appropriately small drill bit. A block of wood under the project makes a useful drilling anvil.

SHARPEN YOUR DULL DRILL BITS

All craftsmen know the importance of keeping their tools sharp, and just like the edges of chisels, axes, knife blades, and saw teeth, drill bits that see a lot of use also get dull. While it is sometimes easier to replace old dull bits with new sharp ones, it can be quite expensive, especially with the larger bits. It makes sense to keep your existing supply of bits sharp and in good order. Sharpening dull twist drill bits is not necessarily a difficult task, and there are several ways of doing it.

Probably the most common technique is to simply touch up the bit's tip freehand on a grinding wheel or bench-top belt sander. This takes steady, well-supported hands and close attention to detail. It is particularly tricky with a high-speed grinding wheel because the steel in the bit tends to overheat quickly, and the cutting tip you are trying to sharpen can be destroyed easily. It helps to keep a can of water close at hand, where the tip can be submerged frequently to keep it cool. Also, to produce finer cutting edges at the leading end of the bit, it works best to use a wheel with a fine-grit surface rather than a comparatively coarse grinding surface.

(I should point out here that this discussion focuses on sharpening common twist drill bits. Spade, auger, Forstner, countersink, and other specialty bits should also be kept sharp, but in my experience, it is easier to restore some of their more intricately angled cutting surfaces with small flat files.)

If you use this freehanded technique to sharpen a twist bit on a grinding wheel, be sure to progress slowly and carefully, keep the radius to the point even all the way around the tip of the bit, and avoid pressing any part of the bit sharply into the wheel. Doing so would likely ruin the bit, possibly damage the wheel, and present a safety hazard by potentially grabbing the bit out of your hands or flinging dislodged grinding wheel chunks at high speed. I wouldn't even consider doing this without wearing safety glasses.

The main concerns when sharpening a drill bit,

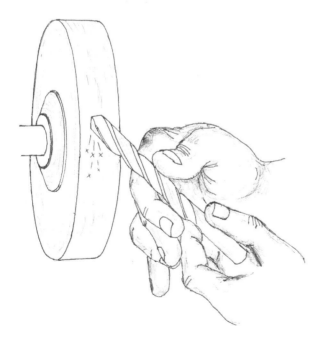

Sharpening a drill bit on a grinding wheel. Keep a can of water close for cooling.

Sharpening a spur of an auger-type drill bit with a small flat file.

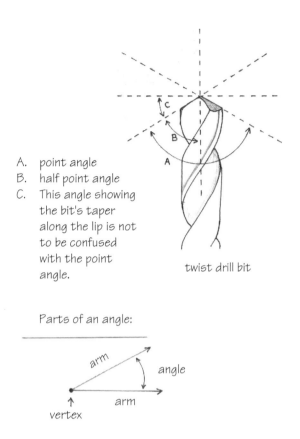

A. point angle
B. half point angle
C. This angle showing the bit's taper along the lip is not to be confused with the point angle.

twist drill bit

Parts of an angle:

arm

angle

arm

vertex

The point angle of a drill bit.

Using a protractor to measure the angle of a drill bit point.

besides progressing slowly, include observing all the angles and edges carefully before grinding, striving to preserve any original angles, and keeping everything as even and symmetrical as possible. The angle of the taper at the point of the bit, known as the point angle, is an important consideration. There are several other important angles associated with drill bits, including the clearance angle, the lip angle, the notch wheel angle, the primary and secondary chisel angles, and the web angle, but for now let us focus primarily on the point angle to keep things as simple as possible for this discussion.

As noted in *Mechanical Trades Pocket Manual* by Carl A. Nelson, the recommended general-purpose point angle for twist bits is 118 degrees. Bits for drilling into very hard or tough materials usually have a blunter taper, such as 135 degrees, while bits intended for drilling into wood or other soft materials can be practical with steeper point angles of anywhere from 60 to 100 degrees.

If you use a protractor to measure the point angle of a bit, it is essential to line up the proper

corresponding edges carefully for an accurate measurement, and then to understand exactly which angle you are measuring. In the photo above, we see the angle of one side of the bit's tip, or half point angle, being measured. The protractor reading is approximately 59 degrees, so the full point angle is 118 degrees in this case.

When you are checking the point angle with a protractor as shown here, make sure you rotate the bit a full 360 degrees on its axis while keeping the shaft at a consistent, parallel position in relation to the protractor's arm. In this way, you can observe any variance from the cutting lip on one side of the bit to the other.

Perhaps one of the most important considerations when sharpening drill bit tips is the relief. Simply put, the relief is the area directly behind the cutting lip or edge of the bit (not shown in the accompanying illustrations due to its rather subtle appearance). Removing some of the relief area provides better clearance for the bit as it bores through material.

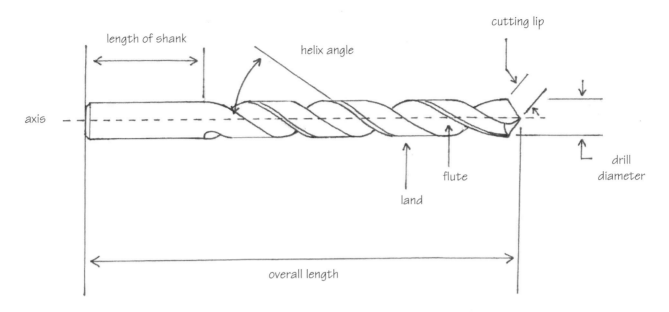

Anatomy of a twist drill bit.

The Craftsman drill-bit grinding attachment for sharpening drill bits from 1/8 to 3/4 inch in diameter.

Note the groove worn into the face of this grinding wheel.

Tools are available to make the task of grinding the point of a bit more consistent and generally easier. Various grinding attachments marketed by General, Craftsman, and other tool makers are essentially bit holders that help guide the point to a grinding wheel at the proper angle for the proper bit rotation during sharpening.

A grinding wheel that gets used a lot will occasionally develop uneven surfaces or grooves in the face along its most used sections. While you're sharpening your drill bits, you might also take a moment to perform a bit of grinding wheel maintenance. It is often beneficial to true up, or "dress," the face of a grinding wheel that has grooves or worn edges, using any of the wheel-dressing tools or stones you can buy for this task. I have had good success with Delta's grinding wheel dressing stone.

Another convenient tool for sharpening drill bits is the type that works much like an electric kitchen knife sharpener, or perhaps even more like an electric pencil sharpener. This tool has its own electric motor and small grinding wheels on angles inside, and it requires the operator to feed the point of the bit into the device as prescribed to grind the point at a fixed generic angle. A number of products that employ this basic concept have been marketed over the years, and I have found they work fairly well for medium-sized twist drill bits, and they are certainly fast and easy to use.

EXPEDIENT GUIDES, STOPS, JIGS, PUSHERS, AND FENCES

Every craftsman at some point comes to the realization that he has only two hands but could surely use more, and that's where these invaluable little helpers come in. Many of the creative projects I work on involve the use of makeshift guides or jigs of one type or another. I might need special guides to keep my tools or work materials properly aligned, or various oddball jigs to help me accomplish a myriad of tasks from bending metal to holding materials or tools in odd positions for specialty operations. Sometimes these expedient setups are created quickly on the spot and used only once, but they allow a particular task to be executed effectively and are thus worth the effort.

Using a dressing stone to true up the wheel.

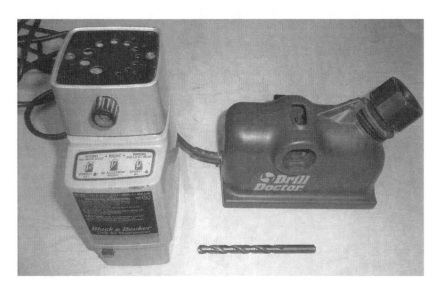

Two common electric bit sharpeners: one from Black & Decker, the other the famous Drill Doctor.

The key to creating successful jigs, guides, and similar setups is to think ahead about the various steps of a given project and contemplate the necessary tasks well before you get to them. That will usually suggest the most practical sort of aid you will need, and you can then go ahead and set it up before getting too far into your project.

Guides are useful for keeping your tools aligned during cutting operations or for positioning the

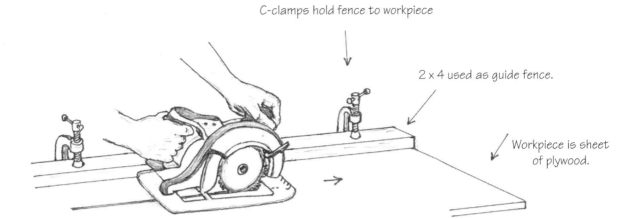

C-clamps hold fence to workpiece

2 x 4 used as guide fence.

Workpiece is sheet of plywood.

Ripping a board—making a straight, guided cut with a circular saw and 2 x 4 fence.

A miter box uses slots as tracks to guide the miter saw blade for angled cuts.

workpiece itself in some specific alignment or arrangement. Anyone who has ever attempted to cut a straight line in a board with an unguided handheld saw of any type knows just how difficult such a task can be.

A common example of a type of guide is the simple miter box, with slots crisscrossing at different angles that keep a miter saw in its track at a specific angle during the course of a cut. The slots serve as guides for the saw blade, and the walls of

the box help keep the work in the proper position during the sawing.

Another common example of a guide is an ordinary template. Technically speaking, templates are guides for the marking tools used to duplicate the various shapes contained in them.

Expedient stops are often necessary to keep one or a series of workpieces in a particular position. They can be in the form of an indexing system to maintain accurate spacing, or a gauge to present the desired length of some part of a workpiece. Workbenches, vises, and stands can often be modified to accommodate any variation of needed stops. These might consist of vertical pegs that fit or screw into holes or are otherwise affixed to a bench top wherever needed, or they might just be simple blocks of wood clamped in place, where they prevent the work from sliding too far one way or another.

Jigs can include any apparatus that helps facilitate a specific operation of one kind or another. There is some sort of jig for just about every conceivable workshop task. In this vast category we have bending jigs, straightening jigs, clamping jigs, doweling jigs, routing jigs, dovetailing jigs, boring or drilling jigs, sanding jigs, squaring jigs, centering jigs, bottle-cutting jigs as we discussed earlier, and a myriad of others.

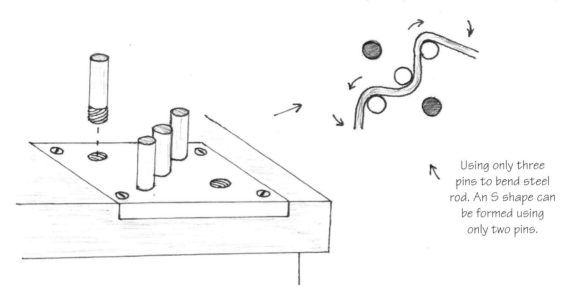

Top view: pins form bending jig.

Using only three pins to bend steel rod. An S shape can be formed using only two pins.

Steel plate is inset into workbench with threaded holes to receive removable stop posts or bending pins.

Using a Vise Grips-type hold-down clamp as a simple kind of clamping jig for drilling.

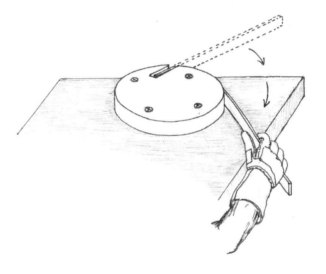

Bending jig for strap iron. For bending tube, conduit, or pipe, take the sheave out of a pulley and set it up as a makeshift jig, just as shown here.

Jigs can be as complex or as simple as might be devised and practical for the task at hand. For example, a jig for bending strap iron will require a notch or catch in which to hook one end of the stock or workpiece and a pivot block, post, bar, or other stationary fixture over or around which the work can be bent.

A turning fork, like the forked hardy I occasionally use in my anvil for bending hot bars of iron, is another example of a bending jig. Yet another good example is the little wire-bending jig popular with jewelry makers. These are typically constructed of cast aluminum and contain several raised blocks of various shapes around which sections of metal wire can be bent, in addition to several holes to accommodate vertical bending pins.

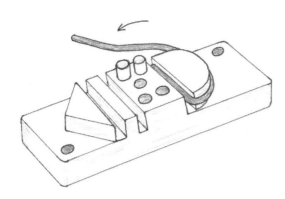

Typical wire-bending jig used in jewelry making.

Using a simple wooden pusher to keep hands clear of the blade of a table saw.

A straightening jig might be comprised of thick, perfectly straight, flat-sided steel blocks that can be forced against the work on opposite sides, perhaps with large vise jaws or clamps, in order to sandwich it and flatten out any bends or bumps. Alternatively, one end of the stock or workpiece could be caught in a sturdy notch and straightened out by hand, using the leverage force available within human hands and arms. Any contraption that aids the craftsman in any such effort would fit my definition of a straightening jig.

Pushers and push sticks allow you to safely manipulate a workpiece into or around a cutting tool, such as a table saw or band saw. In some cases, such as with miter gauges, they can be used to set a

This homemade miter gauge consists of a plastic protractor, wooden block shaped to match it, and the steel guide bar made of common strap iron attached with screw and wing nut.

prescribed angle for a board being fed into a power saw blade. They are especially important because they keep your hands and fingers safely clear of a saw blade or other cutter, as well as keep the workpiece feeding into the cutter at the proper angle. Most types of pushers are relatively simple and easy to make.

I consider a guide fence in this context as a device that functions like a stop as well as a type of guide, especially along one side or edge of the work. Table saws make use of rip fences to help keep the work oriented on the table. Another example of a type of guide fence is a board temporarily nailed or clamped along the side or edge of another board that is to receive special cutting from a handheld router or plane, which forces the tool to cut only along a prescribed channel—a task that would be difficult to attempt freehand.

The majority of handy little guides and jigs are really easy to fabricate from common materials. Think of a scrap board clamped to another to create a makeshift guide or fence as just described, a couple of bolts screwed into a tabletop to serve as stops or bending posts, sections of angle iron mounted as an angle rest for a tool, or some other simple innovation assembled in a hurry and employed to improve your methods of operation. You just have to use your imagination and get creative.

COVER THE JAWS OF YOUR VISE

Here's another standard trick that is almost too basic and obvious to include here, but I mention it more as a reminder than anything else. Whenever I neglect to employ it, I usually regret doing so.

My bench vise probably sees more use than any other single tool or piece of equipment in my shop, and a quick and simple precaution when clamping a workpiece in it is to cover the grid of the hard steel jaws with a softer type of material to prevent marring or damaging the surfaces of your workpiece.

Plates of sheet brass bent at 90 degrees to conform to the top and faces of your vise jaws serve this function well. You can buy these jaw covers ready made (good ones are sold by Brownells), or you can easily make them yourself from two small pieces of sheet brass. Scraps of soft plastic (heated to form fit), angled aluminum, or even pieces of lead might also serve this purpose if brass is in short supply.

Another simple trick is to fold a piece of thick leather or rawhide around the work to be secured in the vise jaws. I do this often, because I usually have plenty of scraps of heavy cowhide on hand, and this is quick and easy. If you don't have a supply of leather or cowhide, even a thick cotton shirt will protect the surface finish of your workpiece from the jaw teeth.

CIRCLES FOR THE MAKESHIFT HOBBYIST

I would bet that the majority of my makeshift projects have involved making or using circles in one way or another. I've cut narrow strips from leather circles in a spiraling progression to the center to obtain a long cord, and I've used existing circles as templates to draw other circles for projects as simple as drawing target rings on paper in order to sight in my guns. I've cut a disk out of sheet metal to serve as the bottom of a homemade frying pan; created numerous circular holes and hole plugs for a multitude of applications; shaped wooden flywheels for primitive hand drills; fabricated all sorts of disks, buttons, wheels, pulleys, spools, washers, and rings from different materials; and plotted angles using the degrees of a circle, to name only some of the innumerable circular applications I've encountered in my endeavors.

Vise jaw covers like these are easily made from sheet brass.

A scrap of soft cowhide can be used to pad the jaws of a vise and protect the work.

We can find volumes of information concerning the circle, but let's just say that it is one of our most fundamental and utilitarian shapes. I will provide a few handy tidbits here pertaining to circles and their uses for the makeshift hobbyist. None of the math involved is at all difficult or complicated.

First, it's important to understand that a circle is simply the two-dimensional shape defined by a closed curve having all of its points equidistant from a common center point. We can use the circle to plot all of our angles. A circle can be divided into 360 degrees, which are the tiny intervals counted around the circumference in a clockwise direction beginning with zero. For convenience, we can start at the top of the circle at the 12:00 o'clock position

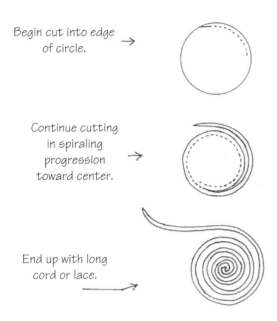

Begin cut into edge of circle. →

Continue cutting in spiraling progression toward center. →

End up with long cord or lace. →

Making cord from circle of leather.

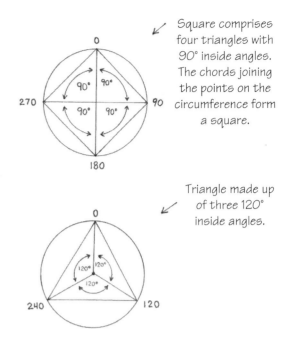

Square comprises four triangles with 90° inside angles. The chords joining the points on the circumference form a square. ↙

Triangle made up of three 120° inside angles. ↙

Shapes from circles.

and progress all the way around and back to the top at 360, which is the same position as the zero.

Some readers may remember from *Makeshift I* (or from learning about it in grade school) that the curved line around the entire perimeter of a circle is called the circumference, that a line segment from the circle's center point to any point on the circumference is called a radius, and that a straight line from one side of the circle to the other that intersects the center is called the diameter, which is equal to twice the length of the radius, or to two radii.

It is also helpful to remember that the circumference of any circle will be 3.1416 times its diameter, so if you know the length of either the circumference or diameter (or alternatively the radius), you could easily calculate the length of the other. This famous circumference-to-diameter ratio of 3.1416 is known as "pi." Calculations based on circumference, diameter, and radius are typically used in measurements involving such things as wheels, pulleys, gears, rings, the ends of cylinders and shafts, and pipes.

One example of how you might find this handy to know is if, say, you needed to tie a rope around the trunk of a tree and you wanted to know how much length of rope you should allow to completely

encircle the tree, with perhaps enough left over to form the necessary knot. Now, let's say that from your side of the tree you were able to roughly estimate its base at approximately 3 feet across. If you wanted to allow about a foot and a half in the running end to form the knot, you would multiply the tree's 3-foot diameter by 3.1416, and you'd discover that you would need almost 9 1/2 feet of rope to encircle the tree base. Add to that the foot and a half of rope for the knot, and you would know to allow 11 feet of rope for your task. Pretty neat how this works, don't you agree?

For plotting angles, think of the center of any circle (also known as the origin of the circle, in geometry) as the vertex of the angle you wish to plot; then orient your protractor and count the degrees on the circumference starting from zero in a clockwise direction to obtain any angle. I realize this will be rudimentary for some readers, but I explain it here simply because it is so incredibly useful for so many routine tasks.

For an example of how we might make practical use of this, most carpenters, cabinetmakers, and other craftsmen need to make and use squares and right angles frequently, and a square is especially easy to make inside of a circle. If you divide the circle's 360 degrees by four, you get 90. All you have to do then is plot four consecutive 90-degree angles that use the origin of your circle as the vertex and connect the four resulting points using a straight edge and a pencil to form the four sides of your square. In geometry, these line segments connecting points on a circle are called chords.

Similarly, using circles to create certain other shapes and polygons is easily accomplished. An equilateral triangle, for example, has three equal sides, and you would create it in your circle by dividing 360 by 3 and then plotting the three resulting 120-degree angles. The pentagon, for another example, is a five-sided polygon. Simply divide 360 by 5; this gives you five individual triangles within the circle, each having a 72-degree inside angle (360 ÷ 5 = 72) and two 54-degree outside angles that use the points on the circle's circumference for their vertices. (If all this talk makes your head spin, just see the accompanying illustration.)

I think it's interesting to note here that the three interior angles in every triangle will always add up to 180 degrees. Hence, in this case we have 72 + 54 + 54 = 180. Also, if you draw a 180-degree angle, the curve of your angle forms a half circle, and the arms of the 180-degree angle line up into a straight line that links the 12:00 o'clock position with the 6:00 o'clock position (assuming you used 12:00 o'clock as your 0 degree starting point), and the two arms of the angle combined give you a diameter line.

We can obtain other polygons within a circle just as we found the square, the triangle, and the pentagon. A hexagon has six sides, so divide 360 by 6 and plot the resulting 60-degree angles in the circle. An octagon with eight sides would be comprised of eight 45-degree angles, and so on. As long as you have a protractor with clear, precise degree markings and a straight edge for drawing the chords that comprise the sides, this is all easy stuff.

Measuring and marking a circle of almost any

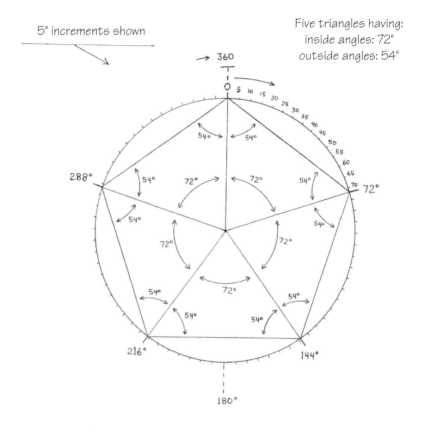

Draw a pentagon from a circle. Use protractor, and divide 360 by 5 to get 72.

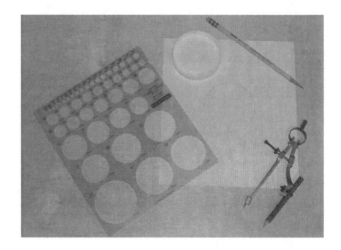

A few common methods for drawing circles.

size is never really a problem. Protractors made of clear plastic make excellent templates for drawing circles, because you can look through them to line things up with markings on your paper. Templates that contain multiple holes for drawing circles of different sizes are also popular.

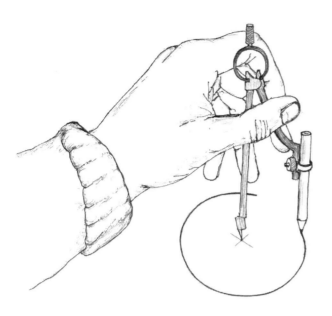

Drawing a circle with a compass.

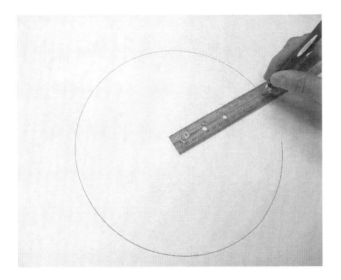

Drawing a circle with a ruler, thumbtack, and pen.

One of the most common methods for drawing quick circles of almost any small to medium diameter is with a compass (or wing divider) that holds a pencil, scriber, or other marking device. This is an inexpensive tool that is available, along with those plastic protractors, in every office supply store or in the school supplies section of your local supermarket. Some have more precision than others, but any can make circles.

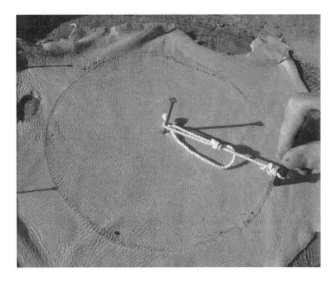

Drawing a circle on a deerskin using only a nail, a string, and a charred stick.

Alternatively, you could make your own expedient substitute compass in several ways. Under primitive circumstances, a piece of string, a nail, and a charred stick can be used to draw a rough circle on a flat, stretched-out animal skin, for example. The neat thing about a string compass is that its working length is easily adjusted by shortening the string if you want to shorten the radius of the swing. The end of the string that ties to the center nail should be looped onto it loosely in order to allow a free and even swing all the way around.

Another simple trick is to use a flat ruler; a thumbtack, nail, or any pointed object pressed downward through a tiny hole drilled through the ruler as the pivot post; and a pen or pencil point through a second hole to mark the circle. The small holes for the tip of the pen can be bored through the thin ruler wherever needed to provide any desired radius within the length of the ruler.

Finally, perfect templates for drawing circles exist in a variety of common items typically found around the house. Such everyday objects as plates, jar lids, coffee mugs, coins, ashtrays, and CDs all fall into this category. Just look around and see what you find.

You also have several options when it comes to cutting circular holes in wood. Holes and circles can be drilled, routed, carved, or sawn, and some of the following methods are useful to keep in mind.

A type of drill bit-like cutter that bores a large hole in wood, called a hole saw, is intended for

Drawing circles on a pine board using a salad plate as the template.

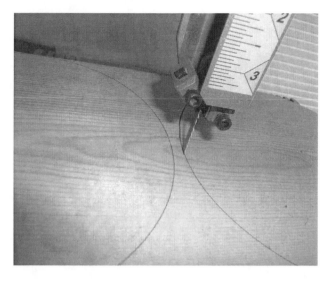

Cutting out circles of wood on a band saw.

cutting larger diameter holes than common-sized twist drill bits can. Many of these circular cutters have a small bit in their center as a pilot drill. Some designs cut out a circular plug that might be saved and used as a disk for some specialty project or another, such as wheels on a little wooden toy car or a small, round chock. Otherwise, just toss the plugs in your supply of kindling for the woodstove or campfire.

Another device for cutting disks out of wood or other materials that is also turned in an electric drill or drill press is a fly cutter, sometimes simply referred to as a circle cutter. The most common style consists of a spindle that accommodates a horizontal bar serving as the swing arm that holds the cutting blade. The center spindle also holds a small pilot bit to help guide the cutter as it rotates. The bar can be adjusted sideways for cutting circles of different diameters. The blade—very similar to a metal lathe cutting bit—is locked into the arm vertically such that it chisels a groove into the workpiece as it swings around.

Fly cutters are capable of cutting more precise circles in wood and other materials than you are likely to accomplish with a band saw, coping saw, jigsaw, scroll saw, or any other method that employs

Miscellaneous circle and hole cutters.

a flat saw blade. When working with a fly cutter, it is best to progress slowly and gradually for the cleanest possible cut. It is also essential to keep your fingers and other body parts clear of that swinging arm, as it twirls around quickly and with a lot of force. Caution is the name of the game whenever working with electric-powered cutting tools.

Cutting a wooden disk using a hole saw and drill press. Save the handy wooden disk for future makeshift applications.

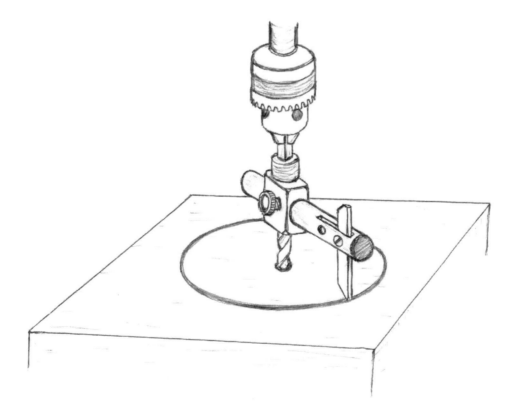

Fly cutter used to cut a disk out of wood.

CHAPTER 7

When You Can't Get
to the Hardware Store

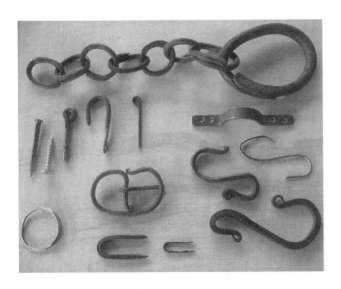

When you can't just go buy common hardware items like chains, nails, screws, hooks, pull handles, staples, buckles, and rings whenever you need them, you might be able to make them yourself.

Anyone who has ever found himself immersed in a creative project or intricate repair knows how frustrating it can be when the necessary materials or essential hardware runs short and more can't be found in the workshop.

In the best-case scenario, an inconvenience like this is remedied with a quick run to the local hardware store for the specialty fastener, hinge, spring, pin, or whatever item is needed. However, I have experienced this predicament *after* the hardware store was closed for the day, or during holidays when the stores aren't open at all. I have also found that certain uncommon hardware items can be hard to find even at the larger stores, requiring ordering them through specialty suppliers.

Another possible predicament is being miles from the nearest town while camping in a remote area, when something like a tent pole breaks or an essential component of a camp stove gets lost, or when a farmer or rancher is out in the hinterland and only schedules his lengthy trips to town for necessary purchases, because spontaneous excursions simply aren't practical as a general rule.

In all these scenarios, a handyman is really forced to make do and find ways to improvise with whatever can be found around the house, campsite, or shop, unless his project can wait until such time when he can buy whatever he needs. This chapter explores various ways to make do on your own, when you can't get to the hardware store.

MAKING YOUR OWN NUTS, BOLTS, AND SCREWS

Several years ago, I challenged myself to make a camp frying pan to carry in my pack, among other items of camping gear I wanted to make, as part of an exercise in self-reliance. The design I came up with included a folding handle made of flat strap

iron that pivoted atop the custom handle mount that I had riveted directly to one edge of the pan. A screw and a wing nut locked the handle in either the folded handle-over-pan position for stowing or in the extended position for using at the campfire. For this project, I decided to also make the screw and wing nut myself, and this was easily accomplished with the thread-cutting tools I had on hand.

Anyone with an assortment of taps and dies for manually cutting screw threads, along with a basic understanding of the process, would have no problem custom-making the sort of special hardware I wanted for my project, as well as any type of hard-to-find nut, bolt, or screw. It simply entails determining the correct thread type and best shaft diameter, and then using the appropriate cutter

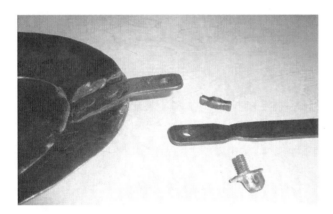

The homemade screw and wing nut for a homemade frying pan.

The pan with its handle attached with the homemade fasteners.

Assorted taps and dies.

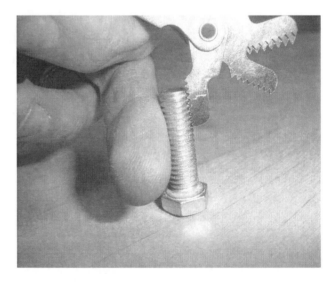

Using a pitch gauge to determine the thread size.

to create the needed threaded fastener and the threaded hole to receive it.

To begin, you need to understand some of the basics of screw threads, as well as the different types of thread-cutting hand tools and how to correctly use each.

Using calipers to measure a bolt's minor diameter in order to match it up with the correct drill bit for making a corresponding nut.

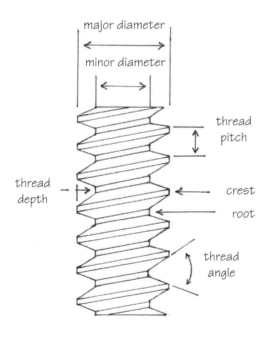

Thread terminology. Pitch diameter, which is between major and minor diameters, is not shown.

The thread on a screw or bolt might be thought of as a spiraling groove around the shaft (or, more correctly, the ridge between the groove) that is technically also an inclined plane wrapping around the shaft. The thread allows more surface area to be in contact between the screw and the screw hole, or likewise between a bolt and a nut, which increases the bearing surface and friction and thus results in greater holding power compared to a straight pin or nail. Readers can refer to the accompanying illustration for basic thread terminology.

A threading die is the cutting tool for making threads on shafts, such as for bolts and machine screws. Dies are available for cutting threads of different types and sizes on shafts of various diameters. They normally are either round or hexagonal and are configured for use with different die holders, called diestocks. The two-handled

Three different styles of threading dies, from left to right: old round die with expandable center plates, split-adjustable round die, and fixed hexagonal die.

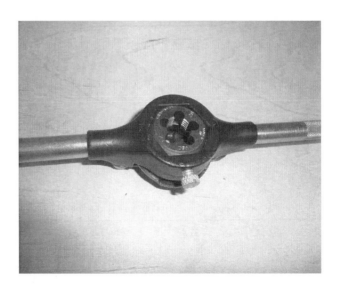

Hexagonal die secured in a diestock, ready for use.

diestock secures the die in position (held fast with a small set screw) for cutting, and it provides a working handle for the die. Dies, like taps, are designated by the size and type of threads they cut (see sidebar).

A thread-cutting tap, or hand tap, is the fluted tool with teeth-like thread cutters that "taps" a hole, i.e., cuts the thread inside the hole. Anything a bolt or screw would screw into can be tapped, usually after drilling a tap hole of slightly smaller diameter. You can even shape and cut around a tapped hole to create a makeshift nut. To do so, drill and tap a hole in a piece of steel of the correct thickness; then cut out a square or hexagon of the proper dimension around the threaded hole to make the nut. I've created threaded nuts having various specialty shapes this way.

There are three basic configurations of hand taps in common use. A bottoming tap has a comparatively blunt-shaped leading end and is intended to cut the thread close to the bottom of a blind hole (i.e., a hole that ends inside the

A typical set of small taps with some corresponding drill bits, purchased from Brownells.

Measurement Standards for Taps and Dies

There are several common measurement standards for taps and dies. The ISO metric (indicated with the letter M) is the standard for general metric screw threads nowadays, established by the International Organization for Standardization in 1947. In the ISO metric standard, individual sizes are identified by the screw's nominal diameter in millimeters, followed by an X and its thread pitch, also in millimeters. For example, the designation M10 X 1.5 indicates a 10mm nominal screw diameter, having thread pitch of 1 1/2 millimeters. Pitch, as you might remember from *Makeshift I*, can be defined as the distance from a point on the crest of one thread on a screw to the same point on the next thread either above or below it, in this case measured in millimeters.

In the United States, the Unified Thread Standard (UTS), previously (before 1949) referred to as American National Standard, is the most commonly used. This includes the Unified Coarse (UNC), also called National Coarse (NC), the Unified Fine (UNF) or National Fine (NF), and Unified Extra Fine (UNEF). The "coarse" and "fine" distinctions denote thread size, or pitch. A screw that conforms to the National Coarse standard will have fewer threads per inch than on a screw that conforms to the National Fine standard.

The American system uses threads per inch (as opposed to thread pitch), in conjunction with the screw's diameter (also in inches or fractions of an inch), to designate tap and die sizes. When screws are smaller than 1/4 inch in diameter, the gauge number of the machine screw is used instead of an inch fraction. For example, a 10–24NC die will cut threads for a #10 machine screw having 24 threads per inch that conforms to the Unified National Coarse standard. Likewise, a die marked 1/4–28 NF will cut threads on a shaft of 1/4-inch diameter, with 28 threads per inch, which conforms to the National Fine standard.

There are separate standards for pipe threads, such as the American National Pipe Tapered Thread (NPT), which are really more special-purpose than the other common thread standards.

The other major thread standard is the British Standard Whitworth (BSW), which includes the British Standard Fine (BSF), British Standard Coarse (BSC), and British Standard Pipe (BSP).

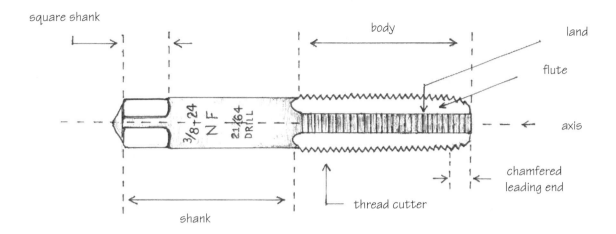

square shank

body

land

flute

axis

3/8·24
N F
21/64
DRILL

chamfered
leading end

thread cutter

shank

Thread-cutting tap.

workpiece rather than going all the way through). A plug tap, sometimes called a second or intermediate tap, is more of a general-purpose configuration and is the most commonly used. It has a slight taper, or chamfer, on the leading end to help guide it and start its cut into the hole. Finally, a taper tap has a longer and more gradual taper than a plug tap and is sometimes used to start the cutting of a thread into an unbeveled hole or in hard-to-cut material.

The tool that holds the tap during cutting is called a tap wrench, and there are several variations. Stock type or bar-handle tap wrenches are for use with medium to large taps, while T-handle tap wrenches are generally more practical for use with very small taps. (Makeshifter aside: if you can't find your tap wrench in the clutter of your shop, Vise Grips or a drill press chuck can be pressed into service to hold the tap.)

The right type of lubricant will facilitate a smoother cut by reducing friction, which will make the cutting easier and reduce the chances of breaking the tap or die. Special cutting oil is preferred, but in its absence, using almost any kind of oil (even olive oil) would be better than cutting the thread into dry steel.

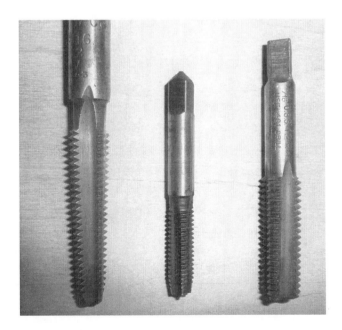

Three different tap types, from left to right: one style of a tapered tap, a plug tap, and a bottoming tap.

A tap secured into a tap wrench for use.

 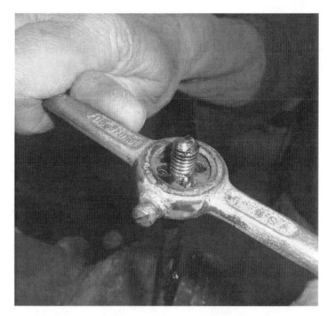

Cutting threads on a screw shaft by hand. Go slow, lubricate the work, and back off occasionally.

Cutting threads by hand can be tricky sometimes, so it needs to be executed carefully. If the tap or die is not started correctly, the thread can be cut on a skewed or uneven angle, and you want to avoid that. Also, excessive torque applied to a small tap can easily snap it off while it's in the hole, because the cutter is of such hard and brittle material. A broken piece of tap stuck down inside a screw hole can be a real aggravation, as anyone who has ever experienced this will tell you.

When cutting threads, it is important to periodically stop the cut and reverse the tool for a partial or full turn to clear away the chips that accumulate, as well as to avoid subjecting the tool to excessive torque stress that builds up. I usually do this at least once or twice before completing every full turn. I've snapped off enough taps in their holes to know how easily it can happen, and removing the broken-off piece can be a hassle. A small brush for periodically brushing away the oily metal chips is another handy piece of equipment.

A good set of taps and dies, or even better, several different sets (both metric and American, for example) belong in every makeshifter's shop, in my

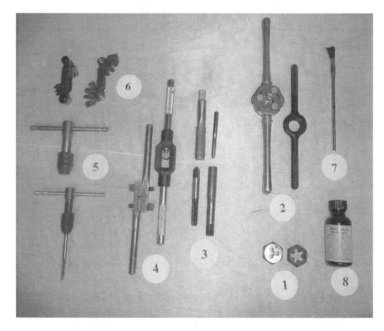

Common thread-cutting tools: 1) threading dies, 2) two styles of diestock, 3) various sizes of hand taps, 4) bar-handle tap wrenches, 5) T-handle tap wrenches, 6) thread pitch gauges, 7) small brush for clearing metal chips, and 8) Do-Drill cutting oil from Brownells.

opinion. Several thread pitch gauges, a drill press or hand drill with a complete selection of bits, a can of cutting oil, and a brush complete the basic setup.

Another important hand tool to keep with the

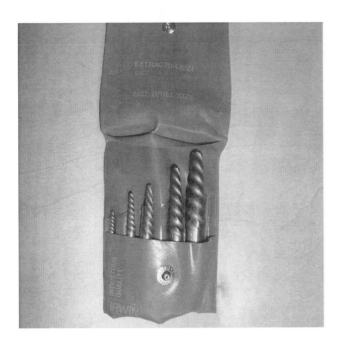

Typical five-piece set of spiral screw extractors.

thread-making equipment is a spiral screw extractor. Screw extractors are normally sold in sets containing several common sizes for helping to remove stuck or broken screws. The extractor is turned into a hole drilled into the exposed part of a broken screw. Once it has a grip, it can then back the broken screw out on its thread. This can be a very frustrating operation, I might add.

With just the tools mentioned here, you won't always have to rely on the hardware store every time you need a particular screw, nut, or bolt. In a pinch, you might be able to fabricate the needed item yourself.

This handy makeshift skill extends to the thread-cutting tools themselves. In *Makeshift I*, we explored how to make our own crude but functional thread-cutting dies out of hard file steel. And my dad still occasionally uses the simple diestock that he fabricated many years ago for a small round die when he didn't have a tool to fit that particular die at the time. It is just a short, square bar of mild steel into which he drilled a hole smaller than the diameter of the die all the way through the center, and then a larger hole (same diameter as the outside of the die) partway into the bar such that the die fits into the bar flush with the surface and rests on the ledge. Next, he drilled a small hole into one side of the bar horizontally through to the larger hole and cut threads into that small hole so he could turn a thumbscrew in as the set screw to secure the die in position. This is a great example of improvising something needed but not conveniently available.

I recently heard of this method to make a homemade tap. Get a good quality steel bolt or a stainless one, which will be "hard" in any form because of the nickel and chrome. Wet grind about the bottom quarter of the threads down (a belt sander with a 220 grit belt works fine) so you have no threads at the tip up to leaving a full thread. Then use a wet grinding wheel to cut the longitudinal flutes the full length of the thread. Cut at least two rows, but four is better on a bigger tap because that gives you twice as many cutting points. Once it's

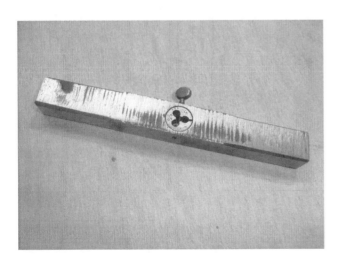 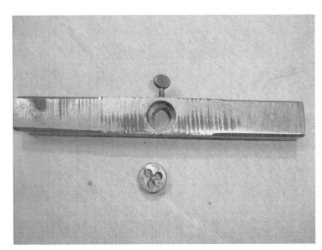

The homemade diestock for the small die, with and without the die in place.

shaped and looks like a store-bought version, sharpen the leading edges with a very fine wheel (diamond is excellent) or by hand with a small round file. There is actually "relief" behind the leading edge of a tap's cutting points, just like on a drill face, but this makeshift method is close enough to work for a homemade tap, especially if you are cutting material softer than steel (aluminum, brass, plastic, wood, etc.).

HOMEMADE WOOD SCREWS

Unlike the cylindrical profile of most bolts and machine screws, wood screws usually have at least partially tapered shafts and are typically pointed at their leading ends. This makes them somewhat impractical to try to make with the same hand tools and techniques that we might use to produce bolts or machine screws. The thread configurations on wood screws also tend to be different than those on bolts and machine screws, as they are intended to screw into unthreaded wood as opposed to a nut with corresponding threads.

Wood screws have been manufactured for literally hundreds of years by a variety of methods. One old method commonly employed by early gunsmiths and tool makers was to file the spiraling thread grooves into the body of the screw with a fine-cut three-corner or triangular file. A scenario where anyone in our era would ever need to sculpt

his own screws by hand may indeed be a rare one, given the commonality and economy of this ordinary fastener, but of course I had to try it for this book.

I decided to make my screw out of a 50d nail of almost 1/4-inch diameter and use the existing head of the nail as the screw head, which would save a lot of time that would otherwise be spent shaping the head. I attempted to copy the basic style of a large wood screw that I had on hand.

After shaping the basic tapered configuration for the screw with my bench grinder (a bastard file would work fine as well), I marked the spiraling pattern for the thread groove around the shaft of the nail with a fine-point felt-tip marking pen. I marked this rather imprecise spiraling line freehanded because I couldn't think of any easier way to do it. This should be perfectly adequate for a homemade wood screw.

Once I had a somewhat evenly spiraling line to follow, it was a simple matter to gradually file the groove around and around with a small three-corner file, stopping periodically to rotate the shaft in the vise as needed. This does require you to carefully follow the line with the corner of the file. I left the screw body attached to the unmodified portion of the nail throughout most of the project, which made it easier to work with because the nail shaft, rather than the screw itself, could be secured in the vise.

The last steps are to snip the screw from the

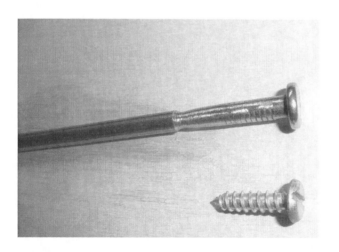

Preparing to simulate a factory-made wood screw, shown here next to the homemade screw body in its earliest stage, having simply been hand filed to the basic shape out of a 50d nail.

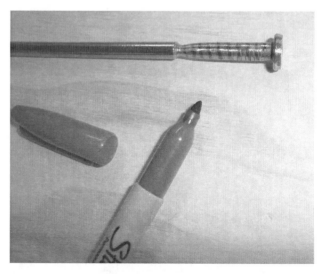

Marking the thread line around the body of the screw.

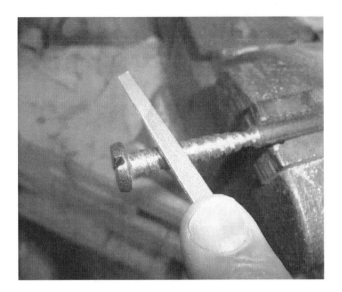

Filing the thread groove around the screw body.

Filing the slot in the top of the screw head. Note how the screw threads in the vise are protected with a thick leather pad.

remainder of the nail and cut the slot in the head (for a slotted screw). I actually started cutting the slot in my screw before filing the threads, but I refined and enlarged it afterward. I started the cut with a hacksaw and then finished it with a very thin, flat metal file. If you do this step after separating the screw from the nail, use a leather pad to protect its threads from the teeth of the vise jaws.

The resulting product is perhaps a bit crude by some standards, but it will be very functional as a large wood screw.

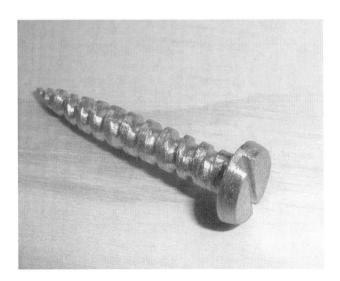

The finished homemade wood screw.

An important consideration whenever using wood screws is that they screw into the wood tight enough to hold, but not so tight as to require excessive torque to screw them all the way in. Too much force applied to a screw can deform either the screw head or the screwdriver tip, and excessive torque can snap off the body of the screw inside the hole, creating a serious inconvenience. Forcing a screw into a piece of wood also has the potential to split the wood.

The key to this process is to predrill the screw hole. When screwing into fairly soft wood, choose a bit diameter that's very close to the screw's minor diameter; this will retain enough material for the thread to dig into and properly hold the screw in position. With very hard wood, the pitch diameter might be more practical as the bit diameter, because it would create a pilot hole with a slightly larger diameter than the root, or inside thread diameter of the screw. The screw could then be turned into the hard wood without requiring excessive torque, as it would if you were turning a screw into a smaller diameter hole in the same hard wood. (For more on minor and pitch diameter, see the illustration on page 131.) Another helpful trick is to lube a wood screw before turning it in, and a bar of soap works as good as anything for this.

Such other styles of screws and bolts as eye screws, wing screws, and thumbscrews can also be made using the same basic techniques just described. To create the eye for an eye screw or bolt, simply heat and bend the unthreaded top section of the shaft into a small loop using a gas torch and two pairs of pliers, or a vise and pliers. A thumbscrew could be made by heating and hammering the top portion of the screw's shaft flat and wide enough to form the paddle-shaped head. For a wing screw, carefully saw the top of the shaft down its middle for a short length; then heat, spread the halves apart with a cold chisel, and fold each half over in opposite directions to create a two-winged screw head. The screw's projecting wings could also be curled into tight loops for style, if desired.

Screwing the homemade wood screw into predrilled wood to attach a pull handle.

Bending eye of screw is best done before cutting threads on shaft. Secure bottom half in vise or grip with pliers on both ends. Heat the bend areas with a propane or MAPP torch.

With pliers or a hammer, bend the top half over to about 90°.

Heat and bend here.

Heat the top quarter of shaft and close the loop for the eye.

Heat here.

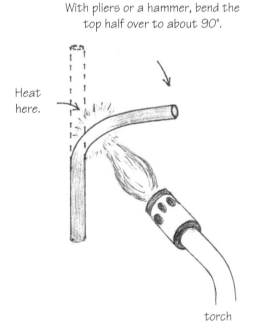

torch

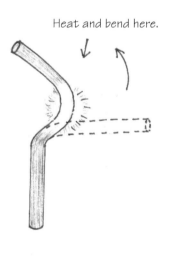

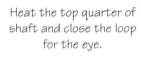

Creating an eye screw or bolt.

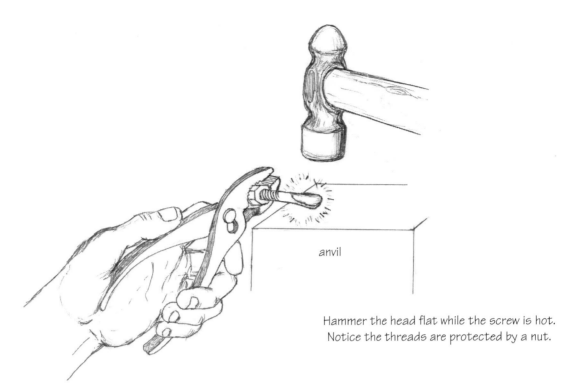

anvil

Hammer the head flat while the screw is hot.
Notice the threads are protected by a nut.

Creating a thumb screw.

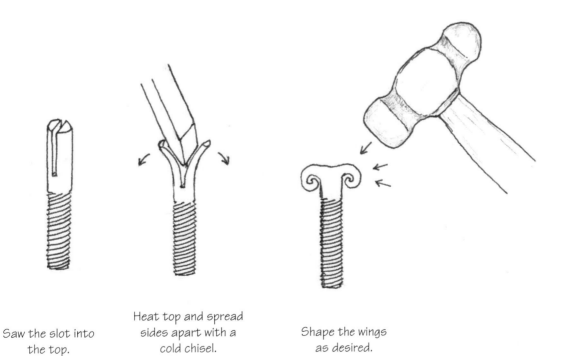

Saw the slot into
the top.

Heat top and spread
sides apart with a
cold chisel.

Shape the wings
as desired.

Creating a wing screw.

MORE COMMON HARDWARE ITEMS THAT ARE EASY TO MAKE

Things like nails and washers are easier to make quickly than screws or bolts, which have to be a bit more precise. Small nails are especially easy to make out of heavy-gauge wire or small-diameter steel rod. Simply cut the stock to the desired lengths, sharpen one end, and use as nails. If a head is desired, it is easy enough to heat the end of a rod or wire with a propane torch and upset that end with light hammer blows to form the head. It's usually not a problem if nails get bent, because they are easy enough to straighten out using a light hammer and a solid surface like a small anvil. You can also make usable flat nails out of thick sheet metal just by cutting their long, tapered configuration out of the stock with a hacksaw or metal sheers.

Washers are similarly easy to fabricate if you've got scraps of sheet metal, a drill press or hand drill, and a bench grinder or files and sandpaper. You merely drill the hole (it's easier for me to get that

part done first) and then cut out the shape of the washer around the hole as needed, using either a hacksaw, tin snips, or a rotary tool with a cutoff disk. Smooth the edges up with files or sandpaper.

If you don't have a supply of scrap sheet metal, look for those round knockouts from electrical boxes, which make excellent raw stock for homemade washers. They are easy to find in debris piles at construction sites or scattered on the floor of a framed but unfinished house in progress.

If you need more than one washer of the same size, use the first one you make as the pattern for additional washers. After the holes are drilled in the stock, simply align them with the hole in the pattern washer and trace the outline of the new ones with a scratch awl or scribe. You could try doing this with a felt-tip pen, but scratching in the metal has the advantage of not rubbing off during the various stages of work.

I have heard about the practice of drilling a hole through a penny or nickel to make an expedient washer, and it would certainly be easy enough,

Cut these shapes out of sheet metal.

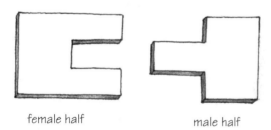

female half   male half

Drill the screw holes.

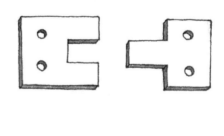

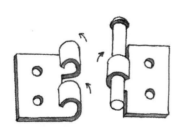

Use hinge pin as forming mandrel for bending extensions.

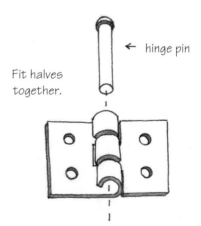

Fit halves together.

← hinge pin

Making a sheet metal box hinge.

although I am not advocating defacing U.S. currency here.

Hinges can be created in a variety of ways, depending on your design requirements. Small box hinges are easy to make from lightweight sheet metal, using mainly files and hacksaws and perhaps a small ball-peen hammer to roll the flat metal into the short tubes that fit over the hinge pin, using the pin as the forming mandrel. A heavy nail might serve as a hinge pin for a box hinge.

Larger, heavier hinges can be created from thicker strap iron or steel bars. A forge for heating the material can really be handy when you have to bend or hammer thicker steel into the desired shape, as the heated metal is much more malleable, but limited bending can still be accomplished without a heat source if you can build a bending jig sturdy enough for the task. Hinges for gates can be made out of round bars of steel, such as cold-rolled 1/2- or 5/8-inch round bar, or even rebar. Form several sections into large staples, closed loops, or eyes, and shape another section like an L. The L section points downward and runs through the pivot eyes, allowing the bent half, i.e., the arm that attaches to a gate or door, to swing freely and open the gate.

You can make chain by forming a series of loops or rings and linking them together. There are numerous variations and sizes of chain types to serve different applications, but creating a series of simple linked rings is a fairly straightforward process, although a repetitive one.

The forge and anvil are the tools for making large-sized chains by hand. Heat lengths of round or square stock in the forge, form them into unclosed rings using a hammer and tongs in conjunction with the horn of the anvil, and forge-weld the individual rings closed after linking them. I find small links of chain easier to work with than larger ones, as they can be quickly heated for bending and forming using just the flame of a gas torch, and most of the forming can be done with needle-nose pliers.

Brackets, latches, braces, wall hooks, retaining bands, and a myriad of other pieces of hardware can be constructed very simply from sections of common strap iron. Mild-steel strap iron is soft enough to be bent into curved loops or folded configurations with the help of sturdy bending jigs or a large wrench in conjunction with a heavy-duty bench vise. This kind of steel is soft enough to be cut with a hacksaw and shaped with a file.

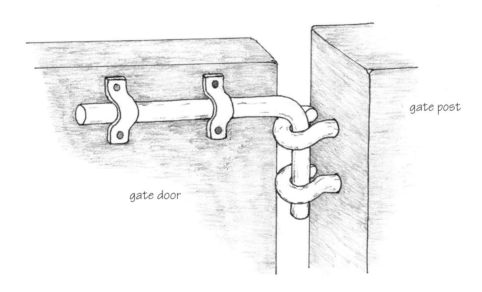

gate post

gate door

Very simple type of hinge.

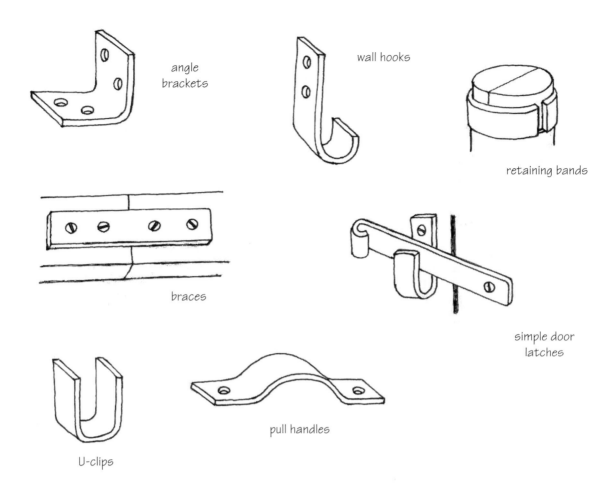

angle brackets

wall hooks

retaining bands

braces

simple door latches

U-clips

pull handles

Simple hardware from strap iron.

WHEN THE NEEDED PARTS ARE MISSING OR BROKEN

How many times have you tried to assemble or use something and discovered that some essential piece was missing? Let's say you just arrived home with a new piece of furniture that came in a box with 40 separate pieces and required assembly, and when inventorying the numbered items listed in the instructions, you discover one tiny piece is simply not to be found among the rest. Or you found a used item at a garage sale that would be perfectly functional except for a broken or missing part. Sometimes a single missing or broken part can render a product inoperable, and this can really be frustrating.

The good news is that very often the essential part can be substituted with something else, or in some instances entirely homemade out of available materials. Many times while I was growing up, I witnessed my dad make things work with parts he'd built himself, and I've found myself doing this on numerous occasions over the years (with varying degrees of success). The key is to be imaginative and keep an open mind.

Having a supply of raw materials on hand is essential if you need to improvise a missing piece or build something from scratch. To acquire needed items, a lot of home workshop do-it-yourselfers turn to hardware stores as their first choice, and for logical reason. Hardware stores, especially the big ones, usually stock dimensional lumber; large spools of rope, hose, chain, cable, and electrical wiring in every gauge and size imaginable; conveniently sorted bins containing thousands of fasteners; every diameter and variety of plumbing pipe and pipe fitting; electrical components; assorted metal stock; a wide assortment of hand, power, and specialty tools; and plenty of other useful materials for projects. Generally speaking, if you need supplies or raw materials for your makeshift projects, you should be able to find most of what you need at your local hardware store when it's open for business.

However, new materials can be rather expensive, and again, for this chapter we are assuming that you cannot get to a hardware store for whatever reason. So, let us explore some alternatives.

It is not difficult to find usable raw materials—probably more than you will ever use—for very low investment. I always keep an eye open for broken broom handles to save as dowel stock, as well as things like odd-sized pieces of lumber, scraps of leather, used tools, assorted fasteners, discarded plastic, and scrap iron and aluminum, and you should develop this habit, too. In a sense, you want to strive to become your *own* hardware store by keeping your own supplies of raw materials and miscellaneous items on hand. Oftentimes when you need this stuff, you *really* need it, so the more you have stockpiled at home, the fewer trips to the hardware store you have to make while you're busy with a particular project.

So, where do you find this stuff?

Yard and garage sales are a logical source for makeshift raw materials and are an excellent place to start. I have acquired more things for my projects

The mixed hardware shown in this photo was purchased at a yard sale, all of it for $1.

from such sales than I could ever list, and all of it was just pennies on the dollar. Look especially for those typical jars or coffee cans loaded with nuts and bolts or other miscellaneous hardware that are usually almost free, as well as used tools and reference books.

Likewise, flea markets and thrift stores can be valuable sources to search for inexpensive materials. It is amazing what kinds of bargains turn up in these places. Again, miscellaneous hardware, tools, and books are good targets here.

Whether you're at a garage sale or flea market, don't forget to consider things like old appliances or larger toys like wagons for their sheet metal scrap value (not to mention all the cannibalized fasteners, springs, bearings, and such). It's really hard to come up with a consistently reliable source for sheet steel, other than buying it at a steel yard or from a supplier, and those are normally rather expensive sources. The scrounged metal I've come across over the years usually came from unusual, one-time sources. Mild strap iron is easier to come by at junkyards and garage sales and from things like discarded bed frames.

Construction sites, especially house remodel projects, generate surprising volumes of materials that you might be able to salvage for makeshift projects. Many of the debris piles at construction sites contain things like scrap pipe, chunks of lumber having odd dimensions, electrical wiring and components, bent nails that could be pulled from boards and straightened, plumbing fixtures, old window frames, kitchen cabinets, doors and door knobs, latches, hinges, and other hardware. Much of the stuff will be damaged to some degree, but sometimes it is possible to salvage, repair, and reuse certain items, especially for makeshift purposes. The contractors generally don't have time to mess with recycling old materials, so they will usually welcome your offer to haul away their junk. Just be careful of hidden hazards like protruding rusty nails and screws, broken glass, jagged splintered lumber, and mold, and make sure you get permission from the property owner or construction manager before you start scrounging through the pile.

Dumpsters yield some very good materials for makeshift projects from time to time and should not be overlooked as a viable source for cheap raw materials. I have pulled repairable office chairs and

A typical construction site debris pile containing usable pieces of wood and materials.

A field-expedient application of a makeshift funnel—using a plastic 2-liter ginger ale bottle to add oil to a car. You could pull into the gas station, buy the soda, drink it, rinse the bottle, cut the top off, and pour the oil right there. In fact, if you bought a bottle of water, you could do all those things *plus* add some water to your radiator!

usable 2 x 4 pine boards from the trash bin in our office parking lot, among other odd items worth saving. I know—I have no shame.

The point is to use your imagination. That broken wooden chair sticking out of the neighbor's trash barrel might contain some hardwood dowels in the legs and frame, as well as good hardwood in other beneficial configurations. Chances are that if you build a lot of wooden crafts in your shop, eventually some of those pieces will come in handy. If you don't have just the right dowel in your stockpile, maybe you can harvest a branch from a tree on your property and shape the needed item from it, or sacrifice an old broom handle for your purpose.

That stack of plastic buckets leaning against the side of your house that your wife has been nagging you to throw away for months might be a good supply of thermoplastic for projects like ax head covers, holsters, and knife sheaths (as we explored in chapter 3). The bicycle your child has outgrown could become the working mechanism of a manually powered machine (as we explored in chapter 2). Perhaps you could salvage the copper wire from the transformer or electric motor in any broken appliances that may otherwise be headed for the dump. And what about that toaster oven with the burned out elements? You may want to save at least all the sheet metal screws before you toss it. (The

thin, chromed sheet metal might only be useful for some very specific application.)

Extend your creativity to makeshift tools as well. If you need a funnel for pouring loose dry goods like sugar, salt, or flour into a jar and the one in your kitchen is too small for the job, form a cone of heavy paper, tape along the outside seam to hold its shape, and trim it up with scissors as needed to create a functional expedient funnel. This technique has worked for me when I wanted to pour coffee creamer from a canister into a smaller jar. For pouring liquids, the bottleneck half cut off a plastic bottle will work as a usable funnel. The point here is that there are usually plenty of alternate possibilities in almost every situation.

This is how a scavenger and makeshifter's mind works. With just about every item we see, we think about how we might use it, how we might build something out of it. We hate throwing most things away, because we imagine how they could be repaired and restored to service or used for other things. When we run across free or cheap supplies that are commonly used in makeshift projects, we tend to hoard them.

The problem is finding enough storage space

A store of mixed hardware items kept on a shelf under a workbench, ready for use.

Spare raw materials kept in a basement crawlspace—wood scraps on the right, miscellaneous pieces of metal, shorter dowels, and PVC on the left. The large, clear plastic jugs holding smaller items are bulk pretzel containers from Costco, rinsed and saved for just such storage purposes.

around your home or shop for all that you might accumulate. I store jars of small hardware items on shelves and under my workbenches. Bulkier items like scrap wood and metal, unused pipe, longer dowels, and so forth need to be stored wherever you can find the room.

I've known people who were not particularly eager to amass jars of screws, piles of lumber, or other raw materials and hardware supplies at their premises, because such stockpiles do take up precious space and can create a cluttered or junky atmosphere if you don't keep things organized. I understand these concerns, and, being the packrat that I am, I know firsthand how unsightly it can get. Some people are naturally better at organizing their stores than others, and I will admit that the organized and orderly arrangement of my supplies has not been high on my priority list. My wife would confirm this.

THE MORE TOOLS YOU HAVE, THE MORE YOU CAN DO

Undoubtedly, the majority of those who read this book will already have some tools—things like hammers, saws, files, wrenches, and pliers. Those who don't should start acquiring at least a few basic implements, and these can be collected little by little and without spending much money at all by shopping for used tools in good condition. Used tools may not be shiny and clean, and some might beg for restoration, but if they're functional or capable of being repaired, they will seem like a godsend when you need them. And at some point in time, you *will* need some basic tools.

There is something else I like to consider about keeping a healthy supply of tools around the house, and that is that with some tools, especially metalworking tools, you can actually fabricate other tools. Using your existing tools to create new or specialized tools will save you plenty a trip to the hardware store, expand your capabilities, and ultimately save you money. This capability to make tools as they are needed, I believe, is at the heart of self-sufficiency, whether you are striving to live an independent life now, or you look to a darker future in which self-reliance becomes the very means of your survival.

As discussed in the previous section, yard sales

and flea markets are wonderful places to find used tools of all varieties for pennies on the dollar. I've acquired literally hundreds of good used tools at yard sales over the years, and I have seen just about every kind of tool I can think of at a sale at some time or another. Such tools as hammers, scissors, screwdrivers, and pliers I see again and again, so I always end up with duplicates and extras when the price is right. Excellent to have on hand for backup or barter.

It might be wise to make a list now, while the hardware stores are still open, of the essential tools the average person will likely need, and then methodically proceed to obtain everything listed. This is where you need to think ahead for the time when, for whatever reason, you won't be able to get to a hardware store.

Making a comprehensive list of necessary tools for the future can certainly be a daunting task. There are simply so vastly many types of tools in existence for so many purposes that it is really difficult to know where to start and where to end. You could put together a lengthy list of tools as you think of them, but without some order to your process, you could find yourself collecting tools for a very long time without ever having achieved any sense of completeness, assuming that this is even possible.

My favorite approach is to categorize the various tool types by their applications or tasks. For example, rather than attempting to cover all the bases by making a shopping list with maybe a dozen or more types of saws, starting with the tiniest precision jeweler's saw and progressing all the way up to a long bar, gas-powered chainsaw, we might simply lump the saws together under the task category of "sawing." So now we have a category under which we can list any type of saw we might need.

When I began to contemplate this approach, I came up with 24 categories that I wanted to try to fill as well as I could with the tools I hoped to find. Some of the tasks are closely related to or overlap with others. Some people, for example, would probably lump chiseling in with the carving and

This collection of tools is but a fraction of what I have acquired recently at yard sales.

planing category. Likewise, some tools could be listed in several categories. A claw hammer can be used for hammering as well as for prying and pulling nails, or the back of an ax head could be used as a hammer. However, I believe this basic methodology has helped me fill in the gaps better than if I didn't apply it. I wanted my list of tasks to be as comprehensive as possible, because I was aiming for maximum flexibility with my tools and shop capabilities.

Here is my list:

1. Abrading, including sanding, grinding, polishing, and honing.
2. Carving, shaving, and slicing. This is where I list knives, razors, and planes.
3. Chiseling and gouging.

4. Chopping, chipping, and splitting.
5. Drilling, boring, and reaming.
6. Filing and rasping.
7. Gluing, painting, and applying coatings and oils.
8. Gripping and holding. This is where I put pliers, tongs, clamps, and vises.
9. Guiding with guide stops, jigs, centers, squares, and spacers.
10. Hammering. I include anvils, mandrels, and forming hardies in this category because they are so often used in conjunction with hammers.
11. Lifting and moving. Includes jacks, ropes, chains, pulleys, hoists, dollies, and carts.
12. Marking with scribes and markers.
13. Measuring and gauging.
14. Prying and wedging.
15. Punching.
16. Sawing.
17. Scraping.
18. Shearing or snipping.
19. Shoveling and scooping.
20. Stitching, sewing, and lacing.
21. Sweeping and brushing.
22. Thread cutting (screw threads).
23. Turning and twisting. Includes wrenches, screwdrivers, sockets, turnkeys, and cant hooks or peaveys.
24. Welding, soldering, brazing, forging, and other hot-metal tasks.

To illustrate my idea of one particular tool category, here we see an assortment of products used for measuring and gauging, including a gunpowder scale, rulers, carpenter's square, micrometer, calipers, firearm caliber bore gauge, kitchen measuring cup and measuring spoons, thermometer, and measuring tapes.

Of course, you might come up with an entirely different categorization system. Here's another possible approach:

1. Workshop
   a. Woodwork
   b. Metalwork
   c. Painting and staining
2. Electrical
3. Plumbing
4. Car repair and maintenance
5. Gunsmithing
6. Gardening
7. Firewood
8. Outdoor camping/survival

Following some kind of category system will provide you with a framework to make your tool selections more organized, thorough, and methodical than without it.

• • • • •

Collecting a comprehensive assortment of tools, as well as your own supplies of miscellaneous hardware and raw materials, is a proactive way to maximize your capabilities and become less dependent on the hardware stores for your do-it-yourself projects. However, I believe that even more important than a person's selection of tools and materials are his or her knowledge, developed skills, and ability to function even with only a minimum of equipment.

One of my favorite motion pictures has long been the original *Flight of the Phoenix* with Jimmy Stewart. In that film, a plane goes down in the remote and harsh Sahara Desert, and the survivors must build an operational airplane out of the remaining plane wreckage in order to return to civilization and save themselves. They are hundreds of miles away from any supply station, so their survival depends entirely upon their makeshift resourcefulness.

I am mindful that this was just a fictional movie, but the whole theme of it—relying on ingenuity to survive under adverse conditions and with limited resources—is not unheard of in real life. People get lost; vehicles break down in remote places; the power grid goes down for an extended period—this stuff happens all the time. And this relates directly to what we are contemplating in this chapter. How would we get along in some situation without the kind of supply lines and infrastructure that most of us are very much accustomed to? How would we adapt when we couldn't simply buy whatever we needed in order to complete essential projects?

Perhaps the biggest factor to influence all this is the mindset of creative innovation. You call on what you've learned through experience and studying, use the skills you've developed, apply whatever tools are available to you, and ultimately invent to some degree your own way of doing what you need to do. Hopefully, this book (as well as the first volume) has helped you become more resourceful and aware in this respect, and ultimately more self-sufficient.

CHAPTER 8

Makeshift True Stories

Plastic trash bag fix to a leaky tent.

I decided to share stories in this chapter mainly to illustrate the value of being able to improvise with makeshift solutions to some of life's unexpected predicaments. Some of the ideas proved very successful, as we shall see, while others would more accurately be described as total disasters. Hence, this chapter is intended for the readers' entertainment more than for instructional purposes, though I do believe worthwhile lessons can be gained from some of the trials and errors you will be reading about. I hope this chapter will inspire more innovative thinking, if nothing else.

MAKESHIFT CAMPING ON LOOP CREEK

About 13 summers ago, my dad and I took a four-day vacation to camp and fish at a perfect little campsite on Loop Creek in Idaho, which in those days was a fairly quiet, out-of-the-way place up the North Fork of the Saint Joe River, roughly 10 miles from the tiny town of Avery.

The day after our arrival was mostly sunny and warm. The evening before, we had set up our four-man nylon tent (which had not been used since our camp trips in the early 1980s) and a nice campfire for cooking, and when morning came we did some fly fishing, plinked with our revolvers, collected firewood, cooked on the fire, and panned for gold (unfortunately, we never found any). The weather was perfect for the first full day.

And then it started raining. And the rain didn't let up much for the remainder of the trip.

It wasn't long before the old tent started leaking in several places. We first noticed the rain getting through the roof sometime during the night, when we discovered our sleeping bags were soaked in spots. I don't remember if it crossed our minds to pack it up and head for home, but in any case we stayed right there and tried to figure out a way to improve our situation. After all, Dad still had a lot of old stories to tell (again).

In the back of his Jeep Wagoneer, Dad kept a canvas duffel bag stocked with an assortment of tools and supplies, and in it he just happened to have several large, heavy-duty plastic trash bags. We opened a couple of those and draped them over the roof of the tent. No more rain came in, so that problem was solved.

When morning arrived, we wanted to heat some coffee and cook up some breakfast, but our fire pit was out in the open. Cooking in a downpour was out of the question—we wanted to stay as dry as possible inside the tent. Cooking inside the tent seemed awkward, considering it had a nylon floor and we lacked a tent stove. The tent model didn't even have a chimney opening.

Warming up a cup of coffee or hot chocolate with the little flame from a candle is a slow process, we discovered, and the drink never really got hot enough to completely satisfy. Suddenly, we remembered the several cans of Sterno canned fuel Dad kept in that canvas duffel bag in his Jeep, mainly for winter emergencies, and we decided to use them to heat up our food and drinks. We scouted the area until we found a flat rock big enough for our purposes, cleaned the mud off, and set it in the middle of the floor inside the tent to be used as our makeshift kitchen table.

The next order of business was to fabricate a tiny stove to make use of the Sterno. We had a few unopened cans of Dinty Moore beef stew in our camp groceries, and we decided to empty the contents of one into our canteen cups and turn the

Cup of coffee heated on stew can stove. Flat rock used as cooking surface to keep the burning fuel off the nylon tent floor.

empty stew can into a small stove.

This is a simple process if you have a few basic tools and materials. Fortunately for us, that canvas bag was well equipped with slip-joint pliers, a lock-blade folding knife, and one essential component of this project: a section of coat hanger wire. That wire happened to be a godsend, as you will see, and ever since I've always kept bits of coat hanger wire in my own vehicle for emergencies, along with parachute cord, duct tape, matches, road flares, plastic bags, large nails, bungee cords, and other odds and ends. You just never know.

With the blade of the small knife and the pliers, we cut and bent a door opening in the side of the stew can to accept a can of Sterno, and then poked enough holes around the sides of the stew can for adequate ventilation to keep the flame burning. With the pliers, we fabricated a grate out of the wire for the top opening of the stew can, upon which we set our metal cups and fry pans for heating and cooking. With this makeshift stove, we were able to heat our drinks, warm up beef stew, and even cook scrambled eggs and bacon, all the while staying dry inside our tent when the weather was wet and cold outside. (By the way, this same little makeshift stew can stove was the subject of my first article ever printed in a magazine. See *Backwoodsman*, Volume 21, No. 1, Jan./Feb. 2000; article titled, "Improvising a Camp Stove.")

We kept the tent's door flap open partway most of the time for ventilation while heating and cooking. I should also mention that cooking and eating inside a tent, or even within the immediate camp area, for that matter, is discouraged by many outdoorsmen because of the risk of drawing wild animals like bears into your camp. While I have been very lucky in the past and have not experienced problems with bears in my campsites, other people certainly have, and this is a valid concern.

CHANGING A FLAT TIRE WITHOUT A JACK HANDLE

My son (who was three years old at the time) and I went on an outing to pick huckleberries with one of my friends and his family on a warm summer Saturday morning. My friend and his son led up the dirt road in their small pickup, and my son and I followed in my Isuzu Rodeo. My friend's wife and their other two kids were already up at the location in the mountains, where the huckleberries were thick.

Maybe a mile or so from our destination, my friend's pickup got a flat tire. Between our two

A re-creation of the expedient jack handle substitution, using Vise-Grip locking pliers. Wedging some sort of rigid rod, like a long-shaft screwdriver, up in the wedge of the handle (above the release lever) might have given us a T handle to turn the pliers easier, but the pliers would need to be tough enough to handle the sideways stress. It takes a considerable amount of torque to turn the screw on a car jack.

vehicles we had everything we needed to change the tire and get the truck rolling again—well, everything *except* a jack handle! I was the one with the jack, a wonderful scissor-type model, but I couldn't produce the handle to turn its screw, no matter how diligently I searched through all my gear. I hadn't even been aware that I wasn't stowing the handle for that jack in the tub of tools I always kept in the back of the Rodeo. What a time to find out!

After contemplating various remedies, we attempted to put air back into the tire with the foot-operated tire pump I happened to be carrying with my tools. The air simply leaked out from the puncture hole almost as fast as we could pump it in, and we weren't in a position there on that mountain road to try to patch a hole in an automobile tire.

We hadn't encountered any other vehicles on our trip, so we knew we were completely on our own with the situation. Somehow we needed to get the jack to do its work so we could get that tire changed.

Suddenly my friend had an idea. He tightened the jaws of a pair of Vise-Grip locking pliers on the jack's screw and started turning it by hand. Sure enough, the wheel started slowly rising off the ground. As slow and difficult as this method turned out to be, it did facilitate the changing of the tire, and I'm not sure how we would have ever gotten the job done without those locking pliers. Needless to say, I later found the jack handle in my garage, and it has remained in my vehicle with its jack ever since.

This whole episode got me to thinking about what I would try to do if I ever found myself in a situation with a flat tire way up in the mountains, off the road and far from any camp or station, without a jack. In such a predicament, I might try wedging a large, flat rock under the frame or axle near the flat tire to support that part of the vehicle, and then excavate the ground with a shovel or trowel directly under the tire until there was enough clearance to pull it off and mount the good replacement.

Assuming that much could be done, I would then fill the dirt back into the hole and pack it down as hard as I could under the wheel. Then I would try to push the support rock out of the way, maybe using a small log or heavy branch such that I could keep safely out of the way of the settling vehicle. If the rock wouldn't budge, I'd excavate some dirt under it until pressure on the frame was released.

Done slowly and carefully, there may not be much danger from the vehicle settling with a lurch and causing injury.

Well, maybe that would work and maybe it wouldn't, but I would sure give it a try if I didn't have a jack or a way to use the jack. I'd be willing to bet that someone somewhere has used this trick successfully at some time or another. It's fun to contemplate these things, isn't it?

MAKESHIFT REPAIR TO A PAIR OF EYEGLASSES

A lady who used to work in the office wore glasses for reading. One day she approached me with her glasses in hand, showing me where the frame had come apart and explaining that she had been unsuccessful in trying to tighten the tiny screw that once held the corner of the frame together.

With the tiny point of my pocketknife, I gave the little screw a few turns and realized that she was not mistaken—the threads were indeed stripped in the frame. She suggested attempting to reconnect the pieces with superglue. I immediately thought about the awkward location on the frame for gluing, the potential mess involved with gluing it up in the office, and the permanent nature of a glued connection.

My experimental idea for a temporary fix was to bind the frame together at that spot with tight wrappings of thread from my emergency sewing kit. I laid a bight of thread across the area to be mended and proceeded to tightly wrap a number of turns over most of it, finally securing it in place by feeding the running end through the tiny exposed eye of the bight that hadn't yet been buried by wrappings and then pulling both ends of the thread taut before trimming off the loose parts. (See chapter 6 for other practical applications of this technique.)

This made a neat and firm expedient connection. Although it may have looked funny, it was very secure and would be relatively easy to remove later without further damage to the frame, as opposed to a glued connection. She wore those glasses with that thread-wrapped fix for months afterward before eventually having the frame replaced.

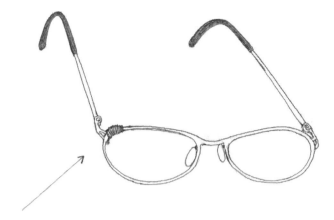

Expedient repair to eyeglasses—binding with thread.

MAKESHIFT WINDSHIELD WIPER REPAIRS

I seem to have had problems far too often with those doggone windshield wipers on cars. The following tales of dealings with faulty wipers should at least provide some amusement for the reader.

The first incident—one of my dad's favorite stories to tell—involved one of the wipers on his Jeep during a road trip he and a friend took maybe 20 years ago.

On their return drive home, they encountered a severe snowstorm. The blizzard conditions progressed to the point where Dad eventually decided to pull onto the shoulder and wait until the visibility improved.

That was when his wiper blade came loose and was thrown free by the wiper arm! Now the bare wiper arm was scraping directly on the windshield glass whenever the wiper motor was running. Suddenly, the whole situation seemed more dire, with the windshield wipers inoperable in their present state and the snowstorm not showing indication of letting up anytime soon.

Without the wiper blade, the drive back would have been treacherous in that kind of weather, so they began searching for it in earnest. Luckily, Dad spotted a narrow slit in the surface of the snow not far from the Jeep. He reached down and pulled out the buried wiper blade! Only a few minutes later, that thin slit in the snow would likely have been covered over and hidden by fresh snowfall.

Now he had the wiper blade, but the little pin that held it securely on the wiper arm was still missing. They needed some way to affix the blade to the arm. It was then that Dad remembered that his friend habitually carried an envelope in his sport jacket pocket containing receipts or checks held together with paper clips. "Say, Clark, would you happen to have a paper clip with you right now?"

Sure enough, Clark handed Dad a paper clip, and with the little paper clip wire, Dad fastened the wiper blade to the wiper arm such that it would function properly. This expedient repair worked so well, in fact, that it remained in place for months, maybe even for a year or two, before Dad finally replaced the old wiper blade with a new assembly and cross pin.

My own story with a makeshift repair to a windshield wiper is perhaps a noteworthy example of what *not* to do. I will describe the whole episode mainly for the readers' entertainment and possibly as a lesson in safety concerning windshield wipers.

Some years ago, the wiper motor on my Isuzu Rodeo started wearing out after its share of winters when I would occasionally run the wipers while they were basically frozen and covered with ice. I learned that doing that tends to put undue strain on the little wiper motor. Pretty soon the wiper arms would slowly swing up and stop without completing their full sweep, because the worn-out motor lacked the power to continue the operation.

I soon learned by experimentation that if I reached outside my driver's side window and over the windshield, I could give the closest wiper arm a gentle tug. This would cause the arms to make one or two full sweeps on their own, powered by the weak motor, before they would stop again. This system worked in the beginning, especially around town at slow speeds, in light traffic, or while waiting for a red light to change to green, and ideally if the rain wasn't coming down in torrents. But I realized I needed a better system.

I looked into replacing the wiper motor and discovered that new ones generally cost considerably more than $50. With my personal finances being what they were, I kept putting off the replacement motor until later, always thinking that I would be

more caught up on my bills in the following month. Funny how the next month rarely ever actually changes our world the way we think it will.

Long before this whole issue with the wiper motor had ever reared its ugly head, I noticed that the screw that held the driver's side wing window to its frame had somehow gotten loose and fallen out, leaving the 3/16-inch-diameter screw hole unfilled. This was another one of those simple little items that I was going to take care of soon but had never gotten around to. It presented no emergencies by any means, since the wing window remained firmly intact even without that screw, and not much cold wind blew through the little screw hole anyway.

I then noticed that the open screw hole was exactly what I needed to feed a string through, which I could tie to the driver's side wiper arm. With this trick, I would no longer have to reach outside an open window during a rainstorm to give the arm a tug to activate the wipers every one or two sweeps. Now all I would have to do was give the string a gentle tug occasionally while sitting comfortably in my seat behind the steering wheel, staying dry with my windows rolled up.

This makeshift arrangement, though it must have looked awfully goofy to other drivers, actually worked pretty well for a while. The biggest problem was that the string kept wearing through due to the friction where it passed through the screw hole, and I was replacing broken strings about every other day during the rainy season. I tried it with different sizes of synthetic cord, but they would all wear out fairly fast as well.

I learned just how dangerous this string-assisted system actually was during a camping trip that involved a 30-mile drive, partly on the freeway over a mountain pass. The trip out in pleasant weather was without incident, but during our drive home, my wife and I found ourselves in a heavy rainstorm. On the long, winding descent of that freeway amidst heavy, fast-moving traffic, the rain started pouring down hard . . . and it was then that my wiper string broke!

I suddenly found myself trying to navigate with basically zero visibility, and I must have uttered every swear word in existence (and invented a few others!) before I managed to ease my vehicle into the slow lane and creep along out of the other cars' way until the rain eased up. That following week, I finally spent the money and replaced the weak wiper motor with a new one.

EXPEDIENT AMMUNITION HAND-LOADING

More than 25 years ago, I traded into an old Smith & Wesson top-break revolver, the S&W standard .44 Double Action First Model. It seemed to be in serviceable condition as far as I could tell, and I could hardly wait to find out how it would shoot. The only problem was that it was chambered for the .44 S&W Russian—a cartridge that had been considered obsolete for many years, and loaded ammunition of that chambering happened to be pretty hard to find in those days.

I was aware that .44 Russian rounds could be fired in a revolver chambered for the more modern and powerful .44 Remington Magnum (as can .44 Special). Their case diameters are the same; the Russian case is merely shorter than the Magnum. Hence, all I needed to do was trim down some .44 Magnum cases to the proper length and then load them as Russians. Obtaining plenty of empty, once-fired .44 Magnum brass was never a problem; the problem was that I didn't have the loading dies for either .44 Russian or .44 Magnum at that time. I also didn't have the proper diameter bullets.

I had to get creative if I wanted to shoot that old revolver. A friend of mine came over, and the two of us came up with an idea. Having a supply of black gunpowder and some soft lead round balls that we had molded for use in a .44 cap-and-ball revolver, we were able to make some expedient hand loads.

First, we positioned the empty magnum cases face up and centered them over the partially opened jaws of a bench vise, and with a nail and hammer, we punched the spent primers out of the primer pockets. (A narrow steel drift punch is a better tool than a nail for this purpose, by the way.)

Next, we shortened the magnum cases to the appropriate length by sanding their mouths down at the bench belt sander. This was the slowest part of the process. We had to check our first case periodically to see when it would chamber in the gun's cylinder, since we didn't happen to have a Russian case on hand for reference. When that initial cut-down case would finally chamber in the

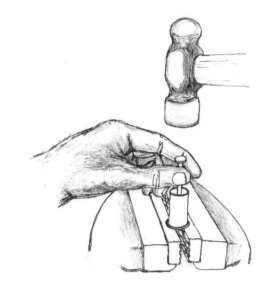

Using a vise and a nail as a punch to de-prime empty revolver cartridges.

gun, we used it as a reference gauge to achieve functional length with the rest of them.

We primed the cases by opening the jaws of the bench vise wide enough to fit the whole case lengthwise, plus enough room for a primer aligned with the primer pocket, and then simply closed the jaws to seat the primers. This is an easier process than might be expected.

I don't remember how many grains of triple-F black powder a .44 Russian cartridge will hold, but it's probably around 20, or maybe even a little more when you're using round balls for bullets, as we were. We didn't weigh the powder charges for this

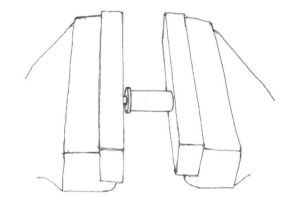

Priming a cartridge in the jaws of a vise.

experiment, but instead we filled the cases just enough to leave room for firmly seating a ball well into the mouth of each case. Black powder is often measured by volume rather than by weight anyway.

Finally, we used the vise jaws to seat the lead balls into the cases the same way we seated the primers. The heavy case walls of the magnum brass would, without crumpling, actually shave off the excess lead around the balls as they were seated down into the mouths, since the balls we used were .454 inch in diameter (if my memory is correct) and .44 Magnum cases are sized for bullets of .429 to .430 inch. Once the balls were seated flush with the mouths of the cases, we applied some lube grease over the front of each, just as is recommended for loading a cap-and-ball revolver, to prevent chain ignition. Black powder is extremely sensitive and easily ignited.

It should be observed here that it is indeed possible to overload a cartridge or gun with black powder, contrary to the popular perception many of us have long had of these "low-pressure" black powder loads. I have heard the famous stories about cap-and-ball revolvers blowing up, like the original Colt Walkers whose chambers would hold up to 60 grains and whose cylinder walls were dangerously thin. I also remember reading somewhere that the famous gun writer Elmer Keith once had a cylinder of a Colt Peacemaker .45 burst while discharging a heavily charged, black powder-loaded cartridge. I'm just saying that if you decide to try makeshift hand-loading yourself, be extremely careful! This can be risky business.

These makeshift hand loads were just plain fun to shoot in that old 19th-century revolver. They worked so well, in fact, that I later tried some black powder hand loads in my Smith & Wesson Model 29 .44 Magnum, with hard cast-lead bullets. Those smoky loads worked well, and I shot some surprisingly tight groups on paper with them.

While we're on the subject of makeshift hand-loading, I have one more story to tell. Back when I was doing a lot of loading for .30-06 about a decade ago, I kept running into problems with the de-capping/case-sizing stage. I repeatedly bent the de-capping pins using my particular set of dies and my loading press. When the die's pin finally got bent to the point that it was no longer serviceable, I headed off to the shooter supply store and bought several

new ones—in fact, I bought every spare de-capping pin they had left in stock, and it didn't take very long until they were all mangled to the point of no return.

Using that die only to size the cases, without the de-capping pin installed, worked just fine as far as that goes, but I learned that using the hammer and nail method to punch out spent primers, as described earlier, is considerably more awkward with a bottleneck rifle cartridge than it is with shorter, straight-walled handgun cartridges.

That was when I realized that the de-capping pins were of the same diameter as a tiny drill bit I had in my toolbox. I don't remember now if this was 1/16th-inch diameter or slightly smaller, but in any case I installed the bit into the die and discovered that it worked quite well.

The drill bit, being much harder, doesn't bend under pressure. It might break easier than a de-capping pin would because it is more brittle, but it won't bend out of shape. I don't remember if I ever broke the bit with that process. Small drill bits are cheaper and more available than are new reloading de-capping pins, so this was an economical as well as convenient substitution.

MAKESHIFT TOY REPAIRS

My son, who is almost four-and-a-half years old as I write this, has his own collection of plastic toys, and they break or lose parts quite regularly. I routinely find myself replacing screws, in some instances fabricating missing pieces (or entire toys like wooden guns or toy sailboats, but that's another story), or more frequently gluing broken items back together.

Earlier this year, the battery compartment door broke off one of his radio-controlled cars, and the batteries would no longer stay in place. The compartment is underneath the car, so it was a challenge trying to keep the batteries in their sockets. Strips of duct tape over the opening proved unreliable; the compartment needed a little door to hold those two AA batteries in place. We could never find the original door that broke off at its hinge.

My solution was to construct a rectangular plate as a substitute for the missing door and tape it in place over the batteries to keep them secured. While searching around the house for some type of rigid material with the proper thickness from which I could make this plate, I came across a clear plastic ruler in one of my junk drawers. It appeared to be exactly the right thickness, but maybe 3/16ths of an inch too wide for the car's battery space. I knew it would be no problem to trim it down to the proper dimensions. After cutting the piece of ruler to the proper length with a coping saw, I used my bench grinder to trim the edges and sandpaper to smooth them up.

With fresh batteries in their sockets, I installed the new cover plate and duct-taped it in place. The little car was once again operational, and the batteries never dropped out again.

CHAPTER 9

Useful Charts and Data for Makeshift Projects

This chapter is provided for those readers who, like me, constantly find themselves in need of a comprehensive reference of basic technical information where they can quickly look up whatever they need to help them invent, design, modify, repair, or fabricate all kinds of things. I hope the following information proves helpful.

MELTING TEMPERATURES OF COMMON METALS

Metal	Degrees Fahrenheit	Degrees Celsius
Pewter †	420	216
Tin	449	231
Lead	621	327
Zinc	786–787	419
Magnesium	1,100	593
Aluminum	1,217–1,218	658–659
Bronze †	1,675	913
Brass †	1,700	927
Silver	1,721–1,761	938–960
Gold	1,945	1,063
Copper	1,981	1,083
Steel (most alloys)	2,500–2,700	1,371–1,482
Nickel	2,646	1,452
Titanium	3,263	1,795
Tungsten	5,432	3,000

† Alloys of pewter, brass, and bronze vary widely in formulation and melting temperature. The book *Working With Metal* (Time-Life Books, 1981), for example, shows the melting temperature for brass at 1,700°F, while Richard Finch shows a temperature *range* for brass' melting point of 1,652 to 1,724°F in a chart in his *Welder's Handbook*.

FRACTIONS TO DECIMALS

Anytime we need to know the thickness of anything less than an inch, it is helpful to be able to convert decimals to fractions or vise versa. Precision measuring tools like calipers and micrometers use decimal readings, but most of us probably think in fractions most of the time. We might be familiar with "three-eighths of an inch," for example, but be totally lost if we saw .3750 on some chart related to whatever we're doing. Or if you have determined that something is .0625-inch thick, it could be worth knowing that it is the same as 1/16-inch thick.

This ability is especially useful when choosing drill bits and fabricating screw threads, but how about gun bores and ammunition? Say you wanted to make a quick-reload bullet block out of hardwood for your muzzleloader of .62-caliber. You could look on your conversion chart and see that you would need to use a 5/8-inch drill bit to make the holes in the block. The useful possibilities of a fractions-to-decimals chart are really endless, in my view.

If you have a calculator or good math skills, here's a handy trick that will get you the same result. Just divide the minor number in the fraction by the major number, and the answer will be the decimal you need. For example, divide 3 by 8 and you get .375.

Fraction	Decimal	Fraction	Decimal	Fraction	Decimal
1/64	0.0156	17/64	0.2656	17/32	0.5312
1/32	0.0312	9/32	0.2812	9/16	0.5625
3/64	0.0468	19/64	0.2968	19/32	0.5937
1/16	0.0625	5/16	0.3125	5/8	0.625
5/64	0.0781	21/64	0.3281	21/32	0.6562
3/32	0.0937	11/32	0.3437	11/16	0.6875
7/64	0.1093	23/64	0.3593	23/32	0.7187
1/8	0.1250	3/8	0.375	3/4	0.75
9/64	0.1406	25/64	0.3906	25/32	0.7812
5/32	0.1562	12/32	0.4062	13/16	0.8125
11/64	0.1718	27/64	0.4218	27/32	0.8437
3/16	0.1875	7/16	0.4375	7/8	0.875
13/64	0.2031	29/64	0.4531	29/32	0.9062
7/32	0.2187	15/32	0.4687	15/16	0.9375
15/64	0.2343	31/64	0.4843	31/32	0.9687
1/4	0.25	1/2 *	0.5	1	1.00

* Fractions divided as small as 64ths are included in this chart only up to 1/2 (0.5). After that, the smallest fractions listed are 32nds.

USEFUL MATHEMATICAL FORMULAS FOR CALCULATING AREA AND VOLUME

To find the *Circumference of a Circle*:
 Multiply the diameter by 3.1416.
To find the *Area of a Circle*:
 Multiply the square of the diameter by .7854, or multiply pi by the square of the radius.
To find the *Surface Area of a Sphere*:
 Multiply the square of the radius by 3.1416, then multiply by 4.
To find the *Volume of a Sphere*:
 Multiply the cube of the radius by 3.1416, then multiply by 4 and divide by 3.
To find the *Area of a Square*:
 Square one side, or multiply the length of one side by itself.

To find the *Area of a Rectangle*:
 Multiply the height by the base.
To find the *Area of a Triangle*:
 Multiply the base by the height and divide by 2.
To find the *Area of a Trapezoid*:
 Add the two parallel sides, then multiply by the height and divide by 2.
To find the *Volume of a Cylinder*:
 Multiply the square of the radius of the base by 3.1416, then multiply by the height.
To find the *Volume of a Cone*:
 Multiply the square of the radius of the base by 3.1416, then multiply by the height and divide by 3.
To find the *Volume of a Pyramid*:
 Multiply the area of the base by the height, then divide by 3.

TRADITIONAL UNITS OF MEASUREMENT

Acre: The common unit of land area measurement used in the United States, equal to 43,560 square feet, or 4,840 square yards. An acre of land can have any shape, but a square acre would have a measurement of 208.71 feet on each side. There are 640 acres in a square mile, also known as a *section* of land.

Cubit: In ancient times, this was the length of one's forearm, or more accurately the unit of measurement usually equal to 18 inches or the longer cubit of about 21 inches (52.5 centimeters) in the ancient Egyptian measure.

Fathom: A unit of length equal to 6 feet. Used almost exclusively to measure depth in water.

Foot: We all know that 12 inches equal the length of 1 foot, and that a foot equals 1/3 yard. This nonmetric unit of measurement is still commonly used in the United States, and it is generally believed that it was originally based on the length of a man's foot. My own feet, by the way, which are admittedly short for a man of my height, actually measure just under 11 inches from the tip of my big toe to the back of my heel, I discovered strictly out of curiosity. Abbreviated as "ft." The common symbol for feet is '.

Furlong: A unit of length equal to 660 feet.

Hand: Also "handbreadth," abbreviated "h" or "hh" for "hands high," the hand is the common unit for measuring horses, equal to 4 inches and based on the width of the average human adult male hand. Generally speaking, a pony measures up to 14.2 hh at the withers; an animal 14.2 hh or taller is a horse.

Hundredweight: Abbreviated as "cwt" for "centum weight," the hundredweight is a unit of weight measurement equal to 112 avoirdupois pounds in the British system, and 100 lbs. in the United States and Canada. English anvils were commonly marked using a three-figure system based on the British hundredweight. The first number indicated the anvil's weight in hundredweights (112 lbs.), the next number to the right (never more than 3) represented quarter hundredweights, or 28 lbs., and the last number represented whole pounds. Hence, an anvil marked as 1-2-3 would indicate: 112 lbs. + (28 x 2) + 3, or 171 lbs. total.

Inch: The inch is a very old unit of measurement that was originally based on the width of the average human thumb. This would be especially useful for anyone with a 1-inch-wide thumb, as he would always have a reference for inch-based measurements with him at all times. I discovered that my own thumb appears to measure exactly 1 inch across. The common symbol for inches is ".

Ounce: There are several common measuring systems that use the ounce unit, and therefore it has several different definitions. There are 480 grains to the ounce in the troy and apothecaries' measuring systems, but only 437.5 grains to the avoirdupois ounce. There are 12 troy ounces in a pound and 16 avoirdupois ounces in a pound. Often abbreviated "oz."

Pennyweight: A unit of measurement commonly used in measuring the weight or, more correctly, the *mass* of precious metals. (Mass is a measure of how much *matter* an object has, while weight measures the *gravitational pull* on an object.) Abbreviated "dwt," the pennyweight is equal to 24 grains, or 1/240th troy pound, or 1/20th troy ounce. It is also approximately 0.0549 avoirdupois ounce, or 1.555 grams.

Pound: The general unit of weight measurement most common in the United States, abbreviated "lb." Both the troy pound and the apothecaries' pound are divided into 12 ounces, while in the more common avoirdupois system the pound is divided into 16 ounces. One avoirdupois pound is approximately equal to .454 metric kilograms, and there are 2.205 pounds to a kilo.

Rod: A unit of length equal to 16 1/2 feet, or 5 1/2 yards.

Span: As an ancient unit of measurement, span is defined on Wikipedia as "the distance measured by a human hand, from the tip of the thumb to the tip of the little finger." In English usage, it is standardized as a unit of length equal to 9 inches.

Yard: The yard (often abbreviated "yd.") is the non-System International (SI) linear measurement equal to the length of 3 feet, or 36 inches. One yard is equal to 0.9144 meters. In the field, walking paces often serve as functional yards for rough, "ballpark" measurements.

HANDY GAUGE REFERENCES

The term "gauge," or "gage," is often used to denote thickness of something, or more precisely the *measurement* of a material's thickness. Today there are several gauge categories in common use, so we have to specify the type of material for which we are trying to determine the proper gauge. Some common examples of gauges are as follows:

Bore gauge: Typically used for shotguns, bore gauge is actually a count of how many lead spheres of a given diameter add up to 1 pound. Hence, there would be 12 lead balls of 12-gauge to the pound, 20 balls to the pound for 20-gauge, and so on. Interestingly, the .410 shotgun, although sometimes referred to as a gauge, is really not a gauge in this sense at all but rather a bore diameter measurement based on the inch.

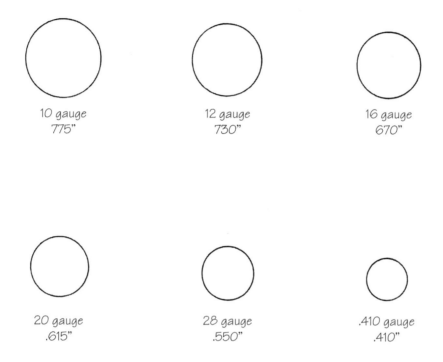

10 gauge
775"

12 gauge
730"

16 gauge
670"

20 gauge
.615"

28 gauge
.550"

.410 gauge
.410"

Shotgun bore gauges.

Circles represent approximate sizes.

Sheet metal gauges: Several different gauging standards have been used for sheet metal, and it can be confusing. Perhaps the two standards most commonly encountered in the United States today are: 1) the United States Standard Gage for Sheet and Plate Iron and Steel, which was established by an act of Congress in 1893 and was based on weight or mass of wrought iron for a specified surface area, and 2) the Manufacturers' Standard Gauge (MSG), which is based on thickness and, for the most part, has replaced the U.S. Standard Gage as an industry standard.

Gauge numbers represent different thicknesses, depending on the type of metal. For example, 10-gauge steel is 0.1345-inch thick, while 10-gauge aluminum is 0.1019-inch thick. Interestingly, while 10-gauge steel measures .1345 inch in the MSG standard, it is .1406 inch thick in the U.S. Standard Gage.

The following chart consists of gauges #3 through #38 of sheet steel and their inch decimal thickness in the MSG standard:

Gauge #	Thickness in inch decimals	Gauge #	Thickness in inch decimals	Gauge #	Thickness in inch decimals
3	.2391	15	.0673	27	.0164
4	.2242	16	.0598	28	.0149
5	.2092	17	.0538	29	.0135
6	.1943	18	.0478	30	.0120
7	.1793	19	.0418	31	.0105
8	.1644	20	.0359	32	.0097
9	.1495	21	.0329	33	.0090
10	.1345	22	.0299	34	.0082
11	.1196	23	.0269	35	.0075
12	.1046	24	.0239	36	.0067
13	.0897	25	.0209	37	.0064
14	.0747	26	.0179	38	.0060

Wire gauges: The two systems in common use for categorizing electrical wiring are the American Wire Gauge (AWG) and Metric Wire Gauge (MWG). Currently, the most used in the United States is, of course, AWG. In this system, the higher the number, the smaller the wire.

Approximate size of wire: Gauge and example application:

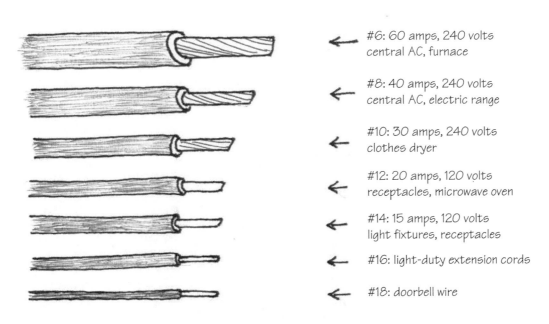

#6: 60 amps, 240 volts central AC, furnace

#8: 40 amps, 240 volts central AC, electric range

#10: 30 amps, 240 volts clothes dryer

#12: 20 amps, 120 volts receptacles, microwave oven

#14: 15 amps, 120 volts light fixtures, receptacles

#16: light-duty extension cords

#18: doorbell wire

Note: Represented here are electrical wire gauges only.

The most common sizes of plastic-coated copper electrical wire gauges (not drawn to exact scale).

Screw gauges: Screws are typically sorted by size, or gauge. The screw's major thread diameter, nominal size, and basic screw diameter (or shank diameter) are measured for the gauge of a screw, and these are all roughly the same dimension. The American National Standard for Machine Screws chart, available in *Machinery's Handbook*, shows the numbering for all machine screws. As far as I can tell, these are basically the same as used for wood screws.

It should also be noted here that screws are commonly designated according to their thread specifications, as was more thoroughly explained in chapter 7.

WOOD SCREW GAUGE CHART

Screw Gauge #	Shank Diameter (Inches)	Fractions
0	0.060	1/16"
1	0.073	5/64"
2	0.086	3/32"
3	0.099	7/64"
4	0.112	7/64"
5	0.125	1/8"
6	0.138	9/64"
7	0.151	5/32"
8	0.164	5/32"
9	0.177	11/64"
10	0.190	3/16"
11	0.203	13/64"
12	0.216	7/32"
14	0.242	1/4"
16	0.268	17/64"
18	0.294	19/64"
20	0.320	5/16"
24	0.372	3/8"

Nail sizes and gauges: Nails are rarely categorized by gauge, which refers to shaft diameter, but are more commonly sorted by their length, expressed with the letter *d*, and sometimes spoken as "penny," which was originally a pound-based designation long ago in England. For example, a 16d common nail measures 3 1/2 inches in length and is commonly referred to as a 16 penny nail. There are approximately 44 16d common nails to a pound.

The gauging of box nails, finishing nails, and other specialty nails will deviate from those of common nails to some degree. The penny sizes of common nails graduate from 2d to 60d, and a nail longer than 6 inches is normally referred to as a spike.

Gauge

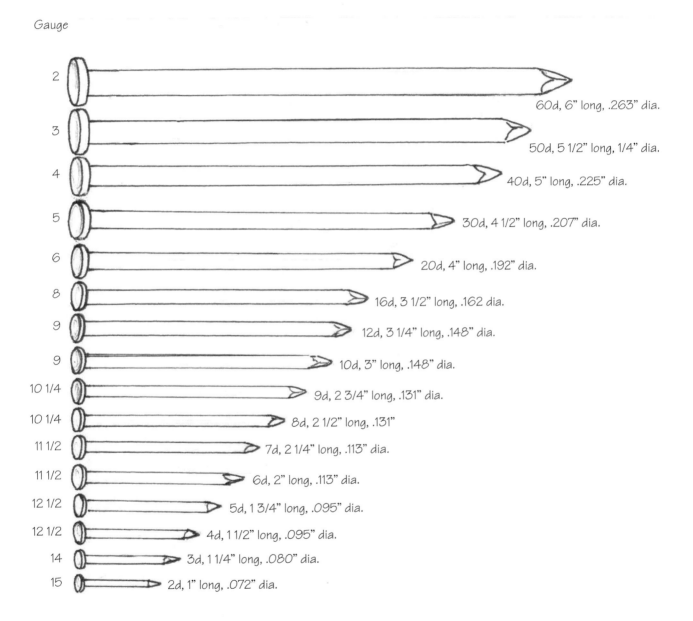

Gauge	
2	60d, 6" long, .263" dia.
3	50d, 5 1/2" long, 1/4" dia.
4	40d, 5" long, .225" dia.
5	30d, 4 1/2" long, .207" dia.
6	20d, 4" long, .192" dia.
8	16d, 3 1/2" long, .162 dia.
9	12d, 3 1/4" long, .148" dia.
9	10d, 3" long, .148" dia.
10 1/4	9d, 2 3/4" long, .131" dia.
10 1/4	8d, 2 1/2" long, .131"
11 1/2	7d, 2 1/4" long, .113" dia.
11 1/2	6d, 2" long, .113" dia.
12 1/2	5d, 1 3/4" long, .095" dia.
12 1/2	4d, 1 1/2" long, .095" dia.
14	3d, 1 1/4" long, .080" dia.
15	2d, 1" long, .072" dia.

Common nails chart (not to scale).

SOME POPULAR AND USEFUL ENGINEERING FORMULAS

Work
$W = F \times D$
where:
W = work
F = force
D = distance

Mechanical Advantage (MA) Formula for Levers
$L/l = R/E$
where:
L = length of effort arm
l = length of resistance arm
R = resistance (weight or force)
E = effort force

(Based on the explanation in Dover Publications' *Basic Machines and How They Work*.)

1st class lever

fulcrum between load and effort

effort force (E)

effort arm (L)

4 feet

fulcrum

2 feet

resistance arm (l)

weight (R) resistance
100 lbs.

$$\frac{4}{2} = \frac{100}{E} \quad E = 50 \text{ lbs.}$$

2nd class lever

resistance arm (l)

2 feet

(R)

100 lbs.

effort force
(E)

load is between fulcrum
and effort

fulcrum

effort arm (L)
8 feet

$$\frac{8}{2} = \frac{100}{E} \quad E = 25 \text{ lbs.}$$

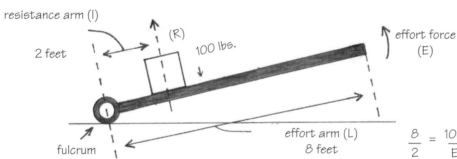

effort force
(E)

100 lbs.

(R)

3rd class lever

effort force is between
load and fulcrum

effort arm (L)
2 feet

resistance arm (l)
6 feet

fulcrum

$$\frac{2}{6} = \frac{100}{E} \quad E = 300 \text{ lbs.}$$

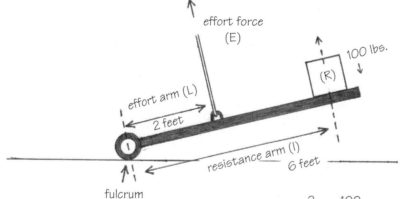

Three types of levers.

Mechanical Advantage Formula Adapted for the Wheel and Axle

L/l = R/E

where:

L = radius of the circle of the turning handle

l = radius of circle of turning axle

R = force of resistance of item being turned

E = force of effort applied to handle

L = turn handle circle's radius

l = radius of axle being turned

R = resistance (weight being raised, in this example)

E = effort force on handle

$$\frac{L}{l} = \frac{R}{E}$$

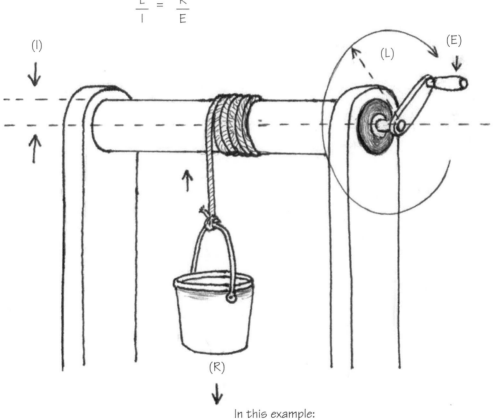

In this example:

6 inches radius of crank handle (L)

3 inches radius of axle (l)

water and bucket weigh 10 lbs. (R)

$$\frac{6}{3} = \frac{10}{E} \qquad E = 5 \text{ lbs. theoretical force required to lift this 10-lb. weight}$$

Wheel and axle.

Ohm's Law

While this volume of *Makeshift Workshop Skills* doesn't deal too much with electricity, the formulas associated with Ohm's Law are perhaps the most important formulas to know for making electrical circuit calculations, as they define the relationships between current, voltage, power, and resistance. I would expect that almost any handyman, appliance repairman, electrician, electrical engineer, electronics hobbyist, or any mechanic who works on automotive electrical systems would agree that Ohm's Law is an incredibly useful thing to memorize.

For example, using Ohm's Law, we can see that E (volts) = I (current) x R (resistance), and therefore we might see something like 12 volts = 2 amps x 6 ohms. Similarly, an example of I (current) = E (volts) divided by R (resistance) might be 2 amps = 12 volts ÷ 6 ohms, and an example of R (resistance) = E (volts) divided by I (current) might be 6 ohms = 12 volts ÷ 2 amps.

I find it easiest to remember these formulas with pie charts. Although you will find variations, the pie charts shown here seem to be the most common. In my view, these charts belong in everyone's reference library.

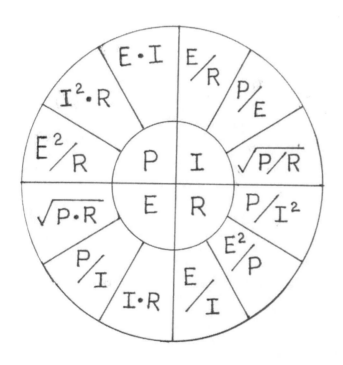

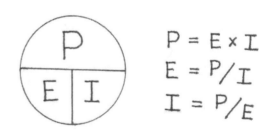

I is Intensity of current in amps.
R is Resistance in Ohms.
E is Electromotive Force in volts.
P is Power in watts.

Ohm's Law pie charts.

Pythagorean Theorem

As we learned in *Makeshift I*, the Pythagorean theorem is particularly useful to know and understand because it can be used to determine distances between points, confirm right angles (to ensure your structure's walls are truly square, for example), or make a myriad of other calculations. In my view, everyone should know and remember it, considering its usefulness.

Essentially, the Pythagorean theorem says that a square formed on the hypotenuse of a right triangle will always be equal to the sum of the squares formed on the other two sides. The hypotenuse is the side opposite the right angle, or the longest side of the triangle. With the Pythagorean theorem, if we know the lengths of any two sides of the triangle, we can find the length of the third side.

This right triangle is bordered on all three sides by squares.

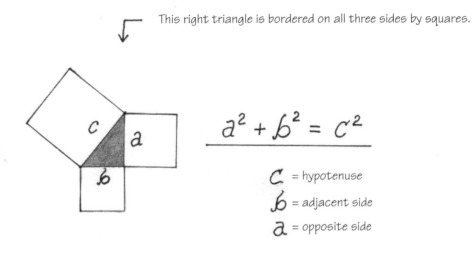

$$a^2 + b^2 = c^2$$

c = hypotenuse

b = adjacent side

a = opposite side

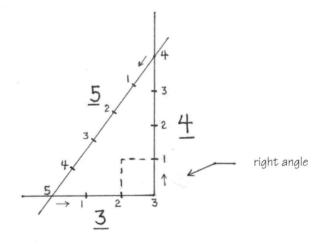

right angle

Use the 3-4-5 rule to confirm a right angle. Measure and mark 3 units (inches, feet, meters, etc.) on one side and 4 units on the opposite side; then measure the hypotenuse across those two points. If it is 5 units, you have a right angle.

Pythagorean theorem.

Useful Mechanical Principles for the Makeshifter

A machine is a device that makes work easier to accomplish, and machines of all kinds help modern people accomplish all kinds of tasks. Muscle-powered, or manual machines, as opposed to gas, hydraulic, steam, or electrically powered devices, could become valuable assets when sources of energy are either scarce, prohibitively expensive, or unreliable, especially in a remote environment or anytime after a cataclysmic crisis.

MECHANICAL ADVANTAGE

To fully understand and appreciate how almost any kind of machine or mechanical device works, it is helpful to first have a familiarity with the concept of mechanical advantage (MA), which, as we briefly touched on in *Makeshift I*, measures the relationship between the force applied to a machine (the input) and the force produced by the machine that accomplishes work (the output).

Different kinds of mechanical advantage relationships exist within the various mechanical systems, but here I am mainly talking about the positive mechanical advantages that magnify an applied quantity like force, as opposed to fractional mechanical advantages (which could actually be thought of as mechanical disadvantages). A positive advantage gives you an increase in something, be it force, distance, or speed at the output, but all of this really depends on what you are intending to increase, and the law of energy conservation puts certain restraints on what you can actually accomplish. We will talk more about this shortly. We can define "work" as a force times a distance, and our mechanical advantage can be expressed as resistance divided by effort ($MA = R/E$).

It is important when working with ratios to keep your units the same. If you were trying to determine some kind of inch-based relationship, for example, you would want to use inches throughout your mathematical calculations that strictly deal with linear measure. This rule for keeping things consistent while figuring ratios also applies to quantities like force, unless you are specifically trying to convert one into another. In other words, you should consider the relationship between the input force and the output force of a machine, or an input distance with an output distance, and so on.

It is also helpful to have a solid understanding of the six basic kinds of "simple" machines before getting too deeply into more complex mechanical concepts, since we will be revisiting some of these principles as they apply. These six simple machines are the inclined plane, wedge, screw, lever, pulley, and wheel and axle. They are used extensively in more complicated machines as well. We'll take a closer look at some of these as we move forward in this section.

A relatively fundamental (and extremely useful) technology to know how to calculate the various mechanical advantages for, or at least to understand the basic concept, is the process of transmitting rotary motion from one shaft to another, using either belt-driven pulleys, gears, or sprockets and chains. A homemade manually powered machine might employ one or more of these systems to make use of this MA or to make work easier to accomplish.

Gears, sprockets, and pulleys are related systems in the sense that they all transmit rotary motion from one shaft to another, but they are very different technically. Gears are toothed wheels or shafts that mesh together such that the rotational motion of one acts directly to turn the other. A sprocket is also a toothed wheel, but it is distinguished from a gear by the fact that it does not mesh directly with another sprocket or wheel. Instead, the sprocket is linked to another sprocket by a special chain or perforated belt that is engaged and driven by the teeth on the sprocket. A pulley differs from either a sprocket or a gear by the groove around its circumference, or a flange on each side of the wheel to center a drive belt or rope. Pulley wheels also do not mesh or act together directly; drive belts, bands, ropes, or chains transmit their rotary motion.

In certain applications, such as with the common child's tricycle, it is actually practical to fix the crank (foot pedals, in this case) directly to the wheel's axle, which would also be the drive shaft of this kind of manually powered machine. Such a machine uses no gears, pulleys, or sprockets to transmit rotary motion from one axle to another. One full turn of its pedals yields one complete revolution of its wheel, providing a distance advantage.

This can be visualized more easily with a simple model that simulates the pedal circumference in relation to the wheel's circumference. In the photo on the next page, two cardboard circles of different diameters are affixed so that they turn together. The smaller circle represents the circumference, or one revolution, of

Belts and pulleys: direction of rotation preserved.

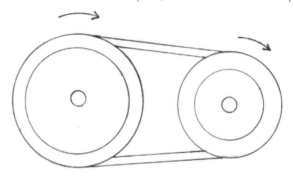

Sprockets and chains: direction of rotation preserved.

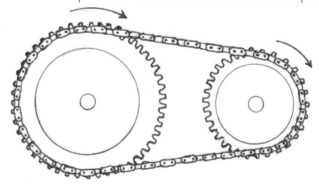

Two gears in mesh: direction of rotation reversed.

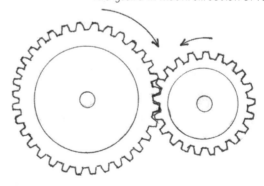

Three basic systems for transmitting rotary motion.

A child's tricycle is an example of a machine that requires no gears, sprockets, or chains.

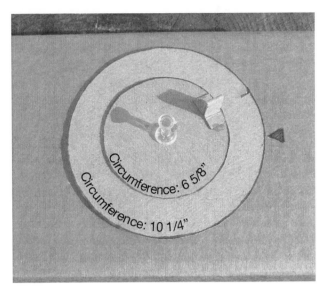

Cardboard disks are used in this model to illustrate the ratio between pedal strokes and wheels.

the pedal stroke, and the larger circle represents the wheel being driven. In this example, I have glued a small fold of cardboard to the outer edge of the smaller wheel to serve as the turn handle, or pedal substitute.

The two circles are thumbtacked to a cardboard box such that they can be turned together freely. A mark on the box and a corresponding mark on the larger circle make it easier to index a full rotation by lining up the marks. You can determine the circumference of each circle either by multiplying the diameter of each by pi (3.1416), or by laying a string on the outside edge of each circle all the way around, marking where the running end touches the standing part, and then straightening it back out to measure the length. The circumference can be thought of, in the context of a turning wheel, as the distance of rotation.

With this model, it is easy to see that a shorter distance pedaled or hand-cranked (length of circumference of the smaller circle) will yield a greater distance traveled (length of circumference of the larger circle that represents the wheel being driven). In other words, the feet move the pedals a given distance in rotation, but the tricycle travels a longer distance down the driveway. In the photo, we see that this model's simulated pedal stroke is 6.625 inches, which will turn the big wheel a distance of 10.25 inches in one full rotation.

GEAR RATIOS

You may remember how to calculate gear ratios from *Makeshift I*. A two-gear machine, or simple gear train, will have a drive gear (also called driver, or driving gear), which is the gear that receives its rotational energy directly from the power source, and the driven gear, which receives its rotational energy from the drive gear. Machines with more than two gears in a gear train also have intermediate, or idler gears, which can be used to change shaft spacing as well as change the direction of rotation.

When you want to determine the number of revolutions of one of the gears in the simple two-gear machine per each revolution of the other gear, multiply the number of revolutions of one of the gears (let's start with our drive gear) by the number of teeth on the same gear, and then divide that number by the number of teeth on the other (driven) gear to find its number of corresponding revolutions.

Hence, if we say that gear A (the drive gear in this example, which also happens to be the larger of the two gears) makes six revolutions, and our count tells us that it has 35 teeth, then, using this formula, we would come up with 210 (35 x 6 = 210). Now we count the teeth on gear B and discover that it has 15 teeth. We can then conclude that gear B will turn 14 revolutions for every six revolutions of gear A,

Miscellaneous small gears saved from broken toys and machines can be useful for your inventions.

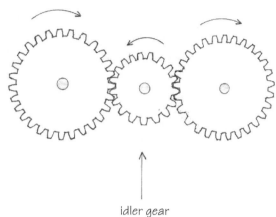

idler gear
The two outside gears turn in the same direction.

Having three gears in mesh restores rotational direction.

because 210 divided by 15 equals 14. And we could then also figure out, using simple division, that for every one full revolution of drive gear A, driven gear B will turn 2.33 times (14 ÷ 6 = 2.33).

It might actually be easier to think of this as simply the number of teeth of one gear divided by the number of teeth on the other gear to find the ratio (in this case 35 ÷ 15 = 2.33). This simplifies things in the sense that we are basing our calculation on only one full rotation of our known gear, but the ratio relationship of revolutions between the two gears is the same. We could write it as 2.33:1, and we might read it as "two and a third to one ratio."

In the illustration at right, we see two gears in mesh. Gear A has 8 teeth while gear B has 12 teeth. If we say that A is the driver and B is the driven, then using the formula described above, we could write our gear ratio as "two-thirds to one ratio." However, if B becomes the driver and A becomes the driven, the ratio would then be "one and a half to one."

At this point, let us observe that there will always be a trade-off whenever we multiply either speed or force—one will be diminished whenever we increase the other. This is that law of energy conservation we were introduced to earlier. When dealing with gear trains, we will have two kinds of ratios to consider. The first is usually referred to as the gear ratio, or sometimes the speed ratio, because it shows how the speed of rotation of the shafts in

the machine will be affected by the relationship of the gear sizes that mesh and transmit rotary motion. The shafts on the smaller gears will turn faster than the shafts on the larger gears, because the smaller gears make more turns for every corresponding turn of the larger gears. And with toothed gears this is easy to figure, as we've seen, by comparing the number of teeth on the gears.

The other kind of ratio we may consider is referred to (usually) as the mechanical advantage

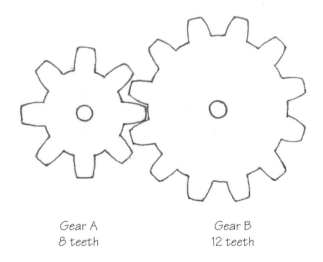

Gear A
8 teeth

Gear B
12 teeth

Two gears in mesh.

(MA), which, in this context, considers the increase in torque (the force that produces rotation) through the system of gears.

Here is where some readers might get confused, as I was for some time. What some people call gear ratio, others might call (incorrectly, I believe) mechanical advantage, but for our purpose here, we will make a distinction between them.

As was previously suggested, the mechanical advantage can be the relationship between an applied force, distance, or speed of the input to the force, distance, or speed of the machine's output. However, when we are talking about the mechanical advantage of a gear train, we are normally concerning ourselves with gaining a force advantage rather than a speed advantage. In other words, our drive gear (input) will be smaller than our driven (output) gear, so that we will gain rotational force (technically, torque) at the output, but we will also get a slower-turning driven (output) gear wheel. A theoretical mechanical advantage, also called an ideal mechanical advantage, ignores any loss to friction, and if we focus on the theoretical for now, we can express this gearing down that *slows* the output of our gear train, using the number of gear teeth to determine the rotational relationship between the gears, this way: the number of teeth on the driven gear over the number of teeth on the drive gear, and this follows the popular formula: MA = Output/Input (MA = Resistance divided by Effort).

By contrast, the gear or speed ratio (as we are using the terminology in this discussion) can be expressed as the drive gear over the driven gear, or Speed Ratio (SR) = Input Gear/Output Gear. Hence, the output gear in this case will make more revolutions per second than will our input gear, and we thus gain a speed advantage at the output, but we also lose some torque in the process.

It might help to think of these ratios as MA = Output Force/Input Force, and SR = Input Distance/Output Distance. Note that in the first ratio, we are considering the output and input *forces* (in this case, torque) and are concerning ourselves with units of force as much as gear wheel revolutions. In the second, we are considering input and output *distance* relationships as interpreted by gear wheel circumference, if we can deviate from counting gear teeth just for a moment to make this point. So, thinking in these terms might help us avoid confusing

the ratios for torque and speed, though both can be important depending on what we want to accomplish.

Interestingly, a two-gear operation will serve to reverse the rotational direction, while a two-pulley belt-driven machine will preserve the same rotational direction. With gears, even numbers of gear wheels in the gear train will reverse direction, and odd numbers of gears preserve the rotational direction (in relation to the direction of the drive gear).

Determining the ratios of gear trains having more than two gears is also a relatively simple process. An easy formula to remember for this is found in Dover Publications' *Basic Machines and How They Work*, prepared by the Naval Education and Training Program Development Center, which says: "The product of the number of teeth on each of the driver gears divided by the product of the number of teeth on each of the driven gears gives you the speed ratio of any gear train."

To reiterate, just remember that, whenever our ratio yields a number greater than 1 (as opposed to some fraction) when we are talking about input over output with these gear relationships (drive gear divided by driven gear), we are looking for the speed advantage. But when we see the ratio as driven gear/drive gear, we are considering a speed *dis*advantage, or a slowing of the axle on the driven gear, which, as it turns out, would also give us an increase of torque in the output.

A compound gear train describes a gear arrangement having more than one gear stacked onto any single shaft. With this kind of arrangement, the total gear ratio will also be the product of the ratios, as described above.

Different kinds of gears serve different applications. The most common is the spur gear, whose teeth are on the outer circumference and perpendicular to the gear's face. Helical gears differ from spur gears in that their teeth are at an angle to their gear faces, which serves to give them more tooth contact area. Bevel gears are useful for transmitting the rotational force on an angle (such as 90 degrees, for example) where the shafts are not parallel. A rack is a kind of toothed straight bar used in conjunction with a pinion (small round gear) to transfer rotational motion into linear motion, or vice versa. Epicyclic, or planetary gear trains, typically used in such applications as automatic transmissions and cordless drills to optimize load distribution,

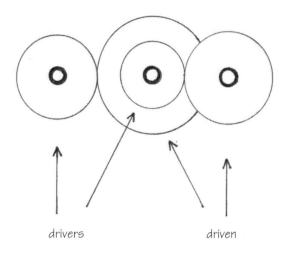

drivers   driven

Circles representing gears in a compound gear train.

An example of a compound gear train.

consist of a planet carrier ring, a ring gear or annulus with inward facing teeth, a center gear called the sun gear, and typically three or four planet gears that orbit the sun gear.

Several more configurations of gears that might be worth further study include worm gears, hypoid gears, face gears, pawl or ratchet gears that allow rotation in only one direction, and herringbone gears, among the numerous other variations of related mechanical devices.

Virtually all gears manufactured today are composed of either some type of metal or a synthetic plastic material such as nylon. However, hardwoods and especially ironwoods have been used successfully in gear construction in the past. Wooden gear movements in old clocks are perhaps the most common examples of this. This presents at least one additional possibility for the makeshift inventor, and certain types of hardwoods might be more accessible and easier to work with than most metals and plastics for the average craftsman.

The main disadvantages of wooden gears are: 1) their comparatively low wear resistance with applications involving substantial amounts of friction, and 2) their tendency to warp or shrink due to climate and temperature changes. My dad built an impressive grandfather's clock in his garage in 1971, basing most of the mechanism on the famous Thomas all-wooden clock design. He cut the gears

out of birch on his old band saw. The clock ran for several years and kept fairly accurate time until one of the gears eventually warped and interfered with its operation. He keeps threatening to isolate the hang-up in the gears someday and replace it to restore the clock to full operation.

One interesting example of a clock with wooden gears that has functioned continuously for almost 300 years is the one made by John Harrison, the

Part of the planetary gear train found in a cordless drill.

Gears made of plastic are not uncommon in small appliances like this alarm clock.

A clock escape gear made of hardwood.

A Thomas wooden grandfather's clock built by Gene Ballou.

18th-century English clockmaker and famous inventor of the marine chronometer. With gears made from lignum vitae ironwood, Harrison's clock, which was built in the early 1720s, still runs in England today, and I understand it keeps remarkably accurate time. My point here is that we cannot entirely rule out using wood for gears.

Before progressing beyond gears in our discussion of transmitting rotary motion, I think it's beneficial to have a familiarity with at least some of the gear-related terminology. For instance, the word "pitch" is encountered when studying gears. Pitch is generally defined as the distance from a point to some corresponding point. When talking about gears, circular pitch is the distance from a point on one gear tooth to a corresponding point on the next tooth along the circumference of the pitch circle, or pitch line, and the pitch circle is the imaginary circle on a gear that makes contact with the pitch circle of any gear it meshes with.

Pitch diameter simply refers to the diameter of one of these imaginary pitch circles, while diametral pitch specifies the number of teeth on a gear per inch of pitch diameter. Gear sizes and proportions are determined either by circular pitch (usually with large gears) or more commonly by diametral pitch.

The tooth of a gear is sometimes referred to as a cog. The length of the gear tooth (or cog) outside of the pitch circle (its height above the pitch line) is

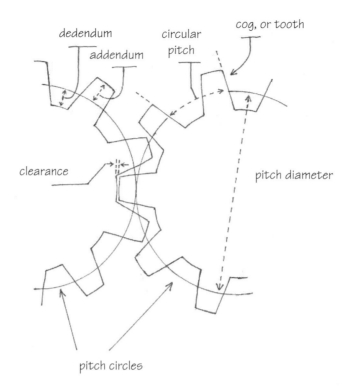

The parts of gears and gear teeth.

called the addendum, and the depth of a gear space below the pitch line is called the dedendum. The clearance of a gear refers to the space of the dedendum of one gear below the addendum of a mating gear tooth.

Another thing to consider about gears is backlash, which, as described by Carl A. Nelson in *Mechanical Trades Pocket Manual, 3rd Edition*, is "the play between teeth that prevents binding." *Machinery's Handbook, 24th Edition*, further defines backlash for purposes of measurement and calculation as "the amount by which a tooth space exceeds the thickness of an engaging tooth." While a certain degree of backlash is beneficial in a gear train, an excessive amount can interfere with the efficiency of the mechanism.

BELT-DRIVEN PULLEYS

Pulleys have one distinct advantage over gears, and that is the flexibility of shaft positioning. Since the pulley wheels don't make contact with one another directly, their shafts can be spaced essentially anywhere within belt-drive range.

However, one downside with pulleys is the possibility of the belts slipping, resulting in power loss. Pulleys depend to a large degree on belt tension for reliable function, and in this respect they are not as efficient as gears.

The good news about pulleys for the makeshift inventor is that pulley wheels will normally be much easier to fabricate from common materials than toothed gears, and they present more flexibility for arrangements. Tolerances are perhaps not as critical with pulleys as they must be with gears, although again, belt tension is always a big issue with belt-driven pulley systems.

You could build an operational pulley arrangement under surprisingly primitive circumstances, and in less time than it would normally take to measure and cut all the teeth on precision gears. You could substitute twisted ropes or straps of leather for V-belts in a pinch, if available materials are limited, and make all your pulley wheels out of wood for an unsophisticated but functional manually powered machine. Even if the wooden wheels warped, they might still work to some extent. A well-balanced pulley wheel might even be made from hardwood by cutting its shape on a wood lathe.

A small pulley wheel will rotate more times than a larger pulley wheel with a given rotational input on either wheel on the drive belt. Calculating the pulley speed ratio is not a complicated process—we are, in this case, working with the differences between the wheel sizes as opposed to a difference in the number of gear teeth.

If our drive or driver pulley—the pulley that is powered directly by a motor or, more likely in our case, manually with a hand crank—is the smaller of the two pulley wheels on the drive belt, then the axle or driven shaft (the shaft on the bigger wheel, in this case) will turn slower than our drive shaft, but the crank will be easier to turn.

If the configuration is reversed and the drive pulley is larger than the driven pulley, then the crank will be harder to turn, but we'll get proportionately more revolutions per minute (rpm) with the output, or driven, shaft.

There are two common methods to change the direction of rotation using pulleys and belts. The first is by putting a twist in the belt. One 180-degree twist in the drive belt will reverse the rotational direction on the driven pulley. This is generally considered practical only with slow-turning pulleys, because there is a high probability that the twisted belt will rub against itself, which would cause

excessive friction. The other possible method for changing rotational direction with pulleys and belts is by placing a third pulley outside the belt loop. A wheel running on the back of a belt will rotate in the opposite direction from the wheels running inside the loop. However, this approach requires at least an additional pulley wheel and shaft, and the desired properties of a V-belt will be lost on the third wheel that turns in the opposite direction from the other two, because it is running on the backside—the flat surface—of the belt.

Standard arrangement—rotational direction preserved.

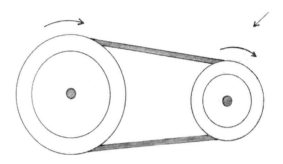

Crossed belt changes rotation.

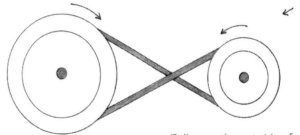

Pulley on the outside of the belt changes rotation.

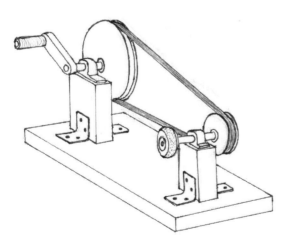

Hand-cranked grinding wheel powered by belt and pulleys. A large wheel turns a small pulley for a speed advantage.

Methods for changing rotational direction with belt and pulleys.

177

A bicycle is one of the most efficient manually powered machines.

SPROCKET AND CHAIN DRIVES

We might think of the bicycle as one of the most efficient and successful manually powered machines ever developed. As already noted, a sprocket is much like a toothed gear, except that it drives a special type of chain whose links engage the sprocket's teeth as opposed to engaging the teeth of another wheel directly, as does a gear.

The sprocket and pedal mechanism from a bicycle lends itself well to a variety of makeshift contraptions (one example is the makeshift forge blower I devised for *Makeshift I*), since the parts and engineering have already been created and refined for the purpose of manually turning a wheel with the minimal amount of effort, saving us an enormous amount of time getting all that business arranged and working properly. Besides, used bicycles are commonly found at yard sales or online and are usually very inexpensive.

One of the main advantages of a sprocket and chain system is that, like a belt, it provides great flexibility for shaft placement, unlike gears that mesh together. Also, the sprocket teeth give the chain drive more positive transmission of force than what is normally available to a pulley and belt system, because a chain is not subject to slipping to the same extent that a belt is.

A final option worth mentioning here is the toothed belt, which combines the best characteristics of a V-belt with the advantages of a chain drive. The sheave has female pockets at the bottom of the groove; the belt has matching "teeth" to engage them. The idea is to provide positive engagement like a chain drive, but with all the flexibility of a V-belt.

DEALING WITH FRICTION

Up to now, we have focused more on the theoretical, or ideal, mechanical advantages provided by some of these mechanical systems. In the real world, however, we have to deal with friction.

Friction can be defined as the resistance to motion, or a force that resists the motion, of objects in contact. Friction reduces a machine's efficiency. You might have to make certain adjustments in your calculations to accommodate the effects of friction in your mechanisms, but this can get rather complicated because there are a number of influencing factors at play. For example, the type of material and texture of its surfaces will have an effect on the amount of friction generated, as will the types, specifics, and amounts of forces present in the moving parts in contact.

Because the variety of possible mechanical movements is so diverse and the variables that influence friction are so varied, it is not always practical to apply any general rule of thumb about friction, such as something like, "just add 20 percent to the input to compensate for friction loss." That might get you by in some of the more basic applications, but others require a more accurate prediction of how the various forces will act upon and affect the system.

In *Basic Machines and How They Work*, I noticed that in the discussion about friction, the attention is actually shifted away from friction directly when it comes to making specific calculations and instead shifts toward considering the *efficiency* of the machine. The generic formula for efficiency is then provided as: Efficiency = Output ÷ Input.

You might remember that this is the same generic calculation for obtaining the mechanical advantage of a simple machine (MA = Output/Input), except that instead of looking for a ratio, here you would convert the fraction into a percentage to determine the efficiency of the machine. It is stated as being "[# percent] efficient" (e.g., 70 percent efficient).

Although friction does have its benefits with certain applications, such as helping knots hold in rope, enabling V-belts to properly transmit rotation from one pulley wheel to another, or keeping nuts tight on bolts, one of the big challenges in mechanical design is trying to find ways to minimize friction between moving parts in contact. This can be accomplished to a degree by making all contact surfaces as smooth as possible; keeping the contact surface areas of moving parts to an absolute minimum while still maintaining adequate support of shafts, wheels, levers, etc.; using lubricants like oil or graphite where appropriate; and using roller or ball bearings whenever possible. If by necessity a machine is to be devised in a primitive situation and only wood is available for the construction, any contact areas between moving parts may be improved by burnishing the surfaces and applying wax (e.g., beeswax), animal fat, or tallow as the main lubricant.

AFFIXING WHEELS TO SHAFTS

Belt-driven pulley wheels and gears are typically fixed to their shafts so that they turn together in most arrangements, and there are several methods by which this can be achieved. Four common methods that come to mind are the setscrew, key, cross pin, and locking ring. Setscrews and cross pins require a raised hub on the gear wheel or pulley around the axle through which the locking devices can pass perpendicularly. The setscrew method will hold much more securely if the shaft has a shallow hole, notch, or other depression at the desired location to accommodate the bottom of the screw, which will lock the wheel into a fixed position on its shaft.

Possibly the simplest and most used system is the key that fits into corresponding slots in both the wheel and axle when in alignment with each other, thereby locking the two rotating parts together.

With some mechanical devices, such as gun locks having hammers and tumblers, certain clock gears, and similar mechanisms, it used to be quite common to employ wheels with square holes in their centers through which squared shanks or

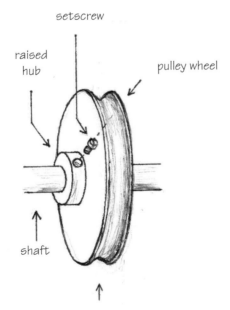

Wheel fixed to shaft with setscrew.

Gear fixed to shaft with key.

Attaching wheels to shafts.

squared sections of the shafts would fit, forcing the wheels and shafts to rotate together.

Another method for fixing a wheel to a shaft, which is perhaps more common with grinding wheels than with gears, is by using a threaded, or at least partly threaded, shaft and using nuts over washers on both sides of the wheel to firm the wheel into position with compression force.

Suggested Resources for Further Study

An assortment of references is as valuable a resource as any tool in a makeshifter's shop.

***Bushcraft: A Serious Guide to Survival and Camping* by Richard Graves (New York: Warner Books, 1978)**
This handy little survival book (not to be confused with another good survival book, *Bush Craft*, by Mors L. Kochanski) provides a wealth of information about expedient, makeshift methods to help a marooned individual or someone in almost any other kind of survival situation. The illustrations are extremely simple, but they are adequate for getting the ideas across. I learned several neat makeshift tricks from this book, such as how to cut the top off a glass bottle using string, kerosene, and a pail of cold water.

***Camping and Wilderness Survival: The Ultimate Outdoors Book* by Paul Tawrell (Lebanon, NH: survivalbook.com, 1996, 2001)**
Paul Tawrell covers an enormous amount of survival and wilderness information in this extensively illustrated volume, and it may actually hold up to the claim of being the "ultimate outdoors book," as I am not sure I have ever seen a wilderness book that was more comprehensive in scope. I do have one

observation about the illustrations. While they are undeniably clear and effective in their purpose, they do seem a bit generic. A lot of them appear similar to or exactly the same as what you will find in many heavily illustrated contemporary outdoor survival books. But this is really a trivial observation of an amazingly extensive resource that I think is well worth having around for its practical information for outdoorsmen and makeshifters alike.

Ductigami—The Art of the Tape: 18 Projects to Make with Duct Tape by Joe Wilson (Ontario, Canada: Boston Mills Press, 2006)

This is an interesting book that provides complete instructions (with clear illustrations and photos) on how to create a wallet, cup holder, apron, baseball cap, and a variety of other interesting products entirely from duct tape. This little book inspired me to become more creative with my own duct tape projects.

Green Woodwork: Working with Wood the Natural Way by Mike Abbott (East Sussex, England: Guild of Master Craftsman Publications, 1989, 1992)

This intriguing book focuses on creating furniture and tool handles out of wood. I am particularly fascinated by the spring-pole lathe it illustrates and describes, which, as we know, makes an effective manually powered machine. The use of natural resources is a main focus of this book and one of the things that makes it especially important for makeshifters.

The Forgotten Arts and Crafts: Skills from Bygone Days by John Seymour (New York: Dorling Kindersley Publishing, 1984, 1987, 2001)

This book, a large and hefty hardcover, is perhaps the most colorfully illustrated how-to book I have ever seen. It almost looks like a huge coffee-table book, but it covers a truly enormous variety of old-world skills and crafts, including such things as basket weaving, rake making, bodging (making wooden chairs), coopering, blacksmithing, linen crafts, leatherwork, wooden boat building, and much more. The artwork alone makes it an impressive book, but I believe this would be a useful resource for anyone interested in learning about traditional crafts as well as for getting ideas about various makeshift projects.

New Fix-It-Yourself Manual by the Reader's Digest Association (Pleasantville, NY: Reader's Digest, 1996)

As I've said before, the Reader's Digest how-to books are of superb quality and contain some of the most complete, clear, and detailed illustrations you will find anywhere. The scope of this particular manual is truly amazing. It explains the tools, hardware materials, and techniques for repairs to your house, furniture, appliances, tools, and even your kids' toys! If forced to select only one household maintenance or repair guide, there is no question in my mind that it should be this book.

How To Do Just About Anything: A Money-Saving A-Z Guide to Over 1,200 Practical Problems by the Reader's Digest Association (Pleasantville, NY: Reader's Digest, 1986)

This is another substantial Reader's Digest book that is definitely worth mentioning here, as it covers so many different things. If you want to learn the basics about how to stitch leather, crochet, knit, weave, scrimshaw, paint, patch plasterboard, saw wood, apply concrete, make metric conversions, nail or screw boards, fix leaky faucets, maintain your bicycle, change a tire on your car, can foods, whittle objects out of wood, tune a guitar, make lean-to shelters, lay bricks, rewire light fixtures, pack a backpack, swim, play marbles, exercise, or do literally hundreds of other activities, this book can teach you how.

The New Handicraft: Processes and Projects, 10th Edition by Lester and Kathleen Griswold (New York: Van Nostrand Reinhold Company, 1969, 1972)

Even though this book is getting old, I still find its content very useful. A hardcover, it is well illustrated and includes many black-and-white photos. It is one of the best I've seen for information about such crafts as leatherwork, ceramics, decorative metal craft, weaving, and braiding. If you come across a copy of this book, I think you will find it worth buying.

The New How It Works: The New Science and Invention Encyclopedia, Volume 1 (Westport, CT: H. S. Stuttman 1987, 1989)

I only have the first volume of this 26-volume set of

encyclopedias, which covers topics alphabetically. However, I hope to eventually collect the other volumes for my library. These books provide quite a lot of information about how various things work, and even about the science behind their invention and manufacture.

Mechanical Trades Pocket Manual, *3rd Edition* by Carl A. Nelson (New York: Macmillan Publishing Company, 1986, 1990)

This is a very handy little softcover manual that provides useful data, charts, and information related to mechanical engineering and the trades. I found the information pertaining to gears, sprockets, chains, pulleys, and belts to be especially helpful in my studies. As its title suggests, this is a pocket manual (it measures 3/4 x 4 x 6 inches; 374 pages), and its compact size makes it very convenient to carry around or keep in your toolbox.

Robinson Crusoe by Daniel Defoe (Mineola, NY: Dover Publications, 1998)

Originally published in 1719 in England, the version I have is the unabridged Dover Thrift Edition. This reprint of the famous classic is a 225-page paperback novel, but an awful lot is crammed into those pages. I paid $2.50 (new retail price) for it at the local bookstore. It is the only work of fiction referenced in this section, but the story's historical and cultural significance, and especially its relevance to our general topic of makeshift expedience, make it worthy of our attention here. Interestingly, its original title in 1719 (according to Wikipedia) was "The Life and Strange Surprizing Adventures of Robinson Crusoe of York, Mariner: Who lived Eight and Twenty Years, all alone in an uninhabited Island on the coast of America, near the Mouth of the Great River of Oroonoque; Having been cast on Shore by Shipwreck, wherein all the Men perished but himself. With An Account how he was at last as strangely deliver'd by Pyrates. Written by Himself."

It is generally believed that the Robinson Crusoe story was inspired primarily by the real-life experience of Alexander Selkirk, the Scottish mariner who was marooned for four years (October 1704 to February 1709) on an island off the coast of Chile. *Marooned: The Strange but True Adventures of Alexander Selkirk, the Real Robinson Crusoe* by Robert Kraske (New York: Clarion Books, 2005) provides a brief biography of Selkirk. Both the real and fictitious castaway adventurers provide considerable food for thought in the realm of self-reliance and adapting to the environment. I find myself wanting to reread the Robinson Crusoe story from time to time to inspire new ideas in my head, among other reasons.

The SAS Survival Handbook by John Wiseman (London: HarperCollins Publishers, 1986)

More than 10 years ago, I bought John "Lofty" Wiseman's survival video and viewed it a number of times. I've long considered it to be among the best survival videos ever created, and his book is also filled with a huge volume of valuable information, much of which could be very useful to any makeshift hobbyist or craftsman. The illustrations are similar to those in the Paul Tawrell book I commented on earlier, but this is nonetheless a useful resource.

Blacksmithing Basics for the Homestead by Joe DeLaRonde (Layton, UT: Gibbs Smith, 2008)

I referenced several good books on blacksmithing in *Makeshift I*, but I recently acquired this one, and I must say that it is a wonderful book on the topic, with infinitely useful tips and very clear, colorful photos and illustrations. This has become my favorite blacksmithing book, and I wouldn't hesitate recommending it as a first book on the subject for anyone just taking up the craft. Joe DeLaRonde also wrote a lengthy chapter in *The Book of Buckskinning IV*, titled "Traditional Blacksmithing," and it was from that chapter that I learned most of what I know about how to forge-weld successfully.

United States Navy Foundry Manual, reprinted by Lindsay Publications (1957 revision of 1944 original)

This might actually be one of the most comprehensive books on metal casting/foundry you will find. While the information it provides is not exactly current, I would venture to guess that most of the processes and methods are not outdated. It is a heavily illustrated softcover book, with black-and-white photos of varying clarity (keep in mind that this is a reprint of an old military manual). Even if you don't work with metal in this way, I believe this could be a useful technical resource for any craftsman or hobbyist's library. By the way, for anyone who is not familiar with Lindsay's Technical Books (as hard as it might be to imagine, I learned about Lindsay for the first time less than a year ago!), now might be a good time to order their current catalog. Every hobbyist, craftsman, inventor, and makeshifter will find a wealth of resources there. Check them out at www.lindsaybks.com.

Making Crucibles by Vincent Gingery (Rogersville, MO: David J. Gingery Publishing, 2003)

Another instructional resource available through Lindsay Publications, this is a short booklet on homemade crucibles for metal casting/foundry, and it covers the topic in considerable depth. Well illustrated with a surprising quantity of clear black-and-white photos for a 59-page booklet. This could be valuable information for the makeshift foundry worker.

The Fiberglass Repair and Construction Handbook, 2nd Edition by Jack Wiley (New York: TAB Books, Division of McGraw-Hill, 1988)

This is the most complete book I have ever seen on the subject of fiberglass. While I am mindful that not every makeshift hobbyist will work with fiberglass, it is nevertheless a handy material to be familiar with for certain projects, and this book provides good information about related ingredients like resins and epoxies as well. I believe anyone (and especially those who read my books) can benefit from such knowledge.

RE/USES: 2133 Ways to RECYCLE and REUSE the Things You Ordinarily Throw Away by Carolyn Jabs (New York: Crown Publishers, 1982)

I found this interesting book in a used bookstore and could not resist buying it. While it does not appear that the author had much firsthand experience with all the suggestions, the ideas are nevertheless numerous, and many of them are quite intriguing. With plenty of sketches and black-and-white photos to illustrate the concepts, this is really a fun book to peruse for numerous common and uncommon makeshift ideas, especially as they apply to recycling used products.

Tough Times Survival Guide, Volumes 1 and 2 (Boulder, CO: Paladin Press, 2009)

These two books cover a considerable volume of information and ideas of potential use to anyone interested in learning more about improvising and adapting, frugal living, surviving off-grid, and related topics. Dozens of authors contributed articles to both volumes.

Making Do, Volume 1: The Poor Man's Forge, featuring Jason Hawk (Boulder, CO: Paladin Press, 2009)

This intriguing video mainly covers how to forge a quality knife from common rebar steel, an inexpensive and easy-to-come-by resource. The lengthy 220-minute video also demonstrates a simple plastic trash bag bellows as part of a crude but functional makeshift forge someone could quickly set up in the field. I wish the trash bag bellows was explained with a bit more detail, but overall this is an entertaining and instructive video that addresses the "make-do" concept quite well. Jason Hawk explains his processes in a straightforward, commonsense manner.

Home Workshop Knifemaking: Making Utility and Defensive Knives on a Budget, featuring Wally Hayes (Boulder, CO: Paladin Press, 2003)

Here is another informative knife-making video that incorporates some intriguing and potentially useful methods and techniques for the makeshift craftsman. I think viewers will be particularly interested in the low-budget knife forge using small gas torches. Anyone interested in makeshift forging or knife making could benefit from watching this video. Approximate running time: 150 minutes.

Periodicals:

Popular Mechanics (New York, NY: Hearst Communications, www.popularmechanics.com)

With a circulation in the millions, this is no doubt one of the most popular guy magazines in America. But it isn't really just a "guy magazine"—even if it is hard for me to imagine any red-blooded American male not being interested in it. It would certainly be inaccurate to characterize this publication as one that caters primarily to *auto* mechanics. While it definitely talks about cars and car engines quite a bit, it also goes into home repairs and other do-it-yourselfer topics, including but not limited to home workshop projects, woodworking, the latest tools and hardware products, cutting-edge technologies in numerous fields, and plenty of other how-to skills and areas of interest. For example, the October 2009 issue is devoted to the self-reliance themes of off-grid living and disaster survival. You can find *Popular Mechanics* in the magazine stand of most supermarkets and large bookstores, or if you want to subscribe, visit the website above.

Backwoods Home (Gold Beach, OR: www.backwoodshome.com)

Backwoods Home (not to be confused with either of two other fine magazines with similar names, *Back Home* or my all-time favorite, *The Backwoodsman*) is printed six times a year and published by its founder, Dave Duffy. Advertised as "America's best self-reliance magazine," topics typically include things like building with logs, growing fruit trees and vegetables, raising chickens and other farm animals, baking bread, alternative energy, guns and shooting, and other preparedness issues. I have long considered it an entertaining and informative magazine.